CHALLENGES TO
THE WORLD BANK
AND IMF

Advance reviews

'This is a very refreshing and thorough critique of today's development orthodoxy represented by the World Bank and the IMF. The combination of iconoclastic perspectives and detailed knowledge of the subject matter makes it particularly powerful.'

Ha-Joon Chang, Assistant Director of Development Studies, University of Cambridge; author, *Kicking Away the Ladder: Development Strategy in Historical Perspective*

'incisive and powerful… *Challenging the World Bank and IMF* is a unique book, providing the reader with a collection of highly professional papers from the perspective of developing countries, covering their economic problems and their relations with International Financial Institutions.'

Claudio M Loser, *Inter-American Dialogue*

'Nowhere is the voice of the developing nations expressed as cogently and powerfully as in these fresh and controversial essays… a gripping reminder of the long road we need to travel before the governance of the world economy becomes truly hospitable to the aspirations of the developing world.'

Dani Rodrik, *Professor of International Political Economy, John F Kennedy School of Government, Harvard University*

'This is a challenging and timely book by a distinguished cast of scholars, analysing the philosophy, governance, political economy and effectiveness of the two premier global economic institutions. It robustly criticizes their unquestioning reverence for free markets, their political economy and governance, and their methodology and effectiveness. Of the recent analyses of the two institutions, this is clearly one of the most rigorous, balanced and coherent. A "must" for development specialists and students.'

Sanjaya Lall
*Professor of Development Economics,
International Development Centre, University of Oxford*

CHALLENGES TO THE WORLD BANK AND IMF

Developing Country Perspectives

Edited by
Ariel Buira

for the G24 Research Program

Anthem Press

This edition first published by Anthem Press 2003

Anthem Press is an imprint of
Wimbledon Publishing Company
75–76 Blackfriars Road
London SE1 8HA

British Library Cataloguing in Publication Data
Data available

Library of Congress Cataloging in Publication Data
A catalog record has been applied for

ISBN 1 84331 140 2 (hbk)
1 84331 141 0 (pbk)

1 3 5 7 9 10 8 6 4 2

Typeset by Regent Typesetting, London

Printed and bound by Bell & Bain Ltd., Glasgow

CONTENTS

The G24

The Intergovernmental Group of 24 for International Monetary Affairs and Development was constituted in 1972 as a result of a mandate given in Lima by the Group of 77 to their Chairman, to consult member governments on the establishment of an intergovernmental group on monetary issues. Its members, nine African, eight Latin American and seven Asian countries are as follows:

Algeria, Argentina, Brazil, Colombia, Côte d'Ivoire, Democratic Republic of Congo, Egypt, Ethiopia, Gabon, Ghana, Guatemala, India, Iran, Lebanon, Mexico, Nigeria, Pakistan, Peru, Philippines, South Africa, Sri Lanka, Syrian Arab Republic, Trinidad and Tobago, and Venezuela.

The purpose of the G24 is to further the interests of the developing countries and their effective participation in the discussions of monetary, financial and development issues at the Bretton Woods institutions and other fora. It seeks to provide technical support to its members and to the G77 in their consideration of these issues. To this effect, the G24 Secretariat, supported by its members and other sources, runs a research program in which academics and other researchers from countries in the North and South address the main issues of concern to the developing world in their areas of competence. To ensure intellectual freedom in their work, the results of their research and the views expressed in the papers presented to the G24 are the sole responsibility of the authors.

LIST OF CONTRIBUTORS

Ariel Buira, Editor, is Director of the G24 Secretariat. He has been Special Envoy of the President of Mexico for the UN Conference on Financing for Development, Ambassador of Mexico, Member of the Board of Governors of the Bank of Mexico and Executive Director of the IMF.

Gerald Epstein is Professor of Economics and Co-Director of the Political Economy Research Institute (PERI) at the University of Massachusetts, Amherst. He is the co-editor of *Globalization and Progressive Economic Policy* and *Macroeconomics After the Conservative Era*, both with Cambridge University Press.

Ilene Grabel is Associate Professor of International Finance at the Graduate School of International Studies at the University of Denver. Grabel is co-author of the book, *Reclaiming Development: An Economic Policy Handbook for Activists and Policymakers* (London, Zed Press, forthcoming, 2004).

Bernhard Gunter is an independent consultant, specializing on issues related to development macroeconomics, poverty and debt. He is currently associated with the New Rules for Global Finance Coalition and the World Bank. Formerly an economist in the World Bank's HIPC unit and a Consultant for the World Bank Institute.

Javier Guzmán studied economics at the National University of México, and did his graduate studies at the University of Louvain and at Yale University. He is currently Director of International Affairs at the Bank of Mexico.

Barry Herman is Chief for Policy Analysis and Development in the Financing for Development Office in the United Nations Department of Economic and Social Affairs. He has headed the team that produced the UN's annual *World Economic and Social Survey*.

KS Jomo is Professor in the Applied Economics Department, Faculty of Economics and Administration, University of Malaya. Jomo is on the Board of the United Nations Research Institute on Social Development (UNRISD), Geneva, and Founder President of the International Development Economics Associates (IDEAs).

Ravi Kanbur is TH Lee Professor of World Affairs and Professor of Economics at Cornell University. He has previously taught at Oxford, Cambridge, Essex, Princeton and Warwick. He has held various appointments at the World Bank including Chief Economist for Africa, and Principal Adviser to the Chief Economist of the World Bank.

Martin Khor is the Director of the International Secretariat of the Third World Network and the author of several books and articles on trade, development and environment issues. He was formerly a Vice Chairman of the UN Commission on Human Rights Expert Group on the Right to Development, and is a consultant to the United Nations.

James Levinsohn is Professor of Economics and Professor of Public Policy at the University of Michigan. He holds the J Ira and Nikki Harris Family Chair in Public Policy. His research interests span international economics, development economics and industrial organization.

Aziz Ali Mohammed is G24 Deputy for Pakistan, former Alternate Executive Director, IMF. Has held senior positions on IMF staff, including Director, External Relations.

Rodolfo Padilla is currently Economic Researcher at the Direction of International Affairs at the Bank of Mexico.

FOREWORD

The research program of the Group of 24 is the world's only research effort devoted to evaluating the international economic system from the perspective of developing nations' needs. Multilateral development banks and other research organizations may put out a larger volume of studies, but their mandate and intended audience are not as clearly defined as the G24's. This makes the papers produced under the auspices of the G24 very special. Nowhere is the voice of the developing nations expressed as cogently and powerfully as in these papers.

This volume continues a tradition of dissemination that has long been part of the G24 agenda. It includes chapters on some of the most burning issues on the agenda: reform of the IMF and its conditionality, debt workouts and restructuring, management of capital flows, efficacy of self-insurance against crises, debt sustainability in the HIPC countries, poverty-reduction strategy papers (PRSP), international public goods, and the Millennium Development Goals and the 'global partnership for development'. Readers will find fresh and controversial perspectives in each of these chapters.

Separating hype from fact and promise from reality has always been a hallmark of the G24 research tradition. If you are doubtful that there exist effective mechanisms for improving the governance of the IMF and its conditionality, read the chapters by Buira. If you believe that the HIPC initiative has a solid chance of placing poor countries on the path of debt sustainability, read the chapter by Gunter. If you think the World Bank's PRSP approach is based on solid economic and statistical reasoning, read the chapter by Levinsohn. If you think financial markets have become so integrated that prudential controls on capital flows have become unfeasible, read the chapter by Epstein, Grabel and Jomo. If you are of the view that the IMF's proposal of a Sovereign Debt Restructuring Mechanism (SDRM) is harmful to 'emerging' economies, read the amended version that is offered in the chapter by Herman.

I hope the reader will not stop with individual chapters but take the volume in its entirety. It is a gripping reminder of the long road we need to travel before the governance of the world economy becomes truly hospitable to the aspirations of the developing world.

Dani Rodrik
May 30, 2003

INTRODUCTION

Ariel Buira

In trying to find their way toward growth and economic and social development, policymakers in developing countries face multiple uncertainties. For most, the major sources of advice of external financial assistance are the Bretton Woods institutions. With large financial resources at their disposal, and their support conditional on the adoption of certain policy prescriptions, the influence of the International Monetary Fund (IMF) and the World Bank (WB) can hardly be exaggerated.

Their influence on economic policy has undoubtedly contributed to the strengthening of the macroeconomic framework of member countries, reducing public sector deficits and public debt accumulation, improving monetary control and reducing the distortions and misallocation of resources brought about by high rates of inflation. In addition, by fostering trade liberalization and privatization of state enterprises, the Bretton Woods Institutions (BWIs) have generally contributed to the growth of exports and the attraction of foreign direct investment. In the face of a number of recent challenges, however, these institutions' neoliberal paradigm would seem insufficient, and needs to be complemented by other elements.

The first of these challenges is posed by the explosive growth of capital markets and their extraordinary volatility, with the consequent potential for the emergence of multiple equilibria in exchange markets – and also for devastating financial crises. While the BWIs recognize these risks, and are trying to improve their capabilities to predict crisis, efforts at crisis prevention have not been successful. As for crisis resolution, the IMF's approaches to in Asia, Russia and Argentina have been controversial. In fact, one of the more successful responses to the challenge posed by the volatility of capital flows has been the introduction in Chile and Colombia, for example, of market-based controls on capital movements, which had been resisted by the IMF for years. These responses illustrate the practical relevance of the 'theory of the second best' by which, when an economy suffers a distortion, welfare may be improved by the judicious introduction of another distortion through some form of government intervention.

A second, related, challenge, which is yet to be addressed, is posed by the massive reversals of previously large capital flows, from the developed to the developing countries. Largely as a result of the failure to prevent the recurrence of financial crises, the increase in the perceived risk of lending to emerging market countries has caused a sharp decline in capital flows to these countries; consequently, they have become substantial capital exporters. At the same time, a number of emerging market economies have sought to insure themselves against the risk posed by the volatility of capital markets by accumulating high levels of international reserves. As a result, emerging markets and other developing countries have become substantial capital exporters, mostly to finance the deficits of the world's largest economy. Little has been done to interfere with this trend, which results in bad allocation of resources for the world economy as a whole.

A third challenge to the prevailing paradigm relates to the contrasting development experiences of Asia and Latin America. The awkward fact is that, despite successfully lowering inflation, strengthening public finances, liberalizing the financial sector, privatizing a significant number of public enterprises and opening to foreign trade and investment, Latin America – the region that has embraced these reforms most enthusiastically and carried them furthest – has grown over the last 10 or 15 years at rates that are half of those observed in the period of state-led development, from 1930 to 1970. Over the same recent period, in contrast, a group of countries in Asia, including China, India, Korea, Vietnam and others, have attained high rates of growth by following a different, more interventionist, model of development that has combined less open capital accounts and protectionism with subsidies and tax incentives. This contrasting performance raises the question of whether the BWIs recommendations were the most appropriate.

In a few broad brush strokes, what is missing in the international financial institutions' paradigm?

Obviously, one must start from what went wrong, or by looking at what was not successful. The first issue is growth, i.e. the failure to attain rapid rates of growth, is the most powerful criticism of their model. This lack of growth has in turn often been accompanied by a lack of concern for income distribution, which worsened in most countries. Additionally, the model failed in employment creation and in the reduction of poverty, which in many cases increased.

Looking at more successful experiences of growth, whether in Asia since the 1980s or in Latin America in earlier periods, one salient difference is the pragmatism with which issues were addressed by policymakers, often lawyers or politicians, without the benefit of a western economics education. These policymakers were prepared to intervene, when it seemed necessary, to provide tariff protection or credits required to attain a given industrial objective, to establish institutions to assist the development of human capital or to promote certain sectors of production.

In contrast, a general characteristic of the approach followed by many economists in the IFIs is an almost reverential respect for the free play of market forces, not as a means to attain certain goals, such as an efficient allocation of resources, but virtually as an end in themselves. Thus, there has been a failure to distinguish between ends and means, a failure of perspective in recognizing what markets can and can not do. Market outcomes are not questioned because, consistently with the prevailing orthodoxy, they are implicitly assumed to be able to provide the optimum economic result.

However, it would be very difficult to argue that markets can or should determine the goals of a society, and indeed, no political philosophy does so. This is because markets are acknowledged to be simply an instrument, an effective mechanism to achieve certain limited goals, but like any mechanism, without moral values, or a vision of society.

Economics, despite its mathematical techniques, remains a social science, one in which policy recommendations are implicitly influenced by the interests, ideologies and values of the policymakers. It is a discipline with few universally accepted truths, and significant and persistent differences with regard to the overall framework. Reflecting the prevailing economic orthodoxy since the mid-1980s, the IMF and the World Bank have adopted an approach that promotes market-oriented policy reforms and relies on market solutions. This is assumed to promote efficient resource allocations every time, but generally lacks the pragmatism required to encourage public action to correct market failures.

While not questioning the role of monetary stability, sound public finances and proper incentives, much contemporary economic thought challenges the foundations and questions the policy prescriptions of neoliberal orthodoxy through its analysis of market failures and the role of institutions, and by questioning the assumption of rationality and consistency of consumer behavior.[1]

Recall that the IMF was set up to combat a market failure, that is, the collapse of domestic demand, and to counter attempts to emerge from this through the adoption of 'beggar-thy-neighbor' policies. It is therefore incumbent upon the IMF to help its member countries avoid recessionary adjustments as a solution to balance of payments imbalances. Thus, among the purposes of the IMF as set out in its Articles of Agreement are:

To facilitate the expansion and balanced growth of international trade, and to contribute thereby to the promotion and maintenance of high levels of employment and real income and to the development of the productive resources of all members as primary objectives of economic policy.

Article I, Section II

and further:

To give confidence to members by making the general resources of the Fund temporarily available to them under adequate safeguards, thus providing them with opportunity to correct maladjustments in their balance of payments without resorting to measures destructive of national or international prosperity.

Article I, Section V

Since economic policy is not an exact science, it is difficult for the policy recommendations of the institutions to escape being influenced by their knowledge of the doctrines and interests of the industrial countries that exert control over them.

The World Bank's history notes that 'economics would become the Bank's hallmark scholarly discipline, and the economists who largely shaped the Bank operations as well as its research were recruited from an array of countries. To a large degree, however, they were the product of the graduate economics departments of English-speaking, but especially, American universities. This fact, as it influenced the Bank's consulting, research, technical assistance and agenda setting, would enhance the US role in the institution beyond the apparatus of formal governance.'[2]

Since the IMF and the World Bank were set up to overcome market failures, how did this intellectual domination of the neoliberal paradigm come about? Two explanations may be suggested. The first is the control of the major industrial countries over the governance of the institutions, their policies, their operations, their resources and their appointment of high officials.[3] The second important factor, a corollary of the first, is the norms imposed by the professionals that take over organizations and structure their activities according to their own ways of thinking:

Like any institution, the Bank has its own self reinforcing culture and its codes which set limits on what can reasonably be believed and discussed if one hopes to be taken seriously and remain a member of the group … Put in the same place several hundred people who have been trained in the same schools to think the same way, recruit them precisely because they have excelled in this training ... (and the) probable outcome will be – at least among economists – monolithic and fundamentalist.[4]

However, this view provides a better description of the IMF than of the World Bank, where the diversity of training and experiences of agronomists, engineers, social anthropologists, sociologists and others provides a greater variety of perspectives.

A fourth challenge to policy recommendations is posed by important differences in the structural characteristics and the institutional frameworks of the developed and the developing countries (as well as between the developing countries themselves). Since economics has to a large extent been developed in the industrial countries, country-specific analyses tend to be based on industrial-country and market-oriented economic models, as well as social and political institutions, in order to ensure the relevance and cultural compatibility of the prescriptions. For instance, economics generally and implicitly assumes that:

1. The rule of law and the courts of justice ensure that contracts are enforced, property rights are protected and that, when loans are not repaid, the courts will ensure that the creditor can recover in an expeditious manner, or if bankruptcy proceedings ensue, will be treated equitably.
2. Domestic markets are highly competitive and not dominated by one or a few firms.
3. The banking system is well capitalized and regulated and provides credit and working capital to meet the needs of profitable enterprises. Also, households are assumed to have access to consumer credit, mortgages and capital markets to provide long-term financing for investment.
4. The labor force is literate, mobile, with a large proportion of skilled workers and professionals.

Making assumptions explicit often suffices to question their validity; contrast these assumptions with the characteristics of a developing region of your choice. There is no need to labor the point by listing the further characteristics assumed in the different sectors. However, different situations must be taken into consideration, since incorrect assumptions may give rise to unexpected outcomes and costly policy mistakes. The recent financial crises in the countries of Latin America and East Asia, which liberalized their capital account prematurely at the insistence of the international institutions, dramatically illustrates this point. Moreover, it also raises the question of whether a commercial interest on the part of major countries,[5] or private domestic interests, may have played a role in promoting over-rapid capital account liberalization.[6] Thus, in examining the policy prescriptions of the IMF and World Bank, it is necessary to think 'out of the box', to take a fresh, pragmatic view of the problems and of their prescriptions and to arrive at an independent assessment.

The chapters that follow, a collection of policy-oriented papers prepared for the Group of Twenty-Four developing country members of the Bretton Woods institutions attempt to do just that. The chapters deal with three broad themes:

- governance and key policies of the Bretton Woods institutions as seen from a developing country perspective
- the management of capital movements and the prevention and resolution of financial crises
- Millennium Development Goals and the provision of global public goods.

1. Governance and key policy issues

The first five chapters in this book address the governance issue by examining a number of assumptions and beliefs associated with the Bretton Woods institutions and their policies. Consider the following propositions that are widely accepted both by informed opinion and by members of the economics profession:

- the governance of the IMF is based on contributions of member countries (or 'quotas') that reflect the importance of the member countries' economies
- the industrial countries underwrite the financial support the IMF provides to the developing economies
- conditionality attached to loans is required to ensure that borrower countries are able to repay the IMF loans.

The following chapters will show, however, that these perceptions are inaccurate: more false than true.

The first chapter, 'The Governance of the IMF in a Global Economy' by Ariel Buira, reviews the governance or power structure of the IMF. Buira discusses the dominant position of the industrial countries holding a majority of the voting power and the requirement of qualified majorities for all-important decisions. This in turn reflects the unrepresentative character of quotas and the marginalization of small economies in the decision-making process. Buira argues that the under-representation of developing countries could be corrected by reducing the over-representation of the European Union. He also addresses the question of whether the governance of the IMF complies with the same standards of transparency, accountability and legitimacy that it prescribes to its member countries.

The second chapter, 'Who pays for the IMF?' by Aziz Ali Mohammed, reviews aspects of the financial governance of the Bretton Woods institutions, focusing on the equity implications of the way in which they distribute their costs. Mohammed finds that while the IMF charges borrowers roughly what it pays its creditor members for the resources used in its regular lending operations, its overhead costs (administrative budget plus addition to reserves) are shared less equitably between the two groups of members. With the overhead costs rising inexorably to meet an increasing number and variety of responsibilities being placed upon the institution – at the instance of the IMF's principal creditors by virtue of their dominant voting power – the under-representation of the IMF's debtors undermines the legitimacy of its decision-making. Mohammed goes on to say that, with regard to the concessionary lending and debt relief operations, some of the funding modalities have involved a substantial contribution by IMF debtors, sometimes under pressure. While this outcome has been accepted as part of an intra-developing country burden-sharing exercise, it has also meant that a significant part of the cost of meeting the IMF's responsibilities to the poorest members of the international community has been shifted from the developed to the developing countries.

The third chapter, 'An Analysis of IMF Conditionality' by Ariel Buira, reviews the nature and purpose of IMF conditionality and, in the light of experience, disposes of the argument that conditionality is necessary to ensure repayment of loans, or in IMF jargon, 'to preserve the revolving character of Fund resources'. Buira raises a number of fundamental political questions relating to conditionality and relates the hardening of conditionality to the decline in IMF resources. This decline, in turn, results in the shifting of balance between adjustment and financing in favor of adjustment and thereby leads to a very high rate of program failure. Buira relates both of these trends to the fact that no industrial country has resorted to IMF support over the last 25 years. He argues that as increased conditionality became dysfunctional, it had to be revised to seek greater country ownership. However, he concludes that, with no increase in resources, the jury is still out on whether IMF measures to streamline conditionality and ensure program ownership have been successful.

Considering that the removal of the debt overhang is a precondition for growth and sustainable development in low-income countries, the fourth chapter, 'Achieving Long-Term Sustainability in all HIPCs' by Bernhard

Gunter, deals with the debt initiative for the Heavily Indebted Poor Countries (HIPC) Initiative. Gunter finds that for various reasons, including overly optimistic export projections leading to insufficient debt relief, HIPC programs generally fail to remove the debt overhang and to provide genuine long-term debt sustainability. He examines the six most crucial problems of the enhanced HIPC Initiative and presents specific suggestions on how its framework could be changed to provide a better basis for debt sustainability. Even after the adoption of such suggestions, however, the long-term debt sustainability of HIPCs would remain fragile. Gunter thus addresses some of the key issues relating to a new aid-architecture and the structural transformation HIPCs would have to undergo to achieve sustainability.

The fifth chapter, 'The Poverty Reduction Strategy Paper Approach: Good Marketing or Good Policy?' by Jim Levinson, considers whether the implementation of the Poverty Reduction Strategy Paper[7] (PRSP) process yields benefits in excess of its considerable administrative costs. In addressing this question, Levinson considers the objectives of the PRSP process, notes its strengths and shortcomings and examines some of the reviews of the PRSP process. Levinson finds that reviews have placed excessive reliance on anecdotal evidence and have been supported by inadequate quantitative analysis. Levinson offers recommendations on how to conduct an objective evaluation of a PRSP.

2. Managing capital movements and preventing crises

The next three chapters deal with the theme of the management of capital movements and the prevention and resolution of financial crises. The first of these, 'Experiences in Capital Account Management' by Gerald Epstein, Ilene Grabel and KS Jomo, uses the term 'capital management techniques' to refer to policies of prudential financial regulation and controls on international capital flows to achieve national economic goals. Epstein, Grabel and Jomo examine the experiences of several developing countries that employed various capital management techniques during the 1990s. The authors find that by employing a diverse set of these techniques, policymakers in Chile, Colombia, Taiwan Province of China, India, China, Singapore and Malaysia were able to achieve critical macroeconomic objectives. These included: preventing maturity and locational mismatches; attracting favored forms of foreign investment; reducing overall financial fragility, currency risk, and speculative pressures in the economy; insulating themselves from the contagion effects of financial crises and enhancing the autonomy of economic and social policy. The paper examines the structural factors that contributed to these achievements and considers the costs associated with the capital management techniques employed. Epstein, Grabel and Jomo conclude by considering the policy lessons of these experiences and the political prospects for other developing countries that wish to apply them.

The recent literature has reviewed a variety of indicators that can be helpful in the prediction and prevention of financial crisis. Chapter 7, 'The Accumulation of Reserves in the Prevention of Financial Crisis' by Javier Guzman and Rodolfo Padilla, specifically considers the ratio of international reserves to short-term external debt. While the authors provide evidence on the usefulness of this ratio in predicting economic crises, they also deepen the analysis of the limitations faced when using the ratio. The chapter contributes to the discussion on the advantages of this ratio, which can provide reasonable coverage in the event of economic shocks, and analyzes the adjustments that could be introduced to increase its usefulness as a tool for crisis prevention. An important result of this analysis is that, beyond a certain point, the accumulation of reserves, which can be very costly, does not provide significantly increased protection against capital account crises.

In 'Strengthening Sovereign Lending Through Mechanisms for Dialogue and Debt-Crisis Workout: Issues and Proposals', Barry Herman considers that a positive future for foreign private-lending to developing countries requires a reduction in perceived risk. This could be achieved through mechanisms for more permanent debtor-creditor 'conversation' and an accepted and effective 'bankruptcy' approach to orderly workouts from unavoidable sovereign defaults. At a time of negative capital flows to the developing countries, Herman fears that current reform proposals, particularly the Sovereign Debt Restructuring Mechanism (SDRM) of the IMF, would increase uncertainty and borrowing costs, and he suggests certain revisions to overcome these problems. Most importantly, however, the author argues that in view of the shortcomings of the SDRM, a premature consensus around it could rob the international system of measures for increasing investor and citizen confidence.

3. Millennium Development Goals and the provision of global public goods

The last two chapters refer to the Millennium Development Goals and the provision of global public goods. In 'Developing a Global Partnership for Development', Martin Khor focuses on the eighth Millennium Development Goal, how to 'develop a global partnership for development'. Khor reviews the need for an appropriate approach to the integration of developing countries in the world economy. He questions the dominant, but eroding, paradigm of rapid capital-account opening and foreign investment and trade liberalization in order to avoid financial crises and dislocation of the domestic productive system. Khor suggests developing countries take a pragmatic approach to liberalization and globalization, that they be selective in order to maximize benefits to themselves. In focusing on international trade and multi-lateral rules under the World Trade Organization (WTO), Khor addresses the problems of commodities, the non-realization of the benefits expected from the Uruguay Round, and problems related to current trade negotiations and the governance of the WTO.

The last chapter, by Ravi Kanbur, 'International Financial Institutions and International Public Goods: Operational Implications' notes that global international financial institutions (IFIs) increasingly justify their operations in terms of the provision of international public goods (IPGs). This is partly because there appears to be support among the rich countries for expenditures on these IPGs, in contrast with the 'aid fatigue' that afflicts the channeling of country-specific assistance. But do the IFIs necessarily have to be involved in providing international public goods? If they do, what are the terms and conditions of their engagement? How does current practice compare to the ideal? And what reforms are needed to move us closer to the ideal? Kanbur attempts to answer these questions within the framework of the theory of international public goods and in the light of the practices of international financial institutions, the World Bank in particular. For the World Bank, Kanbur draws a series of specific operational and resource reallocation implications from his reasoning.

* * *

Editor's Note: These chapters are shortened versions of papers prepared for the Group of Twenty-Four. The full papers may be found on the web at www.G24.org. They represent views of the authors and not those of any government. I am grateful to David Cheney for his valuable editorial suggestions and to Tom Penn and Noel McPherson of Anthem Press for coordinating production of this book.

The Editor

Notes

1 See, for instance, the writings of Amartya Sen, Douglas North, Joseph Stiglitz and Daniel Kahneman, to mention only recent Nobel laureates.
2 Devesh Kapur, John Lewis and Richard Webb, 1997, *The World Bank, Its First Half Century*, vol. 1, p. 4, The Brookings Institution.
3 While the IMF includes nationals from most member countries, there is a longstanding

predominance of nationals from industrial countries among management and senior officials (as listed in the IMF's International Financial Statistics, 26 out of 31 in 1996, 22 out of 29 in March 2001, and 26 out of 32 in April 2003).

4 George and Sabelli 1994, quoted by Miller-Adams 1999, p. 29.

5 See Global Contagion Series 1999, a narrative by Nicholas Kristof with David Sanger, *New York Times*, Section A, p.1, column 1, headline: 'How U.S. Wooed Asia to Let Cash Flow In', 16 February.

6 Fortunately, a more pragmatic approach is now taken by the BWIs on this matter.

7 Countries receiving assistance under the Poverty reduction and Growth Facility (PRGF) must prepare PRSPs, in collaboration with the IMF and World Bank, which lay out their development strategy.

1

THE GOVERNANCE OF THE IMF IN A GLOBAL ECONOMY

Ariel Buira[1]

Abstract

The chapter reviews the elements that constitute the power structure (basic votes, quotas and the qualified majorities) by which the IMF is governed, following the commitment made by all participants in the Monterrey Consensus to increase the voice and participation of the developing countries and transition economies in the Bretton Woods institutions.

It finds that the small economies have been marginalized as a result of the relative erosion of basic votes and that quotas are far from representative of the size of members' economies. As a result, developing economies are under-represented while certain industrial countries, notably those in Europe, are over-represented. It finds that the governance of the IMF does not meet the standards of transparency and accountability needed to ensure the legitimacy of its decisions and the proper use of the resources at its disposal.

Finally, the question is addressed of how the decision-making process can be reformed to attain political legitimacy without weakening the credibility in financial markets.

1. Introduction

Following the commitment of all participants in the Monterrey Consensus to increase the voice and participation of developing countries and transition economies in the Bretton Woods Institutions, the issue of governance has come to the fore of the IMF and World Bank. The Monterrey commitment was renewed in the IMFC and Development Committee communiqués of

12–13 April 2003, and has been reflected in recent administrative steps to strengthen the capacity of African constituencies.

Moreover, since 1997, following the Executive Board's approval of the Guidance Note on Governance, the IMF has increased its attention to governance issues among its member countries. The promotion of transparency and accountability are at the core of the IMF's efforts to ensure the efficient use of public resources, as well as the domestic ownership of IMF-supported reform programs. In recent years the IMF has developed instruments to help countries identify potential weaknesses in their institutional and regulatory frameworks that could give rise to poor governance, and to design and implement remedial measures well beyond the extent envisaged in 1997.

With resources of over $300 billion and an expanded mandate, the IMF is possibly the most powerful of all international institutions. In view of its great influence, two questions on the quality of its own governance arise:

1. How to attain the adequate voice and representation of all members in the decision-making process of the institution?
2. Does the IMF meet the standards of transparency and accountability needed to ensure the legitimacy of its decisions, the ownership by member countries of the programs it supports and the proper use of the public resources at its disposal?

Since the power structure of the World Bank closely parallels that of the IMF, the fundamental question to be addressed, in this connection, is this: how can the decisions of these international financial institutions (IFIs) attain political legitimacy and help secure a greater ownership of economic programs without weakening their credibility in financial markets or their efficiency in attaining their policy goals?

To answer these questions, one must first understand the IMF's voting structure and the rules by which it is governed. This requires a review of the role of basic votes and quotas in the determination of the current distribution of voting power and the requirements of special majorities and how they affect political control and accountability.

2. Votes and decision-making

At the Bretton Woods Conference in 1944 a compromise solution was adopted between two proposed approaches for determining voting power: one that related it solely to members' contributions or quotas, and the other that based it solely on the legal principle of the equality of states. The compromise reached based voting rights on a combination of the two: it gave each member country one vote for every $100,000 of quota plus 250 basic votes. Basic votes, and the voice in decision-making they give smaller countries, were also considered to be necessary in view of the regulatory functions of the IMF in certain areas.[2]

But, with the nearly 37-fold increase in quotas since then, the share of basic votes in the total has declined from 11.3 to 2.1 per cent, despite the quadrupling of the IMF's membership. This has substantially shifted the balance of power in favor of large-quota countries, away from the compromise agreement contained in the IMF's Articles of Agreement that sought to protect the participation of small countries in decision-making. With the passage of time, inflation and growth have combined to increase the size of quotas, but as the number of basic votes has remained constant, small countries' participation in the total has declined; indeed, the basic votes of original members fell to 0.5 per cent of total votes. Today, as a result, quotas ('shares' in the case of the World Bank) are virtually the sole determinant of voting power, and basic votes have little significance.[3] Consequently, the voice of small countries in discussions has been substantially weakened and their participation in decision-making made negligible. The developing countries have advocated the need to increase the number of basic votes to maintain a better balance in decision-making, to no avail.

Box 1 reviews two extreme options for the reform of the 'voting' structure of the IMF.

Box 1. Extreme options for the reform of the IMF Voting structure

One country one vote

Applying the principle of the legal equality of states, which is the rule in most international institutions, there would be no weighted voting; all members would have the same say in the affairs of the institution. However, states differ greatly in size and economic power. Thus, if all financial contributions to the IMF were equal, they would have to be set at a very low level – a minimum common denominator – to be accessible to all members. Consequently, the resources of the IMF would be insufficient for it to attain its purposes, which would further reduce market credibility of IMF decisions. This could in turn aggravate the adverse effect of the inadequacy of financial resources on members needing IMF support.

If, despite members having equal votes, financial contributions were not equal (but, rather, based on the size of their economies), larger countries that make larger contributions would tend to condition these on the adoption of certain policies, as in the case of the United Nations (UN) and several UN agencies and programs, for example UNESCO, International Criminal Court, Kyoto Protocol on Global Warming, etc. Thus, while politically representative of the membership, the one member one vote principle would not permit the effective functioning of the IMF.

Voting power solely determined by voluntary contributions

If a pure market approach were adopted and voting power were based entirely on voluntary contributions, the control of the institution would be in the hands of a small number of rich member countries. Consequently, the system of decision-making could not be considered representative of the interests of the membership as a whole. The legitimacy of IMF conditionality and its other policies, recommendations and regulatory functions would therefore suffer, as policies would appear as unlikely to take into account the needs and interests of smaller members and of potential debtor countries.

Two possible lending policies could ensue:

- If the goal of shareholders with a controlling majority were the pursuit of profits, the cost of lending could be sharply increased to discourage borrowing by higher-credit-risk members or, more likely,
- loans could be made at 'below market' rates of interest, subject to the acceptance by debtors of certain economic and/or political conditions of interest to the controlling members, but not necessarily in the best interests of the borrowers. Of course, the amounts disbursed would be the minimum necessary to attain their policy objectives.

Rather than a rules-based institution of monetary cooperation to which all members could turn to for assistance in dealing with their payments difficulties, such an IMF would simply be a foreign policy tool of the countries in control.

Given the limitations of the extreme options presented in the box, it appears that extreme solutions are to be avoided if the IMF is to attain a degree of representativeness that would provide the necessary legitimacy and transparency, as well as the market credibility required for international monetary cooperation. This requires voting structures with a fine balance between creditors and potential debtors. To achieve greater representativeness and credibility, certain principles seem to be necessary:

1. The institution should not be seen to be dominated by creditor countries. This seems necessary to ensure accountability, representativeness and legitimacy of decisions and a sense of ownership of programs essential to their success.
2. Debtor and potential debtor countries should have a considerable voice but not an assured majority in decision-making. Leaving aside other considerations, this seems indispensable to secure market credibility of IMF-supported programs.
3. Consequently, the total voting power of creditor and potential debtors should be in approximate balance. This would enhance the probability of each case being judged on its merits.
4. Contributions to the IMF and access to its resources should be closely related to the size of members' economies.
5. The size of the IMF should expand in keeping with the potential need for its resources, that is, related to the expansion of world trade and the growth of international capital movements.

3. Consensus and qualified majorities

Most IMF decisions are taken without a formal vote, simply by interpreting the opinion (or 'sense') of the Executive Board. The IMF's Secretary arrives at this opinion by taking an informal tally of the 24 Executive Directors for or against a decision and their voting power. In practice, this often means an additional loss of influence for the many developing countries represented on the Board by a developed country Director, since the Director's position will normally reflect that of his own country or the majority of the votes in his constituency.[4]

The Articles of Agreement stipulate that some decisions require a qualified majority of the votes cast, that is, a particular proportion of votes. At the Bretton Woods Conference, it was initially proposed that qualified majorities should be required in only two cases (one being quota adjustments). The subsequently accepted Articles of Agreement, however, required qualified majorities, either a 70 per cent or an 85 per cent majority, for decisions in nine areas. With the First Amendment to the Articles of Agreement, the number of these decisions rose to 18; with the Second Amendment, the number rose to 53. 40 of these are Executive Board decisions; 13 are Board of Governors' decisions.

The obvious explanation for the increase is the desire to protect a particular interest that might be affected by such decisions, as decisions subject to a qualified majority can be taken only with the consent of the members having a high proportion of the total votes. Currently, the USA has 17.35 per cent of the total vote, Japan has 6.22 per cent, Germany 6.08 per cent and France and the UK 5.02 per cent each. The Group of Seven (G7) industrial countries have a combined total vote of 47.7 per cent, and together with the votes of the Swiss Director, they account for 50.34 per cent. If the votes cast by the Dutch and Belgian Directors which include those of a number of non-industrial countries are also added, the G7 countries' combined vote exceeds 60 per cent.[5]

The concentration of voting power in the hands of the major industrial countries ensures that they have a controlling influence on IMF policies. Nevertheless, some of them have, in addition, sought actual veto power, either for themselves or for a few countries with similar interests. The result is that decisions on 18 subjects require 85 per cent of the total vote, and can thus be vetoed by the largest member country. 21 other questions must be decided by a 70 per cent majority, and can thus be vetoed by the five countries with the most voting power.

Among the issues that the IMF Executive Board must resolve by qualified majority are: decisions on quota size, rates of charge, exchange-rate arrangements, matters related to special drawing rights (SDRs), policies on access to IMF resources, payments to the IMF, use of the IMF's gold holdings and reserves, management of the IMF's investment accounts, publication of reports, remuneration of creditor positions and temporary suspension of IMF operations. Thus, all significant decisions – those related to the size of the IMF and the use of its resources, to SDRs, gold and the international monetary system – are subject to the will of one or a few countries.

Special majorities have been used to block decisions supported by an absolute majority of votes on increases in the size of the IMF (that is, quota increases) and on SDR allocations, sales of the IMF's vast gold holdings and policies on access to IMF resources. The special-majority requirement has often had the effect of inhibiting the discussion of even the important and difficult issues.

Since voting itself is weighted – and favors the industrial countries in decision-making – special majorities should not be necessary. For various reasons, however, the countries that have favored such majorities have not been prepared to do away with them. But even if these are retained, should any one country have the power to veto decisions on 18 subjects in a multilateral institution for monetary cooperation?

4. Review of quota formulas

Since quotas are the major determinant of voting power in the IMF, any review of the subject must consider the appropriateness of current quota formulae in terms of transparency, the relevance of variables included and the weight given to these, and whether their results reflect the relative positions of countries in the world economy.

The discussion of quotas is necessarily complex, since at the time of the Bretton Woods Conference quotas were assigned several important roles:

- the determination of countries' contributions to the IMF
- that of access to IMF resources
- determination of relative voting power

The logic of having only one formula for determining these different roles has often been questioned. As Raymond Mikesell[6] suggests, and in keeping with the well-known postulate of Jan Tinbergen[7] of having one policy instrument for each policy objective, it makes considerable sense to separate the three functions performed by quotas. However, since at Bretton Woods the membership saw merit in having contributions and access to resources based on the same formula, such a far-reaching departure from the traditional definition of quotas might make change considerably more difficult.

The formula developed by Mikesell in 1943 had the political objective of attaining the relative quota shares that the US President and Secretary of State had agreed to give the 'big four' wartime allies, with a ranking that they had decided. Thus, the USA was to have the largest quota, approximately $2.9 billion; the UK, including colonies, about half the US quota; the Soviet Union a quota just below that of the UK and that of China somewhat less again.

The formula produced by Mikesell to determine each country's quota share, was based on: 2 per cent of national income, 5 per cent of gold and dollar holdings, 10 per cent of average imports and 10 per cent of maximum variation in exports, these last three percentages to be increased by the ratio of average exports/National Income (NI)! With variations in the weight given to these variables, and some changes in the definition (e.g., GDP for NI) of the main variables, the IMF continues to use the original formula to determine quota shares, which is combined with four others that give different weights to the same variables. An element of discretion is used in selecting the formulas to be applied in each case for determining members' quotas and other considerations come into play. Consequently, the determination of quotas lacks transparency and over time has become increasingly unrepresentative of the relative importance of member countries' economies.[8]

Not surprisingly (see Table 1), current quotas do not accurately represent the actual sizes of economies, their ability to contribute resources to the IMF or their importance in world trade and financial markets. Moreover, as quota increases over the years have been predominantly (70 per cent) across-the-board or equiproportional, a large element of inertia has tended to perpetuate the initial quota structure. While current quota formulas are difficult to defend by any reasonable criteria, strong vested interests make change difficult.

Table 1. **IMF quotas and gross domestic products for selected countries**

Country	Quota as of December 31, 2002		Share of world aggregate GDP in **purchasing power parity,** 2002	GDP, 2002 Billions of US dollars converted at market exchange rates
	Billions of Special Drawing Rights	As a proportion of total quotas		
Canada	6,369	2.99	2.01	728
China, People's Rep. of	6,369	2.99	12.67	1,237
Russian Federation	5,945	2.79	2.68	346
Netherlands	5,162	2.43	0.88	449
Belgium	4,607	2.16	0.59	247
Switzerland	3,458	1.63	0.45	268
Brazil	3,036	1.43	2.63	448
Mexico	2,586	1.22	1.90	642
Denmark	1,643	0.77	0.33	172
Korea, Republic of	1,634	0.77	1.78	462

Source: IMF World Economic Outlook Database.

The main reason for the difference between GDPs based on purchasing power parity (PPP) and those based on market exchange rates is that the use of market exchange rates substantially underestimates the GDPs of developing countries. This is because in developing countries the prices and wages prevailing in the tradable goods sector are higher than those in the non-tradable goods sector, a phenomenon generally not found in developed countries. As long as the non-tradable sector represents a substantial part of the economy, the valuation of this sector at market exchange rates pulls down the valuation of this sector below its valuation at PPP-based rates. Therefore, to a large extent, the chosen method of GDP conversion substantially determines the distribution of quotas.

Since the weakness of the available PPP-based GDP data in some countries is no worse than that of some of other data used in the calculations, the goal should be to work toward its improvement instead of its abandonment. The instability and large variations in exchange rates introduce distortions in GDPs when converted at market exchange rates i.e. the 40% variation in the €-US$ exchange rate over the last two years. There are very large discrepancies between GDP estimates based on market exchange rates and those PPP-based estimates; but if all estimates have statistical problems and one measure favors one group while another favors another, as a minimum, would it not be reasonable to consider using both and perhaps averaging them?

5. The size of the IMF

The first question to address would be the adequacy of IMF resources relative to the tasks it has been assigned; in other words, is the size of the IMF, the sum total of quotas, adequate to enable it to fulfill its mission?

Recall that this mission includes:

> To give confidence to members by making the general resources of the Fund temporarily available to them... *providing them with the opportunity to correct maladjustments in their balance of payments without resorting to measures destructive of national or international prosperity.*
>
> Article I, Section V of the Articles of Agreement, [my italics]

In this regard, the first thing to note is the sharp decline in the size of the IMF relative to world trade that took place over the last 50 years (see Table 2).

Table 2. **Total IMF quotas as a proportion of world imports**

(per cent)							
Year	1944	1950	1965	1970	1978	1990	1998	2000
Percent	58	17	15	14	9	6	6	4

Source: IMF Report to the Executive Board of the Quota Formula Review Group and IFS

It would seem that countries with the largest quotas, the creditor countries, have opted to limit their contributions to the IMF.[9] And, since the severity of the adjustment required tends to be a function of the amount of financing available, as the availability of financial support has declined, the adjustment process has become more severe and the rate of compliance with IMF programs has fallen.[10] Therefore, the limited resources available to the IMF aggravate the contractionary nature of the adjustment programs it supports.

Moreover, this decline took place at a time when the importance of capital market flows to emerging market economies rose sharply and their volatility made recipient countries increasingly vulnerable to crises of confidence.[11] This volatility gave rise to reverse flows that in turn led frequently to the emergence of financial crises, where exceptional support was required to prevent the crisis and ensuing recession.

Currently, the resources and access rules of the IMF do not allow it to provide sufficient financing to its member countries suffering from trade imbalances or from volatile capital movements. Contrary to the purposes of the IMF, as set out in Article 1 of its Articles of Agreement, neither do they allow members to adjust without resorting to a sharp reduction in aggregate demand, leading to an economic downturn.

As we have seen in the Mexican, Korean and other crises, IMF resources proved inadequate both in providing the support required by countries that come under speculative attack and in allowing them to 'avoid measures destructive of national and international prosperity'. IMF resources have had to be supplemented from other sources, with a resulting increase in complexity, delays and, at times, unwarranted conditionality demanded by certain creditor countries participating in the financial rescue.[12] In most cases, the countries affected have suffered massive currency depreciation, followed by a deep recession and often a banking crisis (the result of a wave of bankruptcies) while their trading partners have faced substantial losses in exports to them.

6. On reforming the governance of the IMF

The governance of the IMF falls short of its own standards and recommendations to member countries in terms of transparency and accountability. Transparency requires that decisions be the result of an open discussion with broad participation. However, policy decisions are often taken outside the country's political process and financial support made conditional on their adoption.[13] Accountability requires that those making decisions face up to their consequences. Although the current rate of program failures is very high (see Chapter 3 on IMF Conditionality), the IFIs are not held accountable to the member countries that follow their policy prescriptions when, due to design failures or lack of financing, the results fall short of those envisaged. On this point Nayyar comments:

> The IMF has almost no accountability to governments in totality, let alone people at large, when things go wrong. Accountability is an imperative without which the IMF could continue to pursue the interests of a subset of the international community, often to the detriment of the general interest of peoples and governments or the collective interest of the world economy.

Legitimacy requires adequate checks and balances, and that all IMF members participate fully in decision-making. It requires that the views and interests of all IMF members, mostly developing countries and economies in transition, be given due consideration.

It is in the best long-term interest of the IFIs that they reconcile countries' own objectives with the wider interests of the international community. This will not happen as long as decisions are made by a small group of industrial countries, the G7, meeting outside the IMF. Furthermore, the current power structure, with a single country in a dominant position, undermines the IMF's accountability for its decisions and recommendations.

Is reform of the governance of the IMF possible? Or rather, to what extent will the IMF be reformed?

Because of its power structure, the IMF is seen by many observers in developed and developing countries as an instrument of control, imposing austerity on developing countries to protect the interests of western creditors. On the conservative side, the Meltzer Report[14] castigated the IMF for fostering moral hazard by bailing out private financial institutions that invested in emerging markets with large injections of money, thereby absorbing the losses arising from their poor investment decisions.

While these criticisms have created a climate favorable to reform of the IMF, political barriers remain. The challenge is, therefore, to overcome the vested interests and resistance of major industrial countries to giving up control, and of some others to giving up certain 'acquired rights', particularly regarding voting power and representation on the Executive Board. Fortunately, senior officials, both in developing and in major industrial countries, recognize that some measure of reform is necessary, indeed indispensable, to secure the legitimacy of IMF decisions and countries' ownership of Fund-supported programs. Indeed, the 13 April 2003 Development Committee communiqué states:

> Enhancing the voice and effective participation of developing and transition countries in the work and decision-making of the Bretton Woods

Institutions can contribute importantly to strengthening the international dialogue and the effectiveness of these institutions.

Reform is also required, among other things, to increase the transparency of decision-making in the appointment of the IMF's Managing Director.[15] It is required to give a voice in policy discussions to certain groups of virtually disenfranchised countries, particularly African and other low-income countries.

The greater participation of borrowers in decision-making is increasingly perceived as essential for the ownership of Fund-supported programs which, in turn, is required for their success. Recent discussions on the reform of conditionality and the creation of an Office of Independent Evaluation in the IMF may be seen as recognition of this need.

The elements of reforming governance

What elements should a reform of the governance of the IMF include? While such reform is a political issue, experience suggests that certain proposals should be addressed if reform is to succeed:

Restructure the Executive Board

Representation on the Board could be regulated so that an increase in the number of Directors representing developing countries is matched by a corresponding reduction in the number of Directors from industrial countries. The region with the greatest number of representatives on the Board is Europe, which currently holds eight chairs, and a vote some 82 per cent greater than that of the USA (while the GNP of the European Union (EU) is smaller than that of the USA). Thus, Europe would seem to be the obvious candidate for a substantial reduction in the number of votes and chairs it holds (see Table 3). Such a reduction, accompanied by an increasing representation of developing countries, would go far to redress the unbalanced representation of the Board.

Another reason for suggesting a reduction in the number of EU Directors is the process of monetary unification that has resulted in a monetary union among 12 countries, which now have a common interest rate and exchange rate policy vis-à-vis the rest of the world. The large intra EU trade had the effect of increasing the quotas of EU countries. Since the adoption of a single currency makes this akin to domestic trade, if Euro zone quotas were adjusted for this, their decline would be as much as 8 per cent of total quotas. While one might think that all members of the European Monetary Union could be represented by one Director, it would suffice to reduce the number of EU Directors to less than half the current number. For example, couldn't

Belgium, Luxembourg, the Netherlands and the Scandinavian countries be represented by one Director instead of three? Could not France and Germany share a Director? This would of course require a reshuffling of existing constituencies.

Table 3. **Quotas and voting power of selected industrial countries in 2000**

	GNI[1] (PPP)	GNI[1] (billion $) at market exchange rates	IMF Quotas (million SDRs)	Votes
Austria	214	204.5	1,872.3	18,973
Belgium	282	251.6	4,605.2	46,302
Denmark	145	172.2	1,642.8	16,678
Finland	127	130.1	1,263.8	12,888
France	1,438	1,438.3	10,738.5	107,635
Germany	2,047	2,063.7	13,008.2	130,332
Greece	178	126.3	823.0	8,480
Ireland	97	86.0	838.4	8,634
Italy	1,354	1,163.2	7,055.5	70,805
Luxembourg	20	19.2	279.1	3,041
Netherlands	412	397.5	5,162.4	51,874
Portugal	170	111.3	867.4	8,924
Spain	760	595.3	3,048.9	30,739
Sweden	213	240.7	2,395.5	24,205
UK	1,407	1,459.5	10,738.5	107,635
European Union	8,864	8,459.4	64,339.5	647,145
USA	9,601	9,601.5	37,149.3	371,743
Memorandum Items				
World	44,459	31,315	212,666	2,172,350
All Industrial Countries	24,793	24,994	130,567	1,347,885
Developing Countries	19,666	6,321	82,099	824,465

1 In 2000

Source: World Bank, *World Development Indicators,* 2002. *IMF Survey Supplement,* September 2002.

In order to be able to give adequate attention to the needs of the countries it represents, perhaps no Executive Director should represent more than, say, 10 countries. In addition, the staff in the offices of Executive Directors that represent more than one country should be increased significantly, in proportion to the number of countries represented. These measures would permit Directors representing large constituencies to play a more active and effective role in policy discussions.[16]

While important, a stronger voice at the Board for developing countries is not in itself sufficient; to be effective it must be accompanied by increased votes.

Revise quota formulas

To improve the proposed formula, overall quotas should be related to world trade and capital movements, or to world GDP. A first approach would be to ensure that the size of the IMF does not fall below an agreed proportion of world trade or of world GDP. Note that total IMF quotas have fallen from 58 per cent of world trade in 1944 to about 4 per cent today. Simply establishing a ratio of, say, 15 per cent of imports would more than treble IMF resources. This would enable it to reduce the costs of adjustment to members, making the institution far more relevant to their problems. Total quotas could be adjusted more or less automatically at three yearly intervals to keep them from lagging behind the growth of the world economy. Additionally, total capital flows to prospective borrowing countries could also be considered in determining countries' potential need for IMF support.

Restore the role of basic votes to their original function

Basic votes should be increased to an agreed proportion of total voting rights and, in future, should rise in the same proportion as total quotas. The increase in the share of basic votes, since it favors smaller members and reduces the relative position of the larger economies, is a potentially divisive issue for the developing countries themselves. To be acceptable to developing countries as a whole, it would have to be accompanied by a significant increase in the quotas of the larger developing economies through the revision of quota formulas.

Use PPP-based GDP estimates in quota formulas

Using PPP-based GDP estimates in formulas would avoid the current under-estimation of the economic size of developing and emerging market economies. This should also help correct their under-representation on the Board. Increasing the stake of developing countries in the IMF should substantially increase their contributions, consistent with their ability to contribute, and lessen the concern of current creditor countries about the risk of IMF lending.

7. Concluding remarks

Since the distribution of power is a political issue, a realistic approach to the quota formula issue might begin with finding an overall outcome that may be acceptable to both developed and developing countries and then work backward to define precisely how it could be reached (for instance, the weight to be assigned to the two components of voting power – basic vote and quotas – that would produce the desired result). While this may appear to lack objectivity, it is probably the only realistic approach and would be far from unprecedented.

Will the EU and other industrial countries that hold a privileged position be prepared to yield part of their power to the broader membership of the IMF and the Bank? There are strong vested interests against, as well as sound political and economic reasons for their doing so. Much has changed in the political map of the world since 1945. As a number of former colonies became sovereign countries, and the Soviet Union gave way to a number of independent economies in transition, the membership of the Bank and the IMF has expanded from 45 to 184 countries.

The structure of the world economy has also changed considerably since the Bretton Woods Conference of 1944. Developing countries now account for a growing share of the world's output and trade, with China, India, Brazil and Mexico among the world's 10 largest economies measured in real terms. Other newly industrializing countries have become major economic players without attaining adequate representation in the IMF and the Bank.

Trade has grown beyond expectations and as official credit flows have declined, the growth of private international financial markets has soared. Vastly expanded international capital markets have created new opportunities, but their volatility poses difficult challenges that the IMF is currently ill equipped to address, except at an enormous cost to the countries themselves.

In the face of the major transformations in the global economic and political order, the IMF needs a more representative and transparent decision-making process to increase its resources and enhance its democratic legitimacy. If globalization is to work for the benefit of all countries, the recognition of the IMF as a truly multilateral institution is crucial. Democratic legitimacy and participation are not contrary to the pursuit of sound policies or the purposes of the IMF.

Appendix

EXECUTIVE DIRECTORS AND VOTING POWER

As of *May 19, 2003*

Director *Alternate*	Casting Votes of	Votes by Country	Total Votes[1]	Per cent of Fund Total[2]
APPOINTED				
Nancy P Jacklin	USA	371,743	371,743	17.10
Meg Lundsager				
Ken Yagi	Japan	133,378	133,378	6.14
Michio Kitahara				
Karlheinz Bischofberger	Germany	130,332	130,332	6.00
Ruediger von Kleist				
Pierre Duquesne	France	107,635	107,635	4.95
Sébastien Boitreaud				
Tom Scholar	UK	107,635	107,635	4.95
Martin A Brooke				
Willy Kiekens	Austria	18,973		
(Belgium)	Belarus	4,114		
Johann Prader	Belgium	46,302		
(Austria)	Czech Republic	8,443		
	Hungary	10,634		
	Kazakhstan	3,907		
	Luxembourg	3,041		
	Slovak Republic	3,825		
	Slovenia	2,567		
	Turkey	9,890	111,696	5.14
Jeroen Kremers	Armenia	1,170		
(Netherlands)	Bosnia and Herzegovina	1,941		
Yuriy G Yakusha	Bulgaria	6,652		

(Ukraine)	Croatia	3,901		
	Cyprus	1,646		
	Georgia	1,753		
	Israel	9,532		
	Macedonia, former Yugoslav Republic of	939		
	Moldova	1,482		
	Netherlands	51,874		
	Romania	10,552		
	Ukraine	13,970	105,412	4.85
Luis Martí	Spain	1,891		
(Spain)	El Salvador	1,963		
Mario Beauregard	Guatemala	2,352		
(Mexico)	Honduras	1,545		
	Mexico	26,108		
	Nicaragua	1,550		
	Spain	30,739		
	Venezuela, República Bolivariana de	26,841	92,989	4.28
Pier Carlo Padoan	Albania	737		
(Italy)				
Harilaos Vittas (Greece)	Greece	8,480		
	Italy	70,805		
	Malta	1,270		
	Portugal	8,924		
	San Marino	420		
	Timor-Leste	332	90,968	4.19
Ian E Bennett	Antigua and Barbuda	385		
(Canada)				
Charles X O'Loghlin	Bahamas, The	1,553		
(Ireland)	Barbados	925		
	Belize	438		
	Canada	63,942		
	Dominica	332		
	Grenada	367		

	Ireland	8,634		
	Jamaica	2,985		
	St Kitts and Nevis	339		
	St Lucia	403		
	St Vincent and the Grenadines	333	80,636	3.71
Vilhjálmur Egilsson (Iceland)	Denmark	16,678		
Benny Andersen (Denmark)	Estonia	902		
	Finland	12,888		
	Iceland	1,426		
	Latvia	1,518		
	Lithuania	1,692		
	Norway	16,967		
	Sweden	24,205	76,276	3.51
Michael J Callaghan (Australia)	Australia	32,614		
Michael H Reddell (New Zealand)	Kiribati	306		
	Korea	16,586		
	Marshall Islands	285		
	Micronesia, Federated States of	301		
	Mongolia	761		
	New Zealand	9,196		
	Palau	281		
	Papua New Guinea	1,566		
	Philippines	9,049		
	Samoa	366		
	Seychelles	338		
	Solomon Islands	354		
	Vanuatu	420	72,423	3.33
Sulaiman M Al-Turki (Saudi Arabia) *Abdallah S Al Azzaz*	Saudi Arabia	70,105	70,105	3.23

(Saudi Arabia)

Sri Mulyani Indrawati	Brunei Darussalam	2,402		
		___		
(Indonesia)	Cambodia	1,125		
Ismail Alowi (Malaysia)	Fiji	953		
	Indonesia	21,043		
	Lao People's Democratic Republic	779		
	Malaysia	15,116		
	Myanmar	2,834		
	Nepal	963		
	Singapore	8,875		
	Thailand	11,069		
	Tonga	319		
	Vietnam	3,541	69,019	3.18
		___		
Ismaila Usman	Angola	3,113		
(Nigeria)	Botswana	880		
Peter J Ngumbullu	Burundi	1,020		
(Tanzania)	Eritrea	409		
	Ethiopia	1,587		
	Gambia, The	561		
	Kenya	2,964		
	Lesotho	599		
	Malawi	944		
	Mozambique	1,386		
	Namibia	1,615		
	Nigeria	17,782		
	Sierra Leone	1,287		
	South Africa	18,935		
	Sudan	1,947		
	Swaziland	757		
	Tanzania	2,239		
	Uganda	2,055		
	Zambia	5,141		
	Zimbabwe	3,784	69,005	3.18
		___		
A Shakour Shaalan (Egypt)	Bahrain	1,600		

Oussama T Kanaan (*Jordan*)	Egypt	9,687		
	Iraq	5,290		
	Jordan	1,955		
	Kuwait	14,061		
	Lebanon	2,280		
	Libya Arab Jamahiriya	11,487		
	Maldives	332		
	Oman	2,190		
	Qatar	2,888		
	Syrian Arab Republic	3,186		
	United Arab Emirates	6,367		
	Yemen, Republic of	2,685	64,008	2.95
WEI Benhua (China) *WANG Xiaoyi* (*China*)	China	63,942	63,942	2.94
Fritz Zurbrügg (Switzerland) *Wieslaw Szczuka* (*Poland*)	Azerbaijan	1,859		
	Kyrgyz Republic	1,138		
	Poland	13,940		
	Serbia and Montenegro	4,927		
	Switzerland	34,835		
	Tajikistan	1,120		
	Turkmenistan	1,002		
	Uzbekistan	3,006	61,827	2.85
Aleksei V Mozhin (Russian Federation) *Andrei Lushin* (*Russian Federation*)	Russian Federation	59,704	59,704	2.75
Murilo Portugal (Brazil) *Roberto Steiner*	Brazil	30,611		

(Colombia)	Colombia	7,990		
	Dominican Republic	2,439		
	Ecuador	3,273		
	Guyana	1,159		
	Haiti	857		
	Panama	2,316		
	Suriname	1,171		
	Trinidad and Tobago	3,606	53,422	2.46
Abbas Mirakhor	Afghanistan, Islamic State of	1,454		
(Islamic Republic of Iran)	Algeria	12,797		
Mohammed Daïri				
(Morocco)	Ghana	3,940		
	Iran, Islamic Republic of	15,222		
	Morocco	6,132		
	Pakistan	10,587		
	Tunisia	3,115	53,247	2.45
Yaga V Reddy (India)	Bangladesh	5,583		
R A Jayatissa (Sri Lanka)	Bhutan	313		
	India	41,832		
	Sri Lanka	4,384	52,112	2.40
Guillermo Le Fort (Chile)	Argentina	21,421		
A Guillermo Zoccali	Bolivia	1,965		
(Argentina)	Chile	8,811		
	Paraguay	1,249		
	Peru	6,634		
	Uruguay	3,315	43,395	2.00
Damian Ondo Mañe	Benin	869		
(Equatorial Guinea)	Burkina Faso	852		
Laurean W Rutayisire	Cameroon	2,107		
(Rwanda)	Cape Verde	346		

Central African Republic	807		
Chad	810		
Comoros	339		
Congo, Democratic Republic of	5,580		
Congo, Republic of	1,096		
Côte d'Ivoire	3,502		
Djibouti	409		
Equatorial Guinea	576		
Gabon	1,793		
Guinea	1,321		
Guinea-Bissau	392		
Madagascar	1,472		
Mali	1,183		
Mauritania	894		
Mauritius	1,266		
Niger	908		
Rwanda	1,051		
São Tomé and Príncipe	324		
Senegal	1,868		
Togo	984	30,749	1.41
		2,171,658[3][4]	99.94[5]

1 Voting power varies on certain matters pertaining to the General Department with use of the Fund's resources in that Department.

2 Percentages of total votes 2,173,313 in the General Department and the Special Drawing Rights Department.

3 This total does not include the votes of Somalia, which did not participate in the 2002 Regular Election of Executive Directors. The total votes of this member is 692 – 0.03 per cent of those in the General Department and Special Drawing Rights Department.

4 Liberia's voting rights were suspended effective 5 March 2003 pursuant to Article XXVI, Section 2(b) of the Articles of Agreement. The total votes of this member is 963 – 0.04 per cent of those in the General Department and Special Drawing Rights Department.

5 This figure may differ from the sum of the percentages shown for individual countries because of rounding.

Source, IMF Annual Report 2002.

Notes

1 This paper draws on earlier work by the author on the subject, particularly 'The Governance of the International Monetary Fund', in *Providing Global Public Goods*, 2002, edited by Inge Kaul et al., Oxford University Press, and 'Reforming the Governance of the Bretton Woods Institutions', in *Financing for Development*, 2002, OPEC Fund Pamphlet Series, no. 33, Vienna.

2 Gold 1972.

3 In the World Bank a majority of the voting rights are vested in a few industrial countries while the principal stakeholders, the developing countries holding a small proportion of voting power provide most of the World Bank's income through the interest they pay.

4 The Articles state that 'all the votes which an Executive Director is entitled to cast shall be cast as a unit'. See IMF Articles of Agreement Art. XII, Section 3.

5 See Appendix.

6 Mikesell 1994.

7 Tinbergen 1952.

8 Switzerland's quota is a case in point.

9 This because of the decline in the size of the IMF's resources despite the high costs of crises for countries that suffer them. I do think it is necessary to enter into a discussion of the 'moral hazard' argument against increasing quotas.

10 Buira 2002. See also Chapter 3, this volume.

11 The volatility of capital flows to emerging market economies is a multiple of that faced by developing countries or industrial countries (see IMF 2001, 'SDR Allocation in the Eight Basic Period–Basic Considerations').

12 Feldstein 1998.

13 Discussing the IMF governance a recent study, Nayyar 2003 states: 'Indeed, its operations and programmes are shrouded in secrecy. The absence of public scrutiny means that there are almost no checks and balances. It is high time that the IMF practices what it preaches about transparency. This calls for a disclosure of information and an independent evaluation of operations. The accountability of the IMF is limited, at best, to finance ministries and central banks, which, in turn, have close connections with the financial community'.

14 Report of the International Financial Institutions Advisory Commission, March 2000.

15 The Managing Director of the IMF is traditionally a European, whereas the President of the World Bank is traditionally an American. There is no valid reason for excluding qualified nationals of developing countries from these positions.

16 The Boards of the IMF and the World Bank approved in April 2003, the addition of three advisors to each of the two Executive Directors that represent a total of 44 Sub-Saharan African countries.

Bibliography

Bhagwati, Jagdish, 1998, 'The Capital Myth' in *Foreign Affairs*, May/June, vol. 77, no. 3, pp. 7–12.

Buira, Ariel, 1995, 'Reflections on the International Monetary System', *Essays in International Finance*, no. 195, Princeton, NJ, Princeton University, International Finance Section.

Buira, Ariel, 1999, 'An Alternative Approach to Financial Crises', *Essays in International Finance*, no. 212, Princeton NJ, Princeton University.

Buira, Ariel, 2002a, 'An Analysis of IMF Conditionality', Oxford University, *Discussion Paper Series*, no. 104.

Buira, Ariel, 2002b, 'The Governance of the International Monetary Fund', in *Providing Global Public Goods*, 2002, Inge Kaul et al., eds, Oxford University Press.

Buira, Ariel, 2002c, 'Reforming the Governance of the Bretton Woods Institutions', in *Financing for Development*, 2002, Vienna, OPEC Fund Pamphlet Series, no. 33.

Feldstein, Martin, 1998, 'Refocusing the IMF', *Foreign Affairs*, March/April, vol. 77, no.2, pp. 20–33.

Gold, J, 1972, 'Voting and Decisions in the International Monetary Fund', Washington, DC, IMF.

Horsefield, Keith J, 1996, *The International Monetary Fund, 1945–1965; Twenty Years of International Monetary Cooperation*, vol. 1, Washington, DC, IMF.

IBRD, Articles of Agreement, 1946, Washington, DC.

IMF, Articles of Agreement, April 1993, Washington, DC.

——, 1984, 'The International Monetary Fund: Its Financial Organization and Activities', Pamphlet Series, no. 42, Washington, DC, IMF.

——, 2001, 'Review of the Fund's Experience in Governance Issues', SM/01/30, Washington, DC, March.

——, 2001, 'SDR Allocation in the Eight Basic Period–Basic Considerations', available on the IMF external website.

——, 2000, 'Country Experiences with the Use and Liberalization of Capital Controls', Washington, DC, IMF Occasional Paper.

——, *IMF Survey*, various issues, Washington DC, IMF.

——, *International Financial Statistics*, various issues, Washington, DC, IMF.

——, 2000, 'Report to the IMF Executive Board of the Quota Formula Review Group', Washington, DC.

Kapur, D, Lewis, J and Webb, R, 1997, 'The World Bank, the First Half Century', Washington, DC, The Brookings Institution.

Mikesell, Raymond F, 1994, 'The Bretton Woods Debates: A Memoir', Essays in International Finance, no. 192, Princeton University, International Finance Section, March.

Miller-Adams, Michelle, 1999, 'The World Bank, New Agenda in a Changing World', London, Routledge.

Mohammed, Aziz Ali, 'Governance Issues in Intergovernmental Groupings of Developing Countries', mimeographed.

Nayyar, Deepak, 2003, 'New Roles and Functions for the UN and the Bretton Woods Institutions', UNU/WIDER, may be accessed online at http://www.wider.unu.edu/publications.

Quota Formula Review Group, 2000, 'Report to the IMF Executive Board', April 28, Washington, DC, IMF.

'Staff Commentary on the External Review of the Quota Formulas', 2000, prepared by the IMF Treasurer's Department in consultation with Legal, Policy Development and Review, Research and Statistics Departments, 6 June, Washington, DC, IMF.

Annex: External Review of the Quota Formulas, 2000, EBAP/00/52 Supplement 1, 1 May, Washington, DC, IMF.

Tinbergen, Jan, 1952, 'On the Theory of Economic Policy', North Holland, Amsterdam.

Woods, Ngaire, 2001, 'Making the IMF and the World Bank More Accountable', in International Affairs, R.I.I.A. vol. 77, No.1, January, pp. 83–100.

World Bank, 'World Development Report 2000', Appendix Tables, Washington, DC.

2

WHO PAYS FOR THE IMF?*

Aziz Ali Mohammed[1]

Abstract

In the context of the financial governance of the IMF, what are the equity implications of the manner in which the IMF distributes the cost of running its regular (non-concessionary) lending operations as well as the modalities of funding its concessionary lending and debt relief operations? While the IMF charges borrowers roughly what it pays its creditor members for the resources used in its regular lending operations, its overhead costs (administrative budget plus addition to reserves) are shared between the two groups of members in a less equitable manner. With the overhead costs rising inexorably to meet an increasing number and range of responsibilities being placed upon the institution – largely at the instance of the IMF's principal creditors by virtue of their dominant majority of voting power – the under-representation of the IMF's debtors undermines the legitimacy of its decision-making. With regard to the concessionary lending and debt-relief operations, some of the IMF's funding modalities have involved a substantial contribution by IMF debtors, sometimes under pressure. While this has been accepted as part of an intra-developing country burden-sharing exercise, it has also meant a significant burden shifting away from the developed countries in the cost of meeting their responsibilities to the poorest members of the international community.

1. Introduction

An important aspect of governance at the IMF relates to the cost of running the institution and the sharing of that cost between the industrial countries

---

* This paper is also published by UNCTAD as G24 Discussion Paper no. 24, United Nations, New York and Geneva (forthcoming).

(the IMF's principal creditors) and low-income countries and emerging market economies (primarily borrowers). Much larger issues of equity are involved with respect to the distribution of quotas (or capital shares) and of voting power in the IMF. This subject has attracted growing attention in recent years. A contribution to the literature by a former Secretary of the IMF from 1977 through 1996[2] concludes that:

> The system of quotas and voting power in the IMF has, over the years, created distortions and lacks equity. A group of 24 industrialized countries controls 60 per cent of the voting power, while more than 85 per cent of the membership – 159 out of 183 IMF members – together hold only 40 per cent of the vote ... The existing imbalance is seen as evidence of the lopsidedness of governance of the international monetary system. Thus a more equal distribution of quotas and voting power between the developing world and the industrial countries should enhance the IMF's governance and credibility ...

Rather than enlarging upon this theme, this chapter takes the fundamental inequity in the system of quotas and voting power in the IMF – and hence in the decision-making power structure – as a given, as a fact of life under which both IMF and its sister-organization, the World Bank Group, must operate at the present time. The focus instead is on the narrower issue of *financial* govern-ance at the IMF, and for purposes of this analysis, burden-sharing is defined to cover equity considerations relating to how the cost of running the institu-tion is distributed between the IMF's creditors and its debtors, and among different groups of debtors. This definition covers a broader set of issues than is encompassed by the existing burden-sharing mechanism in the IMF.

2. Cost of IMF lending through the General Resources Account (GRA)

The financial operations of the IMF are conducted through several channels. The principal channel (in terms of the volume of lending) is the 'General Resources Account' (GRA)[3] through which the non-concessionary transac-tions of the IMF take place. Borrowing countries pay interest on amounts they draw from their credit tranches,[4] with the rate of interest being derived from a formula for setting the *basic rate of charge* for the use of IMF resources. That charge is based on the income that the IMF must earn in order to cover

- the *remuneration* that the IMF pays members whose currencies are used in lending transactions,[5] with *the basic rate of remuneration* equal to the rate of interest on the SDR[6]

- the administrative budget of the IMF
- a target level of net income for addition to reserves.[7]

Based on the net income target, the expected SDR interest rate, projected credit extension and the outlook for administrative expenses, the IMF estimates the basic rate of charge as a proportion of the SDR interest rate.[8] The decision on the rate of charge requires annual renewal, with a qualified majority of 70 per cent of total voting power. For the 2003 financial year (1 May 2002 through 30 April 2003) the basic rate of charge has been set at 128 per cent of the SDR rate.

The IMF's income from charges is supplemented by *surcharges* levied on two sets of transactions. Under the Supplemental Reserve Facility (SRF) – established in 1998 to provide credits to countries encountering capital account crises and under which there are no defined access limits – a market-type rationing device has been adopted. An initial surcharge of 300 basis points (on the basic rate of charge) rises by 50 basis points after one year from the date of disbursement and each subsequent six months to a maximum of 500 basis points. For other GRA transactions, there are annual and cumulative access limits on purchases in the credit tranches and under the Extended Fund Facility (EFF).[9] Since November 2000, however, surcharges have also been applied to these transactions to discourage unduly large use of credit and to encourage prompt repayment. The surcharge is 100 basis points on credits exceeding 200 per cent of quota and 200 basis points on credits exceeding 300 per cent of quota. The income derived from surcharges is applied to IMF reserves directly and remains outside the net income target for the year (which enters into the calculation of the basic rate of charge). The IMF also receives income in the form of service charges, commitment fees and special charges,[10] all borne by the IMF's borrowing members.

3. The burden-sharing mechanism

An upward adjustment to the basic rate of charge and a downward adjustment to the basic rate of remuneration are made for two purposes: to offset losses of income from unpaid charges, and to fund certain precautionary balances designated as Special Contingent Accounts (SCAs). The first of these Accounts, 'SCA-1', was established in 1987 as a safeguard against potential losses resulting from an ultimate failure of members in protracted arrears on the payment of overdue obligations to the IMF. Another Special Contingent Account, 'SCA-2', was established in 1990 as a safeguard against possible losses resulting from purchases made through a special scheme for helping members that had accumulated arrears, whereby they could get back on track under a 'rights accumulation program' (RAP). The allocation of these adjust-ments between the debtors and the creditors of the IMF is designated as the 'burden-sharing mechanism'.

Creditor and debtor members contribute equal amounts, in the aggregate, to the SCA-1, whereas creditors provided three fourths of the amounts contributed to the SCA-2. However, SCA-2 was terminated in 1999 when it reached its target of SDR 1 billion, and the amount was refunded to the contributing members after it was concluded that other precautionary balances in the GRA provided adequate protection against the risks associated with RAP-related credits. The amounts collected to offset losses of income from unpaid charges are also refunded, as and when overdue obligations are settled.[11] Resources accumulating in SCA-1 are to be refunded when there are no outstanding overdue repurchases and charges (or earlier if the IMF so decides).

The burden sharing mechanism raises two equity-related aspects.[12] First, members that are neither debtors nor creditors (so-called 'neutral' members) do not provide contributions under the mechanism. However, the inequity involved at present is not particularly onerous since the 'neutral' countries account for only 6 per cent of total quotas. Second, the distribution of the burden among members diverges sharply from quota shares. The problem has been alleviated –though by no means removed – since 1998, as the IMF has moved to allocate creditor participation in the financing of IMF credit according to relative quota shares for members that are included in the IMF's quarterly financial transactions plan (that is, members with sufficiently strong balance-of-payments and reserves positions).

The quarterly adjustments under the burden-sharing mechanism have been modest to date. In financial year 2002 (ending April 2002), there was an increase of 14 basis points on the basic rate of charge and a reduction of 15 basis points from the basic rate of remuneration to 3.39 per cent and 2.65 per cent, respectively.[13] The Executive Board decided in April 2002 to continue the burden-sharing mechanism. However, it has to be recognized that the risk of loss in future could exceed the capacity of the mechanism because of a constraint mandated by the Articles of Agreement, that is, the rate of remuneration payable to creditors cannot be reduced below 80 per cent of the SDR rate of interest. And if the symmetrical sharing of costs between debtors and creditors continues to hold, the burden on debtors cannot be increased beyond whatever the creditors contribute under the burden-sharing mechan-ism as currently constituted.

4. Additional creditor contributions to burden-sharing

Creditors make an additional contribution to financing the operations of the IMF by foregoing remuneration on a portion of their reserve tranche positions.[14] This unremunerated portion was equal to 25 per cent of the member's quota on 1 April 1978, being that part of each country's quota that was paid in gold prior to the Second Amendment of the IMF's Articles of Agreement.[15] While the unremunerated reserve tranche remains fixed in nominal terms for each member, it has become significantly lower, when expressed as a per cent of quota, as a result of subsequent quota increases. The average is now only 3.8 per cent of quota, but the actual percentage differs widely among members as a result of the differential increases in quotas since April 1978. Jacques J Polak has pointed out that the unremunerated reserve tranches range 'from more than 6 percent of its current quota for the United Kingdom to less than 0.5 percent for Saudi Arabia'.[16]

The unremunerated reserve tranche has featured in past IMF staff presentations on the equity aspects of running the IMF. In a paper on IMF finances to be found on the IMF website,[17] the unremunerated reserve tranche is treated as a contribution by creditors in that the IMF's operational expenses (its cost of raising funds) would have been higher if it had to pay remuneration on that portion of the currencies of creditors used in IMF transactions. The accompanying table shows the figures underlying the computation of the relative contribution of debtors and creditors, including in both cases the respective adjustments under the burden-sharing mechanism. The table starts by excluding the IMF's cost of funds, that is, its payments to creditors, but adds back the *imputed* cost that would have been incurred if the creditors' reserve tranche positions had been remunerated. On this basis, the relative contribution of creditors (based on the total of actual and imputed costs) has steadily declined since financial year 1982 from a peak of 72.3 per cent to 25.0 per cent in financial year 2002, with a corresponding increase in the share attributed to debtors.

Table 1. **Relative Burden on Members of Financing the Fund's Administrative Expenses, Precautionary Balances, and Imputed Interests Costs, FY 1982–2002 1/ (in millions of SDRs and percent)**

	Items in Excess of Remuneration Expense and Cost of Borrowing						Debtor's Share			Creditor's Share			Relative Contribution (in percent) 4/	
FY	Administrative expenses	Net income	Defferred charges	SCA-1	SCA-2	Total actual cost	Charges in excess of net operational expenses 2/	Burden-sharing conribbutions	Sub-total	Imputed costs-NRT 3/	Burden-sharing conribbutions	Sub-total	Debtors	Creditors
1982	153.3	92.1	0.0	0.0	0.0	245.4	245.4	0.0	245.4	641.4	0.0	641.4	27.7	72.3
1983	191.4	65.4	0.0	0.0	0.0	256.8	256.8	0.0	256.8	497.0	0.0	497.0	34.1	65.9
1984	192.8	73.0	0.0	0.0	0.0	265.8	265.8	0.0	265.8	436.4	0.0	436.4	37.9	62.1
1985	224.2	(29.8)	0.0	0.0	0.0	194.4	194.4	0.0	194.4	478.2	0.0	478.2	28.9	71.1
1986	223.4	78.1	0.0	0.0	0.0	301.5	301.5	0.0	301.5	411.9	0.0	411.9	42.3	57.7
1987	190.9	86.0	182.2	26.5	0.0	485.6	276.9	117.7	394.6	349.3	91.0	440.3	47.3	52.7
1988	175.1	49.1	153.7	60.4	0.0	438.3	224.2	107.1	331.3	340.0	107.0	446.9	42.6	57.4
1989	172.7	54.2	224.8	62.9	0.0	514.6	226.9	144.0	370.9	413.6	143.8	557.4	40.0	60.0
1990	188.6	85.5	235.3	65.0	0.0	574.4	274.1	150.2	424.3	502.0	150.1	652.1	39.4	60.6
1991	189.4	69.9	210.3	69.8	142.3	681.7	259.3	181.6	440.9	500.9	240.8	741.7	37.3	62.7
1992	232.2	89.9	190.0	73.4	156.3	741.8	322.1	189.3	511.4	398.0	230.4	628.4	44.9	55.1
1993	263.3	70.6	139.4	78.3	177.0	728.6	333.9	172.1	506.0	342.7	222.6	565.3	47.2	52.8
1994	318.0	74.1	94.1	82.0	161.2	729.4	392.1	139.6	531.7	271.1	197.7	468.8	53.1	46.9
1995	288.3	85.1	96.0	85.2	130.3	684.9	373.4	101.4	474.8	293.8	210.1	503.9	48.5	51.5
1996	301.3	89.3	64.4	92.0	174.2	721.2	390.6	92.0	482.6	271.4	238.6	510.0	48.6	51.4
1997	316.8	93.8	47.4	94.8	58.6	611.4	410.6	82.8	493.4	251.2	118.0	369.2	57.2	42.8
1998	368.5	98.5	48.7	99.4	0.0	615.1	467.0	74.6	541.6	266.3	73.5	339.8	61.4	38.6
1999	392.1	106.7	42.4	107.4	0.0	648.6	498.8	74.8	573.6	243.2	75.0	318.2	64.3	35.7
2000	448.4	267.7	42.4	128.5	0.0	887.0	716.1	85.9	802.0	239.8	85.0	324.8	71.2	28.8
2001	384.6	166.6	48.7	94.0	0.0	693.9	551.2	71.5	622.7	292.1	71.2	363.3	63.2	36.8
2002	530.8	46.2	35.0	94.0	0.0	706.0	577.0	64.0	641.0	148.6	65.0	213.6	75.0	25.0

1/ This table is based on the following assumptions: (a) the Fund's "cost of funds," i.e., its payments to creditors, are excluded, and the table attempts to quantify the relative contributions of debtor and creditor members to financing the Fund's "other costs," which are defined to be equal to the total of the first five items (administrative expenses, net income, deferred charges, SCA contributions) plus the imputed cost of the non-remunerated reserve tranche position; (b) debtor members are assumed to finance administrative expenses and net income (because of the method of determining the rate of charge); and (c) creditor members pay for the imputed cost of the nonremunerated reserve tranche positions (i.e. the table assumes zero holdings of nonremunerated reserve tranche positions by debtor members).

2/ Contribution by debtors through charges in excess of the amount needed to cover remuneration expense and the cost of borrowing. This is equivalent to the total of administrative expenses and net income, excluding income derived from surcharges starting in FY 98, and certain windfall gains from the introduction of a new accounting standard in FY 2000.

3/ Cost of holding the nonremunerated reserve tranche (NRT) is calculated at the average rate of remuneration in effect each year.

4/ Based on the total of actual and imputed costs.

Source. IMF Treasurer's Department

The table does not take account of supplementary charges that are being levied on the larger users of IMF resources. It takes the debtors' contribution as equivalent to *ordinary* charges in excess of net operational expenses, that is, in excess of the amounts needed to cover remuneration based on the SDR interest rate (and the cost of any IMF borrowing). These amounts are not trivial: in financial year 2002, for example, as much as SDR 314 million of income from surcharges was transferred to the General Reserve.[18] This compares with SDR 577 million[19] of regular income from charges (in excess of net operational expense) that is included in the calculation of the debtors' contribution in the table.

The particular approach to measuring and distributing the cost of operating the IMF that is reflected in the table, however, has also been criticized on other grounds. The distribution between the two groups depends on assumptions of how to treat the interest foregone by the creditors on part of their credits. If this is seen as a 'burden' accepted by the creditors, it must also be counted as a deduction from the 'burden' of the debtors. It can also be argued that measuring the debtors' burden on the basis of the excess of the rate of charge over the SDR interest rate overstates the debtors' burden in two respects: first, it fails to consider their opportunity cost (the interest rate at which they could obtain credits in the private markets, assuming that such credits were available), and second, the SDR rate used to determine the basic rate of charge is a composite of short-term rates on the official paper issued by four of the most highly credit-worthy financial authorities in the world. The creditors' share, as calculated in the table, declines in part because of the decline in the SDR interest rate in recent years.

5. Rising cost of running the IMF

Notwithstanding the conceptual issues involved in calculating the distribution of the burden, there is no denying that the costs of running the IMF have risen over time and will continue to increase – both administrative expenses and the build-up of precautionary balances.

The IMF's administrative budget in US dollar terms (in which such expenses are incurred) has risen from $583 million in financial year (FY) 2000 to $677 million in FY 2002, or by 16 per cent over the two-year period. If the cost of capital projects is added, the increase in the same period is 18.6 per cent. The projected increase for FY 2003 is 10.2 per cent, without accounting for capital projects that jump from $61.5 million to $215 million, but the latter amount is meant to be disbursed over three years. Measured in SDR terms and using International Accounting Standards, the increase over the three-year period ending FY 2003 is 30.6 per cent. The annual increases in the administrative budget (even excluding capital projects) are likely to continue in order to meet an increasing number and variety of responsibilities placed upon the institution by the major shareholders, by virtue of their dominant majority of voting power in the institution. Among the new mandates are: the intensified emphasis on financial surveillance; extensive work formulating and monitoring standards and codes; and growing involvement in anti-money-laundering measures and controlling the financing of terrorism. In each of these areas, and under the rubric of poverty alleviation, improving governance, and fostering civil society participation in the development and implementation of adjustment programs, the IMF is constantly expanding the technical assistance it provides to its members, resulting in expenditures that approach one third of its administrative budget.[20]

The second contributor to raising the cost of running the IMF is the imperative to build up its precautionary balances in the face of the increased risks confronting the institution. Among these risks are those associated with the growing concentration of IMF credit, as well as the frequency with which the IMF has been called upon to assist members facing capital account crises. Of particular significance is the large amount of credit extended to a very few borrowers; just three members – Argentina, Brazil and Turkey – accounted for almost two thirds of total credit outstanding in the GRA at the end of 2002, itself reflecting the inadequacy of IMF resources to deal with capital account crises.[21] The IMF will need a substantial addition to its present level of reserves and other precautionary balances, which now total SDR 5 billion.[22] In fact, members have indicated support for a doubling of that level and for the maintenance of the current system of accumulating these balances. Under this the surcharge income and regular net income are placed to reserves and only a fraction is financed – or for that matter, can be financed, given the 80 per cent floor on the rate of remuneration – through the existing burden sharing mechanism.[23] Dealing with these rising costs without placing an inordinate burden on debtors in the GRA becomes the principal burden-sharing issue for the IMF in the coming years.

6. Gold and the GRA

Turning next to ideas for meeting the growing cost of running the IMF, one possibility is the mobilization of IMF gold. The IMF currently carries 103 million ounces of gold on its balance sheet, valued on the basis of historical cost, at a book value of SDR 5.9 billion. There is a 'hidden reserve' element attached to this asset when compared with prevailing market prices (of SDR 26–27 billion). The IMF has been reluctant to tap this hidden reserve in the period following the mobilization that occurred in 1976–80 when

25 million ounces were auctioned to finance the establishment of the Trust Fund to support concessionary (low-cost) lending by the IMF to low-income countries.

During 1999–2000, the IMF conducted two off-market transactions in gold that left its holdings unchanged, in order to generate resources to help finance its participation in the Highly Indebted Poor Countries Initiative[24] (HIPC). It sold the equivalent of SDR 2.7 billion ($3.7 billion) at ruling market prices to two countries: Mexico and Brazil. After each sale, the gold was immediately accepted back by the IMF *at the same market price* in settlement of financial obligations of these members to the IMF. The gold so accepted was included in the IMF balance sheet at the market price of the transaction instead of at the original book value of SDR 35 per fine ounce. However, the equivalent of that original price was retained in the GRA and the proceeds in excess of this amount (SDR 2.2 billion or about $2.9 billion) were taken to the Special Disbursement Account (SDA).[25] These funds were invested, with the investment income made available to finance the IMF contribution to the HIPC Initiative.

The rationale for the off-market transactions was to avoid causing disruption to the functioning of the gold market, but it resulted in a recurring increase in the cost of IMF operations. The IMF holdings of usable currencies in the GRA were lower, and reserve tranche positions higher (on which remuneration must continue to be paid) *than they would otherwise have been* by the amount of the profit (SDR 2.2 billion). This is because Brazil and Mexico paid in gold instead of paying in the usable currencies that would have allowed the IMF to reduce the reserve tranche positions of creditor members. The effect on IMF net income was estimated at SDR 94 million in FY 2001, the first year in which the full income effect of the gold transactions was felt.

While the off-market gold sales were 'one-off' transactions, their consequences for the IMF's income would be of long duration. The relatively large increase in cost would have resulted in a higher rate of charge under normal procedures, but the effect has been mitigated for debtors through the existing burden-sharing mechanism, for example, by requiring members to contribute SDR 94 million to SCA-1. The decision to protect the IMF's non-concessionary borrowers from bearing the full brunt of the negative income effect of the off-market gold transactions (they still bear one half of the cost under the burden-sharing mechanism) indicates a recognition that the burden of helping the poorest member countries (that is, those eligible under the HIPC Initiative) ought not to be shouldered exclusively by other borrowing members, some of whom might be only less poor. It does, however, enable creditor countries to shift one half of the burden that they should bear in meeting their obligations to the world's poorest.

The negative consequences for the IMF's income position of the off-market transactions rule out any chance of resorting to this technique for helping GRA debtors; undertaking straightforward sales in the market would evoke even greater resistance from the interest groups that forced the IMF to choose the off-market route, when the objective was to benefit the poorest countries. Moreover, any transaction involving gold requires an 85 per cent qualified majority of total votes, which gives the USA veto power and allows any small group of large quota countries to assemble the votes required to block a decision.

7. Other proposals for improving burden-sharing in the GRA

If gold transactions are ruled out, the sharing mechanism already in place could be modified. The IMF staff paper cited earlier suggests an alternative on the following lines:

> ... the rates of charge and remuneration would initially be set equal to the SDR interest rate and then adjusted, as under burden-sharing, so as to distribute the burden of financing the IMF's remaining expenses (administrative expense and its additions to precautionary balances, less the effect of the IMF's interest-free resources) on the basis of the aggregate quota shares of debtor and creditor members, respectively ...[26]

The proposal would shift from a 50:50 sharing of costs to 60:40 on the basis of current quota shares between the industrialized members and all other countries, or a higher share could even be assigned to creditors since some major non-industrialized members are also IMF creditors. Recall that IMF creditors had accepted a 75:25 sharing ratio in the case of SCA-2.

The proposal does not deal with the requirement that the downward adjustment to the rate of remuneration must not fall below 80 per cent on the SDR rate of interest set in the IMF's Articles of Agreement. There is, of course, nothing in the Articles to prevent the SDR interest rate itself being lowered below that currently set at 100 per cent of the weighted composite of short-term rates of interest on the currencies in the SDR basket. However, this option has been rejected in the past on the grounds that it would diminish the attraction of the SDR as a reserve asset.

A more equitable solution would provide for the portion of the reserve tranche that would be free of remuneration to be expressed as a uniform proportion of members' current quotas. The proportion would be adjusted periodically to generate an amount of interest-free resources that would permit the rate of charge to remain equal to the rate of remuneration, and the latter, in turn, to remain equal to the market (SDR) interest rate. Thus, creditors and debtors would both receive and pay the market interest rate on their positions in the IMF and the proposal would be robust in the sense that the distribution of the burden of the non-remunerated cost would not be affected by fluctuations in the SDR interest rate or in the level of IMF credit.

This proposal cannot be implemented, however, without amending the IMF's Articles of Agreement. Once the possibility of amendment is accepted, other solutions could also be considered, such as repealing the 80 per cent floor noted earlier. Another possibility would be to apply to the meeting of budgetary costs in the IMF's General Department (of which GRA is a part) the principle already applied in the SDR Department, namely, an annual assessment to cover the cost of operating the IMF charged in proportion to quotas.

8. Concessionary lending

Another aspect of IMF operations bears on issues of burden-sharing, namely, the effort made by the international community to provide highly concessionary financing, outside its quota-funded resources, to the poorer IMF member countries. The basic rationale for this effort is that IMF support for the adjustment efforts of low-income member countries should be made available on financing terms consistent with their debt-servicing capacity.

The first effort was made through the establishment of the Trust Fund, using the proceeds of gold auctions during 1976–80 to provide low-conditionality loans at an interest rate of 0.5 per cent, repayable over a ten-year period, with five and a half years of grace.[27] In 1986, the IMF established the Structural Adjustment Facility (SAF) to recycle the resources being repaid by Trust Fund beneficiaries. These resources were limited in amount, however, and it was felt that stronger adjustment and reform measures than those under the SAF would call for an augmentation of SAF resources. An Enhanced Structural Adjustment Facility (ESAF) was launched in 1987 (and enlarged and made permanent in 1994), with the funds raised from bilateral contributors. Resources amounting to SDR 11.5 billion were raised through September 2001 from 17 loan-providers – central banks, governments and official institutions – generally at market-related interest rates. These resources were on-lent on a pass-through basis through the ESAF Trust (redesignated in October 1999 as the Poverty Reduction and Growth Facility (PRGF) Trust) to 54 of 77 eligible countries.[28] In FY 2002, SDR 4.4 billion in new loan resources were made available to finance future PRGF operations, raising the total loan funds available to SDR 16 billion.[29]

While most loan providers are remunerated at a six-month SDR interest rate, ESAF/PRGF borrowers are charged a concessionary rate of 0.5 per cent. This has required the IMF to find additional resources on a grant basis or by way of deposits or investments placed in the Subsidy Account of the Trust at below-market interest rates. At the end of FY 2002, the Subsidy Account of the PRGF Trust had received bilateral contributions of SDR 2.5 billion.

With the launching of the HIPC Initiative in 1996 and its enlargement in 1999, the IMF established a HIPC Trust, succeeded in September 2001 by the PRGF–HIPC Trust. Its purpose is (1) to enable the IMF to provide assistance in the form of grants or interest-free loans to HIPC eligible countries, and (2) to permit the transfer of subsidy resources from the PRGF–HIPC Trust to the Subsidy Account of the PRGF Trust, in order to subsidize continued PRGF lending after subsidy resources available in the PRGF Trust are fully used. The total subsidy resources required for these two purposes are estimated at SDR 7.5 billion, of which SDR 2.2 billion is needed for the HIPC Initiative and an estimated SDR 5.2 billion to subsidize PRGF lending. Bilateral pledges for meeting these requirements amount to about SDR 3.8 billion and come from a wide cross-section of the IMF membership, demonstrating the broad support for the HIPC and PRGF Initiatives. Altogether, 93 countries have pledged support: 27 advanced countries, 57 developing countries and 9 countries in transition.[30] Most of the contributions from the developing countries, however, derive from the refunds they received from the liquidation of the SCA-2 (referred to earlier), and the contributions of some of them may have been the result of considerable pressure from the powers-that-be in the institution.

The IMF's 'own' contributions, amounting to SDR 2.6 billion, are derived from several sources:

- the net proceeds generated from the 1976–80 gold transactions (mentioned above)
- one-time transfers from Trust Fund/SAF reflows into the SDA
- foregoing compensation for the administrative expenses related to the PRGF operations for the financial years 1998 through 2004 from the Reserve Account of the PRGF Trust
- part of the income from surcharges levied on SRF transactions in 1998 and 1999
- these flows to be supplemented by investment income earned on these contributions.

Of these, foregoing compensation for PRGF-related expenses has a bearing on charges paid by GRA borrowers, since a reduction in reimbursements for

PRGF operations increases net administrative expenditures that enter into the determination of the basic rate of charge. Proposals have been advanced for improved cost recovery for expenses incurred by the GRA initially for running the SDR department and for the IMF's concessionary ESAF/PRGF programs. While the costs for the former are trivial, the same cannot be said for the latter; these are projected at SDR 52 million, or about 10 per cent of the total administrative expenses in FY 2000–01. Hence, the decision not to seek reimbursement for PRGF Trust expenses represented a step increase in administrative expenses that directly raised the charges paid by GRA borrowers.

As noted above, the IMF has already raised the loan resources it needs to maintain a lending rate of roughly SDR 1 billion a year for the next four years through what has come to be known as the 'Interim PRGF'. Beyond the four-year period, it is expected that sufficient funds will have been released from the 'Reserve Account' of the PRGF Trust[31] to establish the 'self-sustaining' PRGF at a level of about SDR 0.7 billion annually in perpetuity.

Less assured is the ability of the Bretton Woods institutions to 'top up' the relief to be made available to eligible HIPC countries to guarantee the sustainability of their remaining debt at the 'completion point'[32] of their poverty reduction and growth efforts. A further mobilization of the IMF's 'hidden reserves' in the shape of its gold holdings has been suggested.[33] But this would require actual sale, not the technique used in 1999–2000; neither approach is considered likely for reasons cited earlier.

9. Summary and conclusions

This chapter has reviewed aspects of the financial governance of the IMF. It has focused on how the cost of running the IMF is distributed between its creditors and debtors in the non-concessional lending operations of the institution through its General Resources Account (GRA) and how concessionary lending by the IMF has been funded. We find the existing burden-sharing mechanism to be deficient in several respects, and conclude that robust proposals for alternative mechanisms for improving burden-sharing would require an amendment of the IMF's Articles.

There are two elements of GRA cost: interest expenses by way of remuneration payments to creditors, and 'other expenses' that include the administrative budget and a net income target for building up its reserves. The basic rate of remuneration is equal to the SDR rate. The IMF covers this element of its cost of funds by setting a basic rate of charge to be paid by debtors on their outstanding borrowing from the IMF as a proportion of the SDR interest rate. The 'other costs' are covered by an addition embedded in the basic rate of charge and through a contribution made by creditors in the form of an interest-free portion of the quota resources they provide to the IMF, designated as the unremunerated reserve tranche. However, the unremunerated reserve tranche, being fixed to a historical base, has meant that the creditor contribution remains constant (or changes with the SDR interest rate) while the IMF's 'other expenses' rise steadily, and along with these, the share paid by the IMF's debtors.

Special provisions under the burden-sharing mechanism have been made to offset losses of IMF income from unpaid charges and to accumulate precautionary balances in Special Contingent Accounts (SCA) additional to the IMF's General and Special Reserves. These contributions are refundable to members who made them when overdue obligations are settled. One of these Accounts (SCA-1) has been built up with creditors and debtors contributing equal amounts through adjustments to the basic rate of charge and the basic rate of remuneration. However, the capacity of the burden-sharing mechanism to achieve a more equitable sharing of the rising costs of running the IMF is constrained by the 80 per cent floor on the rate of remuneration payable to creditors set under the Articles. Unless new sharing mechanisms can be devised, these costs will add ineluctably to the burden on the IMF's GRA (or non-concessionary) debtors. Much of the increase in costs results from an increasing number and variety of mandates imposed upon the institution by the IMF's major shareholders by virtue of their dominant majority of voting power. The corresponding disproportion in representation of the IMF's debtors (mostly developing and transition countries) tends to undermine the legitimacy of the IMF's decision-making.

Turning to the IMF's concessionary lending, the IMF has made various efforts to find the necessary resources for this purpose. These efforts have included two quite distinct episodes of gold mobilization in 1976–80 and 1998–99, and a series of approaches from 1987 onwards to garner bilateral official funding to which developing countries have also contributed, sometimes under pressure. The IMF's debtors have directly provided support by way of voluntarily turning back the refunds received by them from the termination of one of the Special Contingent Accounts (SCA-2), and indirectly through agreeing to decisions to forego reimbursements for the cost of administering the PRGF Trust. The artifice used to protect the interests of gold market participants in the last set of 'off-market' gold sales has also involved a contribution by IMF debtors – through the burden-sharing mechanism – for covering the *continuing* higher level of remuneration expenses that this particular 'one-off' transaction has entailed. While many of the IMF's debtors have accepted these efforts as part of an intra-developing country burden-sharing exercise, it has also meant a certain burden-shifting away from the developed countries in the cost of meeting their responsibilities to the poorest members of the international community.

Notes

1 This paper was prepared as part of the research program of the Intergovernmental Group of Twenty-Four on International Monetary Affairs and Development (G24), with financial support from the International Development Research Centre of Canada (IDRC). It is being published by UNCTAD as no. 24 of the G24 Discussion Paper Series. The views expressed and the designations and terminology employed are those of the author and do not necessarily reflect the views of the G24, IDRC and UNCTAD.

2 Leo Van Houtven, 2002, *Governance of the IMF* – Decision Making, Institutional Oversight, Transparency and Accountability, Pamphlet Series no. 53, IMF, Washington, DC. See also Ariel Buira, 2002, *Reforming the Governance of the Bretton Woods Institutions* in 'Financing for Development', OPEC Pamphlet Series 33, Vienna, Austria, being proceedings of a Workshop of the G24 held in New York, September 2001.

3 Quota subscriptions in the IMF are the basic source of financing for the GRA.

4 There is no charge if a member draws out its 'reserve tranche' (previously known as the 'gold tranche'), which is not considered as a credit from the Fund but rather as the use of the member's own reserves.

5 In addition to remuneration, the Fund must cover interest paid on any sums it borrows from member governments under the General Arrangement to Borrow (GAB) or the New Arrangements to Borrow (NAB). For an explanation of these Arrangements, see IMF, 2001, Pamphlet no. 45 (revised) entitled *Financial Organization and Operations of the IMF*, pp. 72–8. There are no outstanding borrowings at present.

6 The SDR interest rate is a weighted composite of market-determined rates on short-term official paper denominated in the currencies in the SDR basket, namely, the US dollar, the euro, the Japanese yen and the pound sterling.

7 The annual increase in reserves was set at 3 per cent of reserves at the beginning of the financial year for the years 1981–4, 5 per cent for financial years 1985–99, 3.9 per cent for financial year 2000, and 1.7 per cent for financial years 2001–2.

8 A mid-year review is undertaken to establish whether an adjustment to the basic rate of charge is required in view of developments during the year. At the end of the financial year, if net income exceeds the amount projected at the beginning of the year, the basic rate of charge is reduced retroactively; if it falls short of the target, the rate of charge is increased in the next financial year to make up for the shortfall.

9 Access is subject to an annual limit on gross purchases currently set at 100 per cent of quota and a cumulative limit on credit outstanding currently set at 300 per cent of quota.

10 A one-time service charge of 0.5 per cent is levied on each loan disbursement from the GRA. A refundable commitment fee is charged on Stand-By and Extended Fund Facility credits, payable at the beginning of each 12-month period on the amounts that may be drawn during that period, including amounts available under the SRF; the commitment fee is refunded when the credit is used in proportion to the drawing made. The IMF also levies special charges on overdue principal payments and charges that are overdue by less than six months.

11 Cumulative charges that have been 'deferred' since 1986 to the end of April 2002 have resulted in adjustments to charges and to remuneration amounting to SDR 865 million; the cumulative refunds over the same period, resulting from the settlement of deferred charges, have amounted to SDR 994 million. See IMF Annual Report for FY 2002.

12 See Box 7, Pamphlet no. 45, op. cit.

13 ibid.

14 In addition to the unremunerated reserve tranche, the Fund's Reserves and other precautionary balances (now totaling SDR 5 billion) have the effect of lowering operational expenses because they allow the Fund to reduce the amount of currency obtained from creditor members for providing financial assistance to other members. Lower expenses allow the net income target to be met with less income from charges. The rate of charge can therefore be lower than if there were no interest-free resources.

15 As explained in Pamphlet no. 45 (revised), 'The gold tranche was never remunerated historically, so it was natural to set aside this same amount in terms of SDR on this date as the unremunerated reserve tranche'. For countries joining the IMF after 1 April 1978, the unremunerated reserve tranche was calculated as the average, relative to quota, applicable to all existing members on the date that the new member joins the Fund.

16 JJ Polak, 1999, 'Streamlining the Financial Structure of the IMF', *Princeton Essays in International Finance*, no. 216, September.

17 See paper titled *Financing the Fund's Operations – Review of Issues* (04/11/2001).

18 Annual Report, FY 2002 (p. 67).

19 As of 7 May 2003, the SDR exchange rate was 1.399 to the US dollar.

20 Most technical assistance is provided on a grant basis, even though it is no longer meant exclusively for poorer members.

21 If Brazil were to make all purchases under the arrangement approved in September 2002, the Fund's exposure to a single country, Brazil, would rise to SDR 25 billion, or about 40 per cent of total credit outstanding.

22 The recent rollover of large Argentine payments obligations raises questions in regard to this policy.

23 See Concluding Remarks by Acting Chair on the *Fund's Policy on Precautionary Financial Balances* (11/18/02).

24 The initiative is designed to assist eligible poor countries to achieve debt sustainability on condition that the debt relief provided by the international community is used to finance poverty alleviation activities (see 'Achieving Long-Term Debt Sustainability in all HIPCs' in this volume).

25 Funds deposited in the SDA belong to the IMF exclusively and are not part of quota resources.

26 Staff Paper cited in fn. 17 *supra*.

27 Of the $4.6 billion in profits from the gold sales, $1.3 billion was distributed to developing member-countries in proportion to their quotas, while $3.3 billion was made available for concessionary lending through the Trust Fund.

28 The change from ESAF to PRGF is claimed to be more than a change in nomenclature. There is now 'an explicit focus on poverty reduction in the context of a growth oriented economic strategy'. Annual Report, FY 2002, p. 61.

29 With the exception of two developing countries (China and Egypt) all loan resources were provided by developed countries, including five of the G7 countries (the USA and the UK being non-contributors).

30 IMF, 2002, Annual Report, pp. 62–3, are quoted extensively for the numbers in this and the next paragraph.

31 The Reserve Account was set up to provide security to bilateral lenders to the PRGF Trust and to cover the cost of administering PRGF operations. The balance in this Account is projected to be sufficient to cover all outstanding PRGF Trust obligations to lenders by around 2007. Once that point is reached, Reserve Account balances are freed to help subsidize the continuation of PRGF operations.

32 The point at which debt relief provisions are finalized for achieving debt sustainability.

33 See study by Nancy Birdsall and John Williamson (with Brian Deese), entitled *Delivering on Debt Relief From IMF Gold to a New Aid Architecture*, Center for Global Development, Institute for International Economics, April 2002. The study proposes mobilizing IMF gold to cover the IMF share of the cost of deepening and including additional countries in the HIPC Initiative ($9 billion) and the establishment of a contingency facility ($5 billion).

Bibliography

Birdsall, Nancy and Williamson, John (assisted by Deese, Brian), 2002, *Delivering on Debt Relief From IMF Gold to a New Aid Architecture*, Center for Global Development, Institute for International Economics, Washington, DC, April.

Buira, Ariel, 2002, *Reforming the Governance of the Bretton Woods Institutions* in Financing for Development, OPEC Pamphlet Series 33, Vienna, Austria, August, being proceedings of a Workshop of the G24 held in New York, September 2001.

IMF, 2002, Annual Report.

IMF, 2001, *Financial Organization and Operations of the IMF*, Pamphlet Series, no. 45, Sixth Edition, Washington, DC.

IMF, 2001, *Financing the Fund's Operations – Review of Issues* (04/11/2001), available at the IMF website.

Polak, JJ, 1999, 'Streamlining the Financial Structure of the IMF', *Princeton Essays in International Finance*, no. 216, September.

Van Houtven, Leo, 2002, *Governance of the IMF*, Pamphlet Series, no. 53, IMF, Washington, DC.

3

AN ANALYSIS OF IMF CONDITIONALITY*

Ariel Buira[1]

Institutions are not ... created to be socially efficient; rather they, or at least the formal rules, are created to serve the interests of those with the bargaining power to create new rules.

Douglas C North
Nobel Lecture, 1993

Abstract

What is the nature and purpose of IMF conditionality, and is it required to safeguard Fund resources? This chapter reviews these issues and then poses some key questions. For example, can program ownership by a country be made compatible with externally imposed conditionality? To what extent is conditionality of the international financial institutions (IFIs) power without responsibility? What, if any, are the consequences for the IMF of imposing programs that fail more often than not? It looks into the reasons for increased conditionality during the 1980s and 1990s and reviews the recent debate on conditionality. As the number of conditions – in particular structural ones – grew rapidly during the 1980s and the 1990s, the rate of compliance with IMF-supported programs saw a parallel and sharp decline. The chapter also presents an analysis that distinguishes between different types of external crises: short-term imbalances that result from excess demand and expansionary policies; medium-term structural disequilibria such as those resulting from time lags in production (future supply) from investment spending (current demand); and currency and external crises resulting from sudden reversals of capital flows, noting that different types of underlying causes of imbal-

* This paper is also published by UNCTAD as G24 Discussion Paper no. 22, United Nations, New York and Geneva (forthcoming).

ances call for different sets of policy conditionality. It critically examines the new guidelines on conditionality approved by the Executive Board in September 2000, concludes that they are not much different in substance from the previous ones, and offers some specific suggestions to make them operationally more effective. It also addresses the optimal mix between adjustment and financing. It discusses how the economic and social costs of adjustment may be minimized and find that Fund resources are highly inadequate to enable it to comply with its mandate. Finally, it offers some specific policy suggestions for streamlining conditionality and enhancing program ownership.

1. Introduction

Conditionality is perhaps the most controversial of the IMF's policies. Among the traditional criticisms of Fund conditionality are that it is short-run oriented, too focused on demand management, and does not pay adequate attention to its impact on growth and the effects of the programs it supports on social spending and income distribution. In particular, fiscal and monetary policies, the core of Fund-supported programs, are seen as too restrictive, having a strong deflationary impact, to the point where the essence of the correction of the external payments imbalance comes from deflation.

Following the sharp rise in Fund conditionality in the 1990s, criticisms of conditionality have also tended to center on its loss of focus, on its imposing an excessive number of structural conditions and on its trying to do too many things at the same time, that is, expanding Fund influence beyond its areas of competence. The Meltzer Report[2] states that 'detailed conditionality (often including dozens of conditions) has burdened IMF programs in recent years and made such programs unwieldy, highly conflictive, time consuming to negotiate, and often ineffectual'.

Similarly, The Council of Foreign Relations Task Force Report[3] finds that:

> Both the Fund and the Bank have tried to do too much in recent years, and they have lost sight of their respective strengths. Both need to return to basics... (The Fund) should focus on a leaner agenda of monetary, fiscal and exchange rate policies, and on banking and financial sector surveillance and reform.

Martin Feldstein[4] considers that:

> The Fund should resist the temptation to use currency crises as an opportunity to force fundamental structural reforms on countries, however

useful they may be in the long term unless they are absolutely necessary to revive access to international funds.

Feldstein adds that 'The fundamental issue is the appropriate role for an international agency and its technical staff in dealing with sovereign countries that come to it for assistance'. It is important to remember that the IMF cannot initiate programs but develops a program for a member country only when that country seeks help. The country is then the IMF's client or patient, but not its ward. The legitimate political institutions of the country should determine the nation's economic structure and the nature of its institutions. A nation's desperate need for short-term financial help does not give the IMF the moral right to substitute its technical judgments for the outcome of the nation's political process.

This chapter will review the origins and purpose of conditionality, its nature and evolution over time and consider whether conditionality is required to safeguard Fund resources. It will look into the reasons for increased conditionality during the 1980s and 1990s, and review the recent IMF debate on conditionality and the proposed changes in Fund practices. It will distinguish between short-term imbalances that result from excess demand and structural disequilibria and the new type of financial crises associated with short-term capital movements, asking whether different problems call for different conditionality. The paper will discuss how the economic and social costs of adjustment may be minimized and whether Fund resources are sufficient to enable it to meet its mandate. It also lists below a number of issues related to conditionality that merit careful consideration that are not addressed in this chapter.

2. Some unresolved questions on conditionality

Apart from the numerous economic policy issues to which conditionality gives rise, there are a number of important political and philosophical questions that have yet to be addressed fully and openly by the Fund (and other International Financial Institutions) such as:

1. Can program ownership by a country be made compatible with externally imposed conditionality? Can externally imposed policies or values become internalized in recipient countries?
2. Is conditionality compatible with democracy? Can governments be held domestically accountable and responsible for the effects of policies imposed from outside? Who are governments accountable to, their electorate or some external institution in which they are under-represented?[5]

3. To what extent is IFI conditionality power without responsibility?
4. Should economic policy decisions that affect all be taken outside the domestic political process?
5. Are the transparency and accountability of governments, which the IFIs consider essential to good governance, compatible with conditionality?
6. Since the political viability of an adjustment program is related to the depth of a crisis, the actions of the government, and to the amount and timeliness of external support, when can inadequate financial support by the international community be considered responsible for its failure?
7. Governments and IFIs are prepared to intervene in the affairs of third-party countries, but are they prepared to take political responsibility for the policies or measures they sponsor?
8. Since the majority of Fund-supported programs are not completed successfully, what if any are the consequences for the Fund and its staff of imposing programs that fail more often than not?
9. Should capital market liberalization take place before liberalization of the state?

3. The nature and purposes of conditionality

Conditionality may be defined as a means by which a party offers support and attempts to influence the policies of another in order to secure compliance with a program of measures; a tool by which a country is made to adopt specific policies or to undertake certain reforms that it would not have undertaken, in exchange for support.

In the context of the IMF, conditionality refers to the policies a member is expected to follow in order to secure access to the financial resources of the Fund. These policies are intended to help ensure that the member country will overcome its external payments problem and thus be in a position to repay the Fund in a timely manner,[6] so that the Fund's resources can be available for other countries in balance-of-payments difficulties.

Therefore, the rationale for conditionality is to ensure the 'revolving character' of Fund resources, whereby the Fund is repaid over a stipulated period of time, normally three to five years. Under Article V, Section 3(c) of the Agreement, the Fund must examine the member's representation to determine that the requested repayment would be consistent with the Articles of Agreement and the policies on the use of Fund resources.

The Articles also provide that requests for 'reserve tranche purchases' (i.e., drawings that will raise Fund holdings of a member's currency up to 100 per cent of quota) may be considered as automatic and will not be subject to challenge. Additionally, the Fund's attitude to those drawings that raise currency holdings to 125 per cent of a member's quota, referred to as the 'first credit tranche', is generally a liberal one, provided that the member is making a reasonable effort to solve its balance of payments problems. Since 1955, the conditionality applied on the use of Fund resources increases when drawings go beyond the first credit tranche, i.e., when Fund's holdings of a member's currency rise beyond 125 per cent of its quota. These are referred to as drawings in the upper credit tranches and require substantial justification.

At the heart of conditionality lies a process of negotiation; the Fund offers its financial support in exchange for a government's commitment to effect particular changes in the member country's policies. A larger country in a stronger financial position has more numerous financing alternatives, as well as a higher-quality economic team; it is thus less likely it will have to accept policy conditions it does not like. Other things being equal, the greater the asymmetry in power between the country and the Fund, and the greater the country's need, the more likely it will need to accept fully Fund-prescribed conditionality.

Is conditionality intrusive? When a country elects to approach the Fund for support the relation would appear to be a voluntary one, similar to that prevailing in any contract among equals. However, governments are not normally monolithic. There are often differences of view and tensions to be found within them, particularly between the 'spending ministries' and the financial authorities, in particular, the ministry of finance and the central bank. Note that the differences between the finance minister and others may not be merely technical, related to economic policy matters, but may also reflect different political interests and views. The intervention of outside forces, as in the form of IFIs offering financial support in exchange for the adoption of certain policies, may tip the balance in favor of the 'financial' view. The above argument suggests that, although a country may not have to enter into a dialogue with the Fund, when it does, in so far as external elements seek to influence the outcome of the domestic policy discussion, conditionality is intrusive.

Considering that governments often harbor policy differences among their ministries, the support of the Fund for its natural counterparts (finance ministries and central banks) holding the 'financial' view raises the issue of program ownership, i.e., who owns the program? Is it owned by the government as a whole or simply by the finance ministry? Does the Fund seek to further its own views by supporting its allies?

Is conditionality coercive? The answer would appear to depend on the circumstances prevailing in each case. For instance, a country with good access to international financial markets and generally good macroeconomic fundamentals, (say Korea, China or Mexico) will be in a strong negotiating position vis-à-vis the Fund; it will thus not be compelled to accept unpalatable conditions in exchange for financial support. On the other hand, if the same country is in the midst of a deep financial crisis, with a low level of international reserves and no access to external credit from other sources, it may be compelled to accept conditions that, in better circumstances, it would have considered politically unacceptable. However, too often, countries turn to the Fund only when their situations compel them to do so.

Within broad limits, conditionality is a relationship of power. On this relationship, Paul Volcker has stated: 'When the Fund consults with a poor and weak country, the country gets in line. When it consults with a big and strong country, the Fund gets in line'.[7]

Thus, the answer to whether conditionality may be considered to be coercive appears to depend on the asymmetry of power between the member and the Fund, and is largely determined by the country's need and its alternative sources of finance.[8] The answer depends on whether the country has any real options available to it. Indeed, a country facing a balance of payments crisis will often not be able to obtain any external financial support from markets or other IFIs unless it first reaches an agreement with the Fund (consider Argentina between February and December 2002).

Conditionality can be said to be coercive when the cost of not accepting the conditionality is so high that a country has no choice but to accept conditions that make it do things it would not otherwise, particularly as countries have a strong preference for avoiding the costs of default.

At its best, conditionality is a form of paternalism, by which a country is guided to act in its own best interests rather like a parent or a teacher guiding a child. This may appear to be the case more often in programs associated with the Highly Indebted Poor Country (HIPC) Initiative, where certain states lack the technical knowledge and/or financial resources to pursue good policies and the IFIs have both the expertise and resources to assist the country.

The Fund, however, has no particular expertise in the fields of poverty reduction or developmental strategy, fields that are the Bank's primary responsibility. However, it has been unwilling to remove itself from these fields, perhaps to show it has a social conscience. The Fund should probably withdraw from this field and stick to its original simplified mandate, giving advice and technical help in its own areas of competence.

At its worst, conditionality implies the imposition on a country of an alien policy agenda that contains elements not necessary for overcoming the payments crisis and which may have been suggested by a third party, but may not be in the country's best interest. At its best, well focused, limited and technically sound conditionality may make a valuable contribution to restoring the country's external viability, particularly when the economic program is 'owned' by the country. However, there are a number of related issues that merit careful consideration.

4. The rise and fall of structural conditionality

While conditionality has been the subject of much discussion since the Fund's inception, its evolution and the changes to which it has been subject over the last 20 years bear looking into.

The Fund and Bank have modified their lending policies over time, in step with changing international economic conditions and the evolving economic orthodoxies. In fact, in the 1980s and 1990s, a significant increase in the number of conditions can be observed. Kapur and Webb have observed that:

> the average number of (IMF) conditions rose from about six in the 1970s to ten in the 1980s (Figures 1 and 2). In the Bank's case the average number of conditions rose from 32 in 1980–3 to 56 by the decade's end.[9]

The number of conditions continued to rise during the 1990s, with the increase centered on structural conditionality.

Figure 1. **Average Number of Structural Conditions per Program Year 1/**

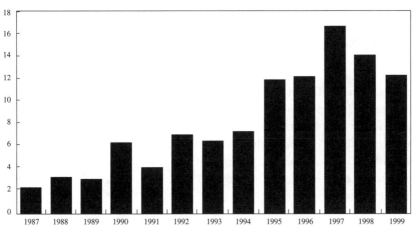

Source: International Monetary Fund, MONA database and country papers

1 Total number of structural performance criteria, benchmarks, prior actions, and conditions for completion of review in stand-by, EFF, and SAF/ESAF/PRGF-supported programs, adjusted for differences of program length.

Figure 2. **Average Number of Structural Conditions per Program Year by Type of country 1/**

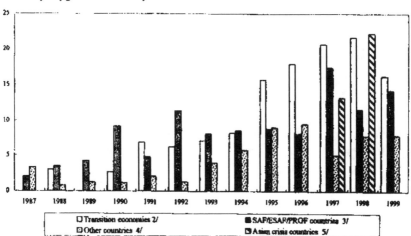

Source: International Monetary Fund, MONA database; and country papers

1 Total number of performance criteria, prior actions, conditions for completion of review, and structural benchmarks per program, adjusted for difference in program length.
2 As defined in the World Economic Outlook, covering former centrally planned economies in Eastern Europe, FSU countries, and Mongolia
3 Countries with SAF/ESAF/PRGF-supported arrangements, excluding tranition economies.
4 Residual group, encompassing programs in countries that do not fall into any of the other categories.
5 Indonesia, Korea and Thailand.

The number of structural policy commitments (prior actions, structural benchmarks, conditions for program reviews and performance criteria) in Fund-supported programs peaked during the Asian crisis.[10] The programs with Korea included 94 structural conditions at their peak; with Thailand, 73 and with Indonesia, 140. In addition to these, a number of other, traditional quantitative performance criteria had to be met: relating to fiscal, monetary and exchange rate matters.

As well as fulfilling an instrumental role in triggering disbursements, compliance with performance clauses or targets also has a double confidence-building role: from the country to the financial markets and from the institution to its major shareholders. As Kapur and Webb pointed out, 'multiplying the number of reforms per loan appeared to increase the reform mileage …that could be gotten from limited policy loan money'.[11]

However, the result of the proliferation of conditions left a lot to be desired. First, there was a loss of transparency and increased uncertainty as to program compliance on the part of the countries and their access to Fund financial support. Would a country that had met, say, 47 out of 60 policy commitments (performance criteria, prior actions and structural benchmarks) be considered in compliance and allowed to disburse? Second, as a general rule, the more conditions in a program, the less likely the authorities felt a strong commitment to, and ownership of, the program, which diminished the chances of successful program completion. Third, the high and increasing proportion of program failures gave rise to questions about having ever more comprehensive and ambitious programs that were not complied with.

The analysis of program compliance since the 1970s suggests an inverse relationship between the number of performance criteria and program success. The reasons for this appear obvious: the greater the number of performance criteria, structural benchmarks and other targets, the greater the chance that some will not be met. Thus, more modest and more realistic programs centered on certain key issues, those critical to economic performance and the achievement of the program objectives, are more likely to command political support and ownership by the authorities, thereby improving their chances of success.

By the mid-1990s, faced with the failure of structural policies to secure such objectives as higher rates of growth, the reduction of poverty and an improved distribution of income, the IFIs rediscovered the role of government. They then sought to improve governance in member countries, in particular through increased transparency, greater accountability and reduced corruption. To this end, in addition to the traditional macroeconomic concerns, both the Fund and the World Bank encouraged reform of public institutions by adding governance-related conditions, including cutting expenditures on arms and strengthening civil society and the rule of law. Since there was no ranking of importance, trying to keep track of so many commitments and variables must have overwhelmed the authorities of a developing country in the midst of a crisis. Conditionality had clearly gone too far and the program results (Table 2) soon confirmed that the approach had become dysfunctional.

5. Does conditionality safeguard Fund resources?

As noted earlier, conditionality is justified as a means to ensure the 'revolving character' of Fund resources.[12] Conditionality necessarily implies a lack of trust in the country's own judgment by those who 'know best'; consequently, the use made of the resources provided by external sources such as the IFIs is to be monitored to ensure that these are not wasted. On occasions, it would appear that the purpose of conditionality is to tie the hands of governments of recipient countries. This would seem particularly true during political transitions such as those in Brazil and Turkey, where strict conditions and careful supervision were added to ensure that the financing provided would be used as intended and repaid on schedule. Proponents of conditionality argue that the mere fact that the country is in balance of payments difficulties shows that it is unable to manage its own economic affairs.

However, considering the experience of other creditors, that is, commercial banks, bond holders and development finance institutions that do not normally require the adoption of an adjustment program by debtor countries, one may well wonder whether conditionality is necessary or whether it is the debtor countries' own desire to protect their creditworthiness that actually secures repayment to the Fund. After all, conditionality ends when the program which it underpins ends, while repayments fall due at a later time; over an extended period of 3 to 5 years after the date of disbursements in the case of stand-by arrangements, and of 4 to 7 years in the case of Extended Fund Facility (EFF) loans.

There can be no question that the resources of the Fund should be preserved for the benefit of all member countries. However, the emphasis placed on 'preserving the revolving character of Fund resources' can be carried too far, giving rise to a conservative bias. This gives priority to achieving a prompt external adjustment to permit a prompt recovery of the resources lent by the Fund, which is inconsistent with the purposes of the Fund, as stated in its Articles of Agreement. Recall that these include the 'promotion and maintenance of high levels of employment and real income and to the development of the productive resources of all members as primary objectives of economic policy' (Article I, Section (ii)). In fact, while the Articles do not provide any indication as to the speed and nature of the adjustment to be followed, Article I's further statement of the Fund's purpose as 'providing (members) with opportunity to correct maladjustments in their balance of payments without resorting to measures destructive of national and international prosperity', Article I, Section (v), clearly suggests that the priority of the founding fathers is to protect the level of economic activity and, consequently, that deflationary adjustment should be avoided to the greatest extent possible.

Nevertheless, countries with Fund-supported programs often perceive these to be unduly restrictive, as the 'preservation of the revolving character' seems to take first priority. This is compounded by the limited Fund financing in support of the adjustment program and the optimistic assumptions frequently made by the staff regarding the availability of external financing.

However, constructing a program around unduly optimistic assumptions on the amount of external financing available to the country, and the limited amount of Fund financing, may put at risk the viability of the program. This may be contrary to the purposes of the institution, which refer explicitly to the maintenance of high levels of employment and to providing members with opportunity to correct maladjustments in their balance of payments without resorting to deflationary adjustment.

One may wonder whether this apparent 'creditor bias' in program design gives rise to the restrictive, short-term nature of Fund-supported programs so frequently criticized by developing-country members. Could it also lead to the repeated use of resources by some members that could not successfully complete the required adjustment during the life of the program?

The argument that conditionality is essential to secure repayment and thus 'preserve the revolving character of Fund resources' is weakened further by the high failure rate of Fund-suppported programs. As shown in Table 2, less than half of Fund-supported programs succeed in the sense of full implementation of the program. Indeed a recent Fund study by Mussa and Savastano found that if you consider the disbursement of 75 per cent or more of the total loan as the test measure of compliance with Fund policy conditionality, less than half (45.5 per cent) of all Fund-supported programs during 1973–97 would meet the test.[13] Furthermore, with the increase in structural conditionality observed in the 1990s, the rate of compliance declined markedly after 1988, and dramatically in 1993–7, when only 27.6 per cent of 141 arrangements could be considered in compliance.

When the rate of compliance of programs falls below half, and all the more when it falls to less than a third, it can be argued that the whole rationale and the relevance of conditionality come under question. Note that, despite the very low rates of program success or compliance, members have continued to repay the loans received from the Fund; this should be taken as evidence that the traditional argument underpinning conditionality is of dubious validity (Table 2).

Table 2. The declining rates of compliance with Fund-supported programs

Percentage of IMF loan actually disbursed under each arrangement, distribution by quartiles

All Arrangements	(1) x<0.25	(2) 0.25=<x<0.50	(3) 0.50=<x<0.75	(4) 0.75=<1.0	(5) Fully Disbursed	(6) (4)+(5) 0.75=<x	(7) Number of Arrangements
1973–7	36.5	7.1	5.9	5.9	44.7	50.6	85
1978–82	19.4	16.1	10.5	12.9	41.1	54.0	124
1983–7	12.9	15.8	19.4	7.9	43.9	51.8	139
1988–92	17.5	15.1	20.6	14.3	32.5	46.8	126
1993–7	27.0	19.1	26.2	11.3	16.3	27.6	141
Full Period (1973–97)	21.6	15.3	17.6	10.7	34.8	45.5	615
of which							
Stand-By	23.1	13.4	15.0	9.5	39.0	48.5	441
EFF	33.3	22.2	19.0	15.9	9.5	25.4	63
SAF/ESAF	9.0	18.9	27.0	12.6	32.4	45.0	111

Source: IMF, Transactions of the Fund (1998).

6. The new guidelines on conditionality

As approved by the Executive Board 20 September 2002, the IMFs new guidelines on conditionality are a highly commendable effort aimed at improving the effectiveness of conditionality, essentially by recognizing the central importance of:

1. National *ownership* of programs, implying the need for involvement of the member in the formulation of the program and the authorities' assumption of responsibility for its implementation.
2. *Parsimony* in the application of conditions, i.e., reducing the number of conditions and focusing them on those measures considered to be essential to overcoming the problem and critical to the success of the program.
3. *Tailoring* the program to the member's circumstances, i.e., recognizing and addressing the factors behind the balance of payments problem, while allowing the policy adjustments and the mix of adjustment and financing to reflect the member's preferences and circumstances.
4. *Clarity* as to the essential aspects of the program that must be complied with, and the additional measures contemplated whose non-observance does not constitute a breach of the agreement that will impair the country's ability to draw on Fund resources.

However, in substance, the new guidelines are not very different from the previous ones that had been in force since 1979. In fact, although the word 'ownership' was not in use at the time, recall that Guideline 4 stipulated that:

> In helping members to devise adjustment programs, the Fund will pay due regard to the domestic, social and political objectives, the economic priorities and the circumstances of members, including the causes of their balance of payments problems.

As regards the number and content of conditions, recall that the 1979 Guidelines on Conditionality underscored the need to limit performance criteria to the minimum required to assure policy implementation. Guideline 9 stated:

> Performance criteria will be limited to those that are necessary to evaluate implementation of the program with a view to ensuring the achievement of its objectives. Performance criteria will normally be confined to (i) macroeconomic variables and (ii) those necessary to implement specific provisions of the Articles or policies adopted under them.

Performance criteria may relate to other variables only in exceptional cases when they are essential for the effectiveness of the member's program because of their macroeconomic impact.

The current Managing Director of the Fund has clearly seen the wisdom of these principles and the need to review and streamline conditionality, particularly structural conditionality. In the light of the sharp fall in program compliance (Table 2), his decision is very timely.

Why were the guidelines revised? In practice, the 1979 Guidelines had been increasingly ignored by the staff in response to external pressures and to the views of some senior Fund officials. They felt that, when a country came to the Fund for balance of payments assistance, they should avail themselves of the opportunity to push for reforms in a wide range of areas, many of them structural, presumably in the belief that these reforms would benefit the country.

The approval of the new guidelines constitutes an attempt to refocus conditionality by establishing a presumption that every condition included has to be justified. It is an implicit recognition that the previous approach had overburdened programs with conditions, which led to a high rate of program failures. Thus, to the extent that conditionality had become dysfunctional, it had to be revised.

In proposing the new guidelines, the IMF's management is displaying a renewed concern for promoting program ownership as a key to success and seeks to give a new orientation to program design. The new approach would establish the presumption of parsimony and restrict the number of conditions or performance criteria contained in a program to those considered critical for its success. The new guidelines reflect an attempt on the part of management to reform the Fund's operating procedures, an attempt to establish a new attitude among the staff, for the purpose of achieving a higher rate of program success.

The intention:

> ... is to change the mindset with which the staff, management and Board consider whether certain structural measures should be covered under conditionality, shifting from a presumption of comprehensiveness to a presumption of parsimony, and thus putting the burden of proof in each case on those that would argue for the inclusion of additional measures under conditionality.

'Conditionality in Fund-Supported Programs-Overview',
SM/01/60, p. 15.

As the new guidelines state, Fund-supported programs should be directed primarily toward the following macroeconomic goals:

- solving the member's balance of payments problems without recourse to measures destructive of national or international prosperity
- achieving medium-term external viability while fostering sustainable economic growth

The 'new' approach to conditionality is a very welcome one. It seeks to address many of the weaknesses and shortcomings of the previous practice that gave rise to failures and complaints. To be successfully implemented, the new approach will have to overcome considerable ingrained habits in the staff. Recall that operating procedures form part of deeply entrenched habits, and that it is difficult to change one part of a self-sustaining system without modifying the other components. It may take a year or two before we can be certain that the inertia has been overcome and the approach contained in the new guidelines has been fully adopted. After all, the guidelines on conditionality were disregarded in the past, so the proof of the pudding is in the eating.

Take for instance, the stand-by arrangement with Turkey of January 2002. The two-year program contains five performance criteria for 2002 and indicative targets for 2003 and no fewer than 37 structural conditions, in the areas of fiscal policy (2), public debt management (1), banking reform (10), public sector reform (16) and on enhancing the role of the private sector (6). Conditions include 18 prior actions, some required for stand-by approval and others for the completion of subsequent reviews. Such wide-ranging conditionality gives the impression of a lack of clarity as to what is really critical to the success of the program. Moreover, if all these conditions are not met, will the Fund suspend financial support? A program with 42 conditions (5 performance criteria and 37 structural conditions) cannot give the impression of parsimony and of keeping to the critical macroeconomic issues, but rather of wide-ranging micromanagement and lack of focus.

Is the Fund again resorting to micromanaging the economy? Are several of the conditions imposed simply the mapping of the detailed steps to reach a policy outcome? This raises the question of whether the practice of conditionality is in keeping with the new policies. Are all the above conditions really essential for the correction of Turkey's payments imbalance? To the extent that they are not, are the same problems of lack of compliance with the guidelines observed in the past to be expected? It would seem as if, when faced with difficulties in the implementation of a program, the Fund sought to gain credibility by resorting to the introduction of additional conditions.

Let us assume, for the time being, that the new Guidelines on Conditionality will be faithfully applied. Note, however, that a major structural problem remains, which the Fund has yet to address. This relates to the mix between adjustment and financing.

7. Adjustment and financing: a shifting balance

The availability of resources is a major determinant of the nature and speed of the adjustment process undertaken by a country. At the extreme, a country with access to unlimited financing would not have to adjust, and if it were to do so, would be able to postpone adjustment for years. For example, the USA, as a reserve currency country, has this advantage as long as holding dollars as reserve assets remains attractive. Moreover, it may choose among different adjustment paths available, opting for one that is more palatable and less costly in economic and political terms. On the other hand, a country undertaking adjustment with low reserves and very limited financing available to it may of necessity be compelled to adopt very severe, short-term programs that conflict with the goal of maintaining high levels of activity, and be compelled to sacrifice some of its longer-term development goals. Thus, there is often a 'trade-off' between adjustment and financing of imbalances. The role of the Fund should be to seek a 'golden rule', a mix of adjustment and financing that fosters the necessary adjustment while avoiding the severe recessionary and destructive aspects of under-financed programs (in some cases, the Fund may be constrained by previous unpaid borrowing). Since well-financed programs are much more attractive than more severe ones, they would encourage the early correction of imbalances.

Since the harshness of a program and its viability are largely dependent on the amount of financing available, the reduction in the resources of the Fund introduces a bias in favor of increased conditionality and more severe shorter term adjustments. The decline observed in total Fund resources over time, measured as a proportion of international trade or of GDP, would thus appear to have required and been associated with stiffer, more demanding conditionality.

From time to time references are made to the 'catalytic role of the Fund' as a means of justifying its limited financing to members. Since there is no reference in the Articles to a 'catalytic role', this is an odd argument for the Fund to make. Nevertheless, the argument that a member's access to the Fund's resources in the upper credit tranches is regarded by potential creditors and others as an endorsement of the country's policies, and is sufficient to induce additional private capital flows, could be acceptable if, in fact, it assured that financing from the markets was forthcoming. Unfortunately, this is not the case. While the Fund did play a role in inducing capital flows to Latin

America in the debt crisis of the 1980s, empirical studies of the catalytic effect conclude that there is little evidence to support its existence in the 1990s.[14]

Unfortunately, as is often the case, when the conclusion of negotiations on a Fund-supported program does not bring forth market financing in sufficient amounts, the program may be under-financed. Indeed, as Bird and Rowlands point out:

> Structural adjustment is unlikely to succeed if starved of finance. The Fund appears to have assumed, perhaps on the basis of partial and, in the event, unrepresentative evidence, that finance would come from elsewhere, catalyzed by its own involvement. In practice the catalytic effect was largely unforthcoming and IMF programmes showed an increasing tendency to break down. Significantly, the likelihood of breakdown appears to vary inversely with the amount of finance provided by the Fund.[15]

Bird and Rowlands add that 'The premise of a universally positive catalytic effect will lead to inappropriate conditionality and will have adverse consequences for its effectiveness'.[16] However, while other IFIs often condition their financial support for countries on their having an agreement with the Fund, a policy that gives rise to 'cross conditionality' and greatly strengthens the Fund's negotiating position, this is not the usual meaning of the 'catalytic effect'.

At times, some observers, particularly in creditor countries, take the view that the hardships of adjustment that result from poor policies are in some sense deserved. It may be appropriate to note that the Articles do not envisage a morality play in which those who err fall from grace and are punished. In any event, questions could be raised regarding the morality of punishing the entire population of a country, particularly the poor and the unemployed who invariably bear the brunt of adjustment, for the failings of a government or for external factors such as downturns in terms of trade, international recessions or contagion and changes in the markets' appetite for developing country assets.

Table 3. **The size of the fund as a percentage of trade and GDP**

Year	1944	1965	1970	1990	1998	2000
Ratio of Quotas/Imports	0.58	0.15	0.14	0.06	0.06	0.04
Ratio of Quotas/GDP	0.04	0.02	0.02	0.01	0.01	0.01

Source: IMF, International Financial Statistics

Could the decline in Fund resources be related to the observed hardening of conditionality? Or, more to the point, can an undue hardening of conditionality be avoided in view of the relative decline in Fund resources? The declining trend of Fund resources suggests that total resources were probably insufficient to allow the Fund to provide adequate support to member countries without a hardening of its conditionality. This begs the question: should adjustment programs be constructed around access to Fund resources? Should conditionality be determined by the availability of resources when these have diminished sharply over time? Or, in keeping with its purposes and nature as an institution for international cooperation, should Fund resources increase in line with its members' needs, in view of the expansion of international trade and the volatility of capital movements?

If the answer to this last question is yes, one must ask: Why have quota increases not kept pace with these trends? Recall that the majority of Fund member countries usually favor quota increases. A quota increase however, requires an 85 per cent majority under the weighted-voting system. What countries limit the increase in Fund resources? Is the growing schism between creditors and prospective debtors relevant for the analysing of trends in the size of the Fund and the evolution of conditionality?

Finding conditionality unacceptable, no industrial country has resorted to Fund support since the late 1970s. The last such occasion was when Italy and the UK requested Fund assistance under the (lower-conditionality) Oil Facility. Indeed, these countries have developed a network of swaps, monetary cooperation arrangements and other sources of balance of payments support. As a result, only developing countries and economies in transition have resorted to Fund support in the last 24 years.

As the size of the Fund has declined and average quotas have fallen to the equivalent of 3.7 per cent of current payments, can IMF financial support be provided to members that is sufficient to sustain a mixture of adjustment and financing and that allows members to undertake a non-deflationary adjustment process, i.e. non-destructive of national and international prosperity? Given the small size of quotas, the answer to this question is likely to be negative.

Moreover, note that as countries become more open to trade and capital movements, their vulnerability to a loss of confidence increases, giving rise to large, sudden capital outflows, irrespective of whether this is a result of domestic policy errors or of external developments. Access limits appear to have been abandoned on an 'ad hoc' basis in dealing with capital account crises in countries of systemic or strategic importance; Killick[17] considers that such countries as Brazil, China, India, Egypt, Korea, Mexico, Russia and Turkey are always a special cases.[18] This ad hoc access policy is discretionary and discriminatory, since it does not apply equally to smaller countries nor does it help them resolve the more traditional type of payments imbalances. Moreover it is not transparent, as it does not allow members to know before-hand what amount of support they may receive from the Fund. Furthermore, at times, such assistance comes with questionable conditions imposed by countries that contribute to the financial rescue package.[19]

The problem of the limited size of the Fund is aggravated by the fact that quota formulas generally underestimate the size of developing country economies, and therefore the resulting distribution of quota shares short-changes developing countries. Their share of a small Fund is made even smaller than it would be if quotas fairly reflected the size of their economies.

As the 1979 Guidelines on Conditionality stated, conditionality is to be non-discriminatory and therefore equal treatment is to be given to all member countries. However, since conditionality is ultimately the result of a negotiation, there is little question that the larger, systemically important countries with access to financial markets and strong economic teams generally have a stronger negotiating position and can get a better deal than small, low-income countries. Indeed, the financial situation of the country at the time of the negotiation is a major influence on the outcome of the negotiation.

Are the conditions and policies required to obtain the financial support of the Fund always essential to the resolution of a country's payments problem and in the country's best interest, or can they be influenced by the political and/or commercial interest of others? At the time of its financial crisis, Korea was required to open up certain services like banking and insurance to foreign investment and to liberalize the imports of certain industrial products, including Japanese cars, in exchange for financial support. Was this liberalization required to overcome Korea's payments problems? Did it in any way respond to third party interests? Major countries have tended to ask the Fund to include certain structural issues of interest to them in program conditionality, despite the injunction in the Fund's Articles (Art XII, Section IV) that members 'refrain from all attempts to influence any of the (Fund) staff in the discharge of (their) functions'. Morris Goldstein cites the Korean and Indonesian programs as cases in point. Eminent economists such as Martin Feldstein and Joseph Stiglitz have expressed similar concerns.[20]

Most Fund policy prescriptions on a fundamental macroeconomic issue are generally sound; for example, bringing stability to a high inflation economy will help restore confidence and improve the climate for investment and growth. However, it is not always clear that all conditions included in Fund-supported programs, particularly the proliferation of structural conditions in recent years, are required to deal with the imbalance at hand, are timely and are unquestionably beneficial for the country in question. Moreover, it may be argued that in certain cases the Fund recommendations have been mistaken. For example, did the rapid liberalization of the capital account and financial markets in emerging market economies propounded in the 1990s always benefit recipient countries, or did it help precipitate financial crisis? Jagdish Bhagwati believes the latter.[21]

8. Excess demand and structural imbalances

When industrial countries face a recession, they normally pursue expansionary fiscal and monetary policies to stimulate demand, as the USA, the UK and others have done recently. On the other hand, with the exception of a few high savers in Asia, emerging market economies are not able to pursue similar expansionary policies to stimulate their economy. Given the volatility of financial markets, they are normally obliged to adopt restrictive fiscal and monetary policies to protect their reserves from a confidence crisis. By pursuing these policies, they aggravate the contraction of domestic and international economic activity. Should the Fund provide financial support to emerging market economies with sound fundamentals in order to allow them to avoid contractionary policies? This seems a case where Fund support could make all the difference. Recall that Article I, Section (ii), on the purposes of the Fund reads:

> To facilitate the expansion and balanced growth of international trade, and to contribute thereby to the promotion and maintenance of high levels of employment and real income and to the development of the productive resources of all members as primary objectives of economic policy.

Should a country facing a balance of payments crisis and a deep recession be required to balance the fiscal accounts at depressed levels of activity as a condition for Fund support? Is this consistent with the purposes of the Fund, or will it simply exacerbate the downturn?

As fiscal revenues decline with economic activity, an economy in recession will normally run a fiscal deficit. Should the Fund distinguish between the cyclical and the structural component of a deficit to avoid pushing the economy deeper into recession? Should the Fund provide support to a well-constructed program that would secure fiscal balance at a modest but positive growth rate?

The conditionality prescribed for the use of Fund resources requires that the member adopt an adjustment program to deal with the external imbalance. This means that the Fund requires the member to adopt measures to restore a sustainable balance between aggregate demand for, and the aggregate supply of, resources in the economy. The policies adopted for this purpose and the particular policy instruments chosen should vary with the nature and size of the imbalance. But since the most frequent situation is that of an imbalance arising from an unsustainable expansion of aggregate demand, the traditional Fund program relies on a demand management approach, i.e., essentially reducing aggregate demand to restore external balance.

This usually entails the limitation of public expenditures and the increase in public-sector revenues to reduce or eliminate the expansionary impact of public-sector financing requirements and the limitation of domestic credit expansion. While this is, of course, the right approach to deal with excess demand, fiscal adjustments required by Fund-supported programs are often unduly severe and thus have an unnecessarily restrictive impact on economic activity and growth. This is often the result of the underestimation of the impact of reduced public expenditure on private-sector activity and invest-ment. Moreover, cuts in spending tend to focus on investment and social expenditures, such as health and education, that benefit the poorer sectors of the population, which undermines the potential for future growth. The reason for this is that governments find those expenditures easier to cut than wages and other current expenditure. Additionally, the deflationary impact of lower levels of public spending may also be compounded by the limitation of net domestic credit to the private sector that programs usually include to limit aggregate expenditure.

Deflationary policies are suitable for dealing with excess demand and may restore external balance, but they are not suitable for increasing supply or overcoming production imbalances. Nor is demand management always the best way to deal with imported inflation. The adoption of supply-oriented structural measures may be successful where large price and cost distortions have to be corrected, as in the case of many economies in transition. However, in the experience of other countries the introduction of structural measures in Fund programs has been rather less successful than was expected (see section below). More generally, the analysis of the effect of Fund programs on member countries shows that while most strengthen the current account and consequently reduce the overall imbalance on the external accounts (which is consistent with the view that the essence of conditionality is deflation), their impact on growth and inflation is not statistically significant.

Obviously, not all imbalances are the result of excess demand arising from expansionary policies. Consequently, a traditional demand-management approach is not the appropriate one for dealing with structural problems where new investment and a reallocation of productive resources are required to improve the supply response of the economy. For instance, consider the investments and the time lag required to develop domestic energy resources, whether hydroelectric or an oil field, which will reduce future imports. Moreover, since such structural adjustments will normally require greater amounts of financing over an extended period than demand management alone, the type of adjustment policies to be followed will often give rise to policy differences and tensions between the Fund and the member country.

Additionally, since the pace of adjustment and its economic and social costs largely depend on the total amount of financing available, the greater availability of financing would allow the country to extend the adjustment process over a longer period. Thus, the nature of the imbalance, the amount of support and the duration of the adjustment process will be issues for discussion and negotiation between the authorities of the member country and the Fund. The answers given by the Fund to these, and other questions embedded in the program, frequently determine whether the conditionality applied in a particular case is seen as appropriate or as too severe and whether the authorities will be committed to the success of the program. The adjustment of an imbalance is not simply an economic problem, but one that will usually have significant social and political repercussions. Its success requires the political commitment of the authorities, and involves technical and political trade-offs.

9. Capital-account crises

In a world of increasingly integrated financial markets and high capital mobility, the loss of market confidence in a country or currency may give rise to a massive capital outflow, causing a severe financial crisis with international repercussions. Consider Mexico in 1995; Indonesia, Thailand and Korea in 1997; to be later followed by Russia, Brazil, Venezuela, Turkey and Argentina, to name only the best-known cases. Abrupt confidence reversals of this sort have created a new kind of problem for emerging market countries and for the Fund itself. At the outbreak of the Mexican crisis, the Fund's Managing Director characterized it as 'the first financial crisis of the twenty-first century', implying that it required a different response from the IMF. However, the Fund response has been similar to that given to any other balance of payments crisis, except that in some cases it has been quicker and the support larger than traditionally.

The problem with this approach is that, too often, it assumes that the crisis cannot be avoided, should be allowed to erupt and should then be resolved by an economic program backed by large-scale financial support. Implicit in this is the belief that a loss of confidence is caused by poor policies on the part of the affected country and can thus be reversed by strong adjustment measures. These assumptions are questionable. Sudden shifts in short-term capital often appear to be as much the product of weak fundamentals as of speculators' appetites for profit and their often-incorrect interpretation of national or international events. In other words, they may resemble more closely the type of crisis modeled by Maurice Obstfeld than the more traditional payments crises modeled by Paul Krugman.[22] The timing of Fund support is of the essence, since a crisis can often be prevented.

It is widely recognized in the literature, including in Fund papers, that capital flows to emerging markets are often volatile for reasons that may have little relation to country risk. These are the other reasons:

1. Exogenous and unanticipated changes in financial conditions in industrial countries. These can have a severe destabilizing impact on capital importing countries unrelated to their policies. For instance, a tightening of monetary policy that gives rise to higher interest rates (as when Paul Volcker raised US interest rates in 1982, pushing the USA into recession and detonating the Latin American debt crisis) and/or to exchange-rate fluctuations may sharply increase the cost or reduce the availability of financing to developing countries.

2. The pro-cyclical nature of capital flows. Capital tends to flow out of industrial countries when economic activity is at low levels and to return to these countries when economic and business prospects are favorable. Thus markets tend to undermine the creditworthiness of emerging market economies.

3. Financial markets are characterized by information asymmetries and contagion effects. Country risk perceptions often respond to 'herding' behavior rather than serene analysis. But once a run is underway, the self-fulfilling nature of speculative attacks can make it much more risky for the investor to resist than to join the bandwagon. Recent episodes of financial market turbulence show that a country may lose its creditworthiness overnight, leaving the authorities little time to react. In a number of cases this sudden loss of confidence may be unjustified. However, there can be no question that the bandwagon effect can abruptly reduce liquidity across the board, disrupt the economies of capital importing countries, and destabilize the economies of a group of countries or a region. The case of the Argentine crisis is the most recent example of this phenomenon.

Failing to prevent financial crises with large and timely support, the current Fund approach seems to imply that the best way to deal with crises is to let them run their course, then to try to restore confidence by an abrupt change in economic policies coupled with substantial financial support. This approach is unsatisfactory because crises inflict great and immediate damage on the affected country: a sharp contraction of GDP; a fall in consumption, investment and employment and a wave of bankruptcies and banking crisis. Thus, every effort should be made to find a less destructive and costly approach, which would be in line with the purposes of the Fund as reflected in Article 1.

Because the flow of capital crucially depends on the confidence of international investors, timely and ample financial support may prevent a crisis. Therefore, the Fund should be ready to act quickly, at the outset of a speculative attack, before the country falls victim to a financial crisis, rather than coming in after the crisis to pick up the pieces. This would not preclude any exchange rate or fiscal adjustments that may be required in the circumstances, but would simply allow these to take place in an orderly manner.

The key to the approach suggested is for the Fund to sustain confidence by providing, in a timely manner, a large amount of financial support. It would thereby avoid the panic, the overshooting of the exchange and other markets and the recession that occurs as a result of the loss of confidence in the currency.

While the creation of the Contingency Credit Line (CCL) in the Fund would appear to recognize the validity of the above argument, the fact that, despite the occurrence of several financial crises in the three years since its establishment, the CCL has not been used by any member country, indicates it has failed the test of the market. Members may feel that Fund support is not sufficiently certain, nor timely and large enough to protect them from a speculative attack leading to a crisis. Given the small size of quotas, financial support that is little more than a normal day's trading in the exchange market, as in the Mexican case, is not likely to impress the financial market. Therefore, the shortcomings in the CCL design should be corrected to make it operational.[23]

10. Conclusion

Conditionality was not always a policy of the Fund. It was introduced in the 1950s as a means of restoring members' balance of payments viability and ensuring that Fund resources would not be wasted; that the institution would be able to recover the loans it extended to member countries. The practice of conditionality was incorporated as a requirement into the Fund's Articles of Agreement only in 1969, as part of the First Amendment of the Articles. For several decades, until the early 1980s, Fund conditionality centered on the monetary, fiscal and exchange policies of members. Over the last 20 years, while the resources of the Fund declined as a proportion of world trade, the number of Fund-supported programs increased steadily. Not surprisingly, the conditionality contained in programs experienced substantial change. The scope of conditionality was expanded well beyond the traditional fields of monetary and fiscal policy and issues related to the exchange system, to encompass structural change in the trade regime, pricing and marketing policy, public sector management, public safety nets, restructuring and privatization of public enterprises, the agricultural sector, the energy sector, the financial sector and, more recently, to issues of governance and others in which the expertise of the Fund is limited.

As the number of conditions, particularly structural conditions, increased gradually during the 1980s, and rapidly during the 1990s, the rate of member countries' compliance with Fund-supported programs showed a parallel and no less remarkable decline. Successfully completed programs, or 'programs in compliance', fell from rates of over 50 per cent in the late 1970s and early 1980s to below *thirty* per cent in the 1990s, when compliance is defined as that which permitted the disbursement of over 75 per cent of the loan and to rates of only 16 per cent if the test of compliance is the full disbursement of the loan. The decline in the relative size of the Fund in relation to needs must have also contributed to the hardening of conditionality.

As a result of the low rates of program compliance, it would be very difficult to argue that conditionality restores external balance and secures the repayment of loans, and that it is needed to ensure the revolving nature of Fund resources. Moreover, as compliance declined, the credibility of Fund programs has been eroded and their catalytic character has become increasingly questionable, which has obvious implications for the size of the Fund.

If conditionality as currently practiced is not effective for 'preserving the revolving character of the Fund's resources', should it be revised? Since conditionality gives rise to many problems and has a number of negative features, the answer is yes. In terms of preserving the Fund's resources, it is worth considering whether the outcome would be any different if the Fund's attitude to requests for its financing were more liberal – say, similar to that prevailing currently for drawings under the first credit tranche, where all that is required for access to resources is that the member 'make reasonable efforts to solve its problems'. Note that first credit tranche programs are characterized by low conditionality and are essentially developed by the member country – and are thus owned by it – a circumstance that contributes to the authorities' commitment to the program. Since the amount provided by the Fund is a small one, phasing and performance clauses are not required in stand-by arrangements that do not go beyond the first credit tranche. Nevertheless, for more significant access to Fund resources, it would be helpful to members to have some indicative benchmarks to guide them in the application of their program over time.

As conditionality has become dysfunctional, its review and streamlining have become unavoidable. In this regard, the initiative of the Managing Director is both necessary and welcome to address the high rates of program failure. The Executive Board has also recognized the problem. Experience and the Fund's own studies show that program success is closely related to local ownership, and that ownership cannot be externally imposed. It must result from internal analysis and discussion, leading to the conviction by domestic actors that compliance with the program is conducive to the attainment of their own objectives. Since conditionality cannot compensate for the lack of program ownership, it can only be helpful to the extent that it fits with the member's goals. What makes for a successful program is the authorities' commitment to its objectives. Conditionality can neither substitute nor offset a lack of ownership.

This suggests that the role of the Fund staff should be more akin to that of an external advisor or consultant. They could help the authorities develop their own programs by helping them identify available paths and policy options when they have the conviction to pursue objectives consistent with the Fund's mandate. Programs, however detailed, are likely to fail when the authorities accept them without conviction as the price they must pay for external financial support in times of need. On the other hand, when the authorities and, more broadly, the society are committed to certain policy objectives, these can be attained without the doubtful 'benefit' of wideranging and detailed conditionality. Although the Managing Director appears determined to streamline conditionality, the inertia prevailing as a result of many years' practice among a generally very competent and dedicated staff may take time to overcome. However, as shown by the new Fund policies toward capital account liberalization, change is under way.

The review of conditionality should lead to increased participation of members in program design in order to secure greater ownership and transparency. Programs developed by the authorities, preferably in broad consultation with social forces, do not require a multitude of performance criteria, structural benchmarks and prior actions to secure compliance. The Fund's attitude to its members should be more liberal, and one of greater trust, akin to what is currently required for drawings under the first credit tranche. The Fund should need no more than a reasonable program focused on the essentials, usually centered on the Fund's core areas of competence: fiscal, monetary and exchange rate policies. Provided the member shows its clear understanding of the issues and a commitment to a sound program, Fund support should be made available. Flexibility regarding the measures to be adopted and their timing should be allowed to permit the member to respond to changing circumstances. This approach should serve members better and safeguard Fund resources more effectively than the onerous conditionality practices of the 1990s that resulted in such poor program compliance.

As Fund resources have declined steadily over the last half century in relation to all relevant variables (trade, GDP and capital flows), and in the absence of other sources of finance, the mix between adjustment and financing, a major determinant of program success, has shifted toward less financing and more severe adjustment. Obviously, this discourages countries from coming to the Fund at an early stage of their imbalances, and must both contribute to the lack of program ownership, and be responsible for the high rate of program failures.

The changing conditions of the international economy and the recurrence of financial crises call for a review of the resources of the Fund and of the nature and character of its operations. The Fund's own governance and members' contributions and participation in decision-making should also be revised to secure the adequacy of its resources so that it can fulfill the role it is mandated to play in avoiding the recessionary adjustment that is 'destructive of national or international prosperity'.

Appendix I

THE ORIGINS OF CONDITIONALITY

When the IMF was established as an institution for monetary cooperation there was no reference to conditionality. Indeed, the concept of conditionality did not appear in the original Articles of Agreement. This concept was not to be introduced until several years later, in an Executive Board decision in 1952 and much later incorporated in the Articles, as part of the First Amendment.

Writing in January 1944, before the Bretton Woods Conference, Lord Maynard Keynes described the views of the US government on the future character of the IMF as follows:

> In their eyes it should have wide discretionary powers and should exercise something of the same grandmotherly influence and control over the central banks of member countries, that these central banks in turn are accustomed to exercise over the other banks within their own countries.

The US delegation was well aware that, as the countries of Europe embarked on their postwar reconstruction, the USA would be the only substantial net creditor to the Fund for some time to come. On the other hand, the UK negotiators were under explicit instructions from Winston Churchill's War Cabinet that a deficit country should not be required to introduce:

> a deflationary policy, enforced by dear money and similar measures, having the effect of causing unemployment; for this would amount to restoring, subject to insufficient safeguards, the evils of the old automatic gold standard.[24]

Keynes believed that as a result of the Anglo-American discussions on this and related matters:

> the American representatives were persuaded of the unacceptability of such a scheme of things, of the undesirability of giving so much authority to an untried institution, and of the importance of giving the member

countries as much certainty as possible about what they had to expect from the new institution and about the amount of facilities which would be at their disposal.[25]

Keynes believed he had gained agreement for the view that the Fund should 'be entirely passive in all normal circumstances, the right of initiative being reserved to the central banks of the member countries'.

The link between a member's policies and the access to Fund resources was adopted by an Executive Board decision in 1952. These concepts were to be incorporated in Article I Section (v) and Article V Section 3(a) of the Articles of Agreement in 1969, at the time of the First Amendment. The amendments by which conditionality was introduced into the Articles began with the reference to its 'temporary' use in Article I. Thus, the fifth purpose of the Fund was amended to read:

> To give confidence to members by making the Fund's resource *temporarily* available to them under adequate safeguards, thus providing them with opportunity to correct maladjustments in their balance of payments without resorting to measures destructive of national or international prosperity.

The last sentence of Article I was changed to read: 'The Fund shall be guided in all its *policies and* decisions by the purposes of this Article'.

The words in italics are the additions to the text introduced in the first amendment. These conceptual additions were reflected and given operational content by the two subsections added to Article V, Section 3, entitled 'Conditions governing use of Fund resources'. Specifically, the addition reads:

> (c) A member's use of the resources of the Fund shall be in accordance with the purposes of the Fund. The Fund shall adopt policies on the use of its resources that will assist members to solve their balance of payments problems in a manner consistent with the purposes of the Fund and that will establish adequate safeguards for the temporary use of its resources.
>
> (d) A representation by a member under (a) above shall be examined by the Fund to determine whether the proposed purchase would be consistent with the provisions of this Agreement and with the policies adopted under them, with the exception that proposed gold tranche purchases shall not be subject to challenge.

The new subsections state that the Fund must have policies based on the principle of conditionality and that all representations made by members, in connection with requests to use the resources of the Fund beyond the reserve (gold) tranche, must be examined and found to be consistent with those policies.

In the discussions in Atlantic City in June 1944, prior to the Bretton Woods conference, the US delegates raised the subject of requiring member countries that requested financial support to give certain policy undertakings to the Fund, which would decide whether the currency purchase was consistent with the purposes of the Fund; this notion was strongly rejected. Virtually all other countries believed that access to Fund resources should be automatic and unchallenged.

Moreover, they felt that Fund intrusion into their internal affairs would be intolerable. Within the prescribed limits, the decision to purchase foreign currency in exchange for the country's own currency could not be challenged; the role of the Fund should be strictly limited. Thus, by the time of the 1944 conference, since the two amendments that had been proposed by the US delegation had been dropped, this matter appeared settled and, since it was not even raised by the US delegation, was not discussed further. Consequently, the original Articles contained no statement that the Fund had to adopt policies on the use of its resources and thus the member country was entitled to make purchases provided that 'it represents that it is presently needed for making in that currency payments which are consistent with the provisions of this Agreement' (Article V Section 3(a)).

Even in the US conception, the Fund was not to interfere in a member country's domestic policies. A valuable insight into US thinking to this effect is provided by a statement by Harry Dexter White in October 1943: 'The Fund's facilities should not be used to finance either a flight of capital or the issue of foreign loans by a country which could not afford to undertake foreign lending'. Again, the Fund would be justified in intervening where a country was using its quota for rearmament. On the other hand, it would not be justified in the case of an unbalanced budget. In general, the Fund would intervene only in extreme cases of violation of qualitative rules and would bear the burden of proof.[26]

As Article IV, Section 5(f) of the original Articles of Agreement stated, as long as the Fund was satisfied that a change in par value of a particular member's currency was necessary to correct a fundamental disequilibrium, 'it shall not object to a proposed change because of the domestic social or political policies of the member proposing the change'. This wording makes clear that the intention of the Agreement as a whole was to preclude Fund interference with domestic policies having social objectives such as the subsidization of food or other essential consumption goods for the protection of low income groups'.[27]

While the USA had lost the battle for giving the Fund supervisory functions, it would not agree to the use of Fund resources without certain additional safeguards. 'The Europeans had the best of the argument, perhaps, but it was the United States that had the resources, and it was the resources that counted, especially in the immediate aftermath of World War II'.[28]

Therefore, it was the need to obtain the financial support and cooperation of the USA that on 13 February 1952, after a number of years of very limited Fund operations, persuaded the Executive Board to accept a proposal by the Managing Director embodying the US concept of conditionality by which:

> ... the task of the Fund is to help members that need temporary help, and requests should be expected from members that are in trouble in a greater or lesser degree. The Fund's attitude toward the position of each member should turn on *whether the problem is of a temporary nature and whether the policies the member will pursue will be adequate to overcome. the problem within such a period. The policies, above all, should determine the Fund's attitude.*' [29]

And additionally:

> ...considering especially the necessity for ensuring the *revolving character of the Fund's resources, exchange purchased from the Fund should not remain outstanding beyond the period reasonably related to the payments problem for which it was purchased from the Fund. The period should fall within an outside range of three to five years.* Members will be expected not to request the purchase of exchange from the Fund in circumstances where the reduction of the Fund's holdings of their currencies by an equivalent amount within that period cannot reasonably be envisaged.'[30]

Appendix II

THE RISE OF STRUCTURAL CONDITIONALITY

Consider the factors behind this explosion of conditionality. Since the early 1980s, as the Thatcher and Reagan doctrines gained ascendancy in the UK and USA, both institutions adopted a more neoliberal economic stance and increasingly favored policies aimed at reducing the role of the state, reducing or eliminating subsidies and of market liberalization and privatization of public enterprises. These views were to be translated into a new type of structural conditionality which, aiming at these goals, was superimposed on the more traditional macroeconomic conditionality. According to former Managing Director Michel Camdessus, the goals included:

> financial market operations organized around objective financial criteria, transparency in industrial conglomerates and in government business relations more generally, the dismantling of monopolies, and the elimination of government-directed lending and procurement programs.

Although this characterization does not describe the history of any industrial country, it reflected the vision of a global market system increasingly advocated by the US business sector and government from the 1970s.

But the change in the conditionality of the International Financial Institutions appears as the result of the combination of several other factors, including:

1) The limited (declining in relation to demand) financial resources of development finance institutions, which reflected a policy shift of major industrial countries away from the provision of public financing to developing countries and in favor of a policy aimed at the 'graduation' of middle-income countries to private financing, a shift that had begun in the late 1970s. This signified that programs and loan requests had to give prominence to purely economic and financial results to satisfy financial markets.

2) The rise of supply-side economics, the precursor of structural adjustment, in the USA. While initially resisted by many developing countries in the early 1980s, policymakers in these countries became convinced over time that there was no alternative to increased reliance on market financing. Moreover, as structural conditionality seemed to match what financial markets required to have confidence in borrowers, it was gradually accepted.

3) A conversion of national authorities in a number of developing countries to the new economic orthodoxy as 'technocrats', usually US-trained economists who favored market liberalization and a smaller role for the state, gained ascendancy in many developing country governments.

4) The Brady Plan that conditioned external debt reductions to policy adjustment programs, emphasizing changes in economic structures as well as macroeconomic balances.

5) The criticism of Fund-supported programs by developing country representatives as too restrictive and demand-oriented and insufficiently concerned with economic growth, which led the Fund to place emphasis on the structural changes 'required' by long-term growth. This became apparent in the Structural Adjustment Facility (SAF), created in 1986, which required applicant low-income countries to submit a three-year program 'to correct macroeconomic and structural problems that have impeded balance-of-payments adjustment and economic growth'. The Enhanced Structural Adjustment Facility (ESAF), established a year later, included similar requirements.[31]

6) The revised Article IV giving the Fund expanded surveillance responsibilities in missions to members that made the staff and Board more aware of structural issues, particularly when these appeared to have a bearing on balance of payments problems.

7) The major structural problems faced by the economies in transition and the far-reaching transformations these countries required to establish market economies.

8) The emergence of the Asian crisis, which led to the proliferation of norms and standards in a number of fields.

Notes

1 This paper was prepared as part of the research program of the Intergovernmental Group of Twenty-Four on International Monetary Affairs and Development (G24), with financial support from the International Development Research Centre of Canada (IDRC). It was first published by UNCTAD as part of the G24 Discussion Paper Series. The views expressed in this paper are strictly personal.

2 The Meltzer Report, 2000.

3 The Council of Foreign Relations Task Force Report, 1999.

4 Feldstein 1998.

5 Buira 2001.

6 See Appendix I.

7 Volcker and Gyoten 1992.

8 Collingwood 2001.

9 Kapur and Webb 2000.

10 Kapur states that, 'There is an understandable skepticism that rich countries are long on norms when they are short on resources, and the increasing resort to norms of governance even as development budgets decline is perhaps not entirely coincidental. As long as the cold war was on, "crony capitalism" in Indonesia was not considered a problem. Nor was it a problem while the East Asian "miracle" was being trumpeted. But when the Asia crisis of 1997–8 erupted, norms of corporate governance were strenuously advanced to deflect attention from broader issues of the nature and quality of international financial regulation'. See D Kapur, 'Processes of Change in International Organization', paper prepared for UN/WIDER n.d.

11 Kapur and Webb 1997.

12 See Appendix I.

13 Mussa and Savastano 2000.

14 See Bird and Rowlands 1997.

15 op. cit.

16 op. cit.

17 See Killick 1998.

18 The staff has had to learn that some countries are more equal than others. But few staff members have taken their objection to political pressures to the point of resignation as did David Finch, the former Director of the Exchange and Trade Relations Dept. who resigned when pressed to reduce conditionality for political reasons (*Financial Times*, 21 March 1987, 'IMF Silent on Resignation').

19 Feldstein 1998.

20 Goldstein 2000.

21 Bhagwati 1998.

22 Krugman 1979; Obstfeld 1986, 1995.

23 Buira 1999.

24 Moggridge 1980.

25 op. cit.

26 Horsefield 1969.

27 Dell 1981.

28 op. cit.

29 Decision no. 10 (52/11), para. 1, emphasis added.

30 op. cit. para. 2, emphasis added.

31 IMF Decision no. 8240-(86/56) SAF, 26 March 1986, see Selected Decisions and Selected Documents of the IMF.

Bibliography

Bhagwati, Jagdish, 1988, 'The Capital Myth', in *Foreign Affairs*, May/June, vol. 77, no.3, pp. 7–12.

Bird, G and Rowlands, Dane, 1977, 'The Catalytic Effect of Lending by the International Financial Institutions', *The World Economy*, vol. 20, no. 7, November.

——, 2001, 'World Bank Lending and Other Financial Flows: Is There a Connection?', *The Journal of Development Studies*, vol. 37, no. 5, June.

Boughton, James M, 1997, 'From Suez to Tequila: The Fund as Crises Manager', IMF Working Paper no. 97/90, Washington, DC, International Monetary Fund, November.

Buira, Ariel, 1999, 'An Alternative Approach to Financial Crises,' *Essays in International Finance*, no. 212, Princeton, NJ, Princeton University, International Finance Section, February.

——, 1983, 'IMF Financial Programs and Conditionality,' *Journal of Development Economics*, pp. 111–36, North Holland Publishing Company.

Collingwood, Vivien, 2001, 'Between Consensus and Coercion: Defining the Parameters of Political Conditionality', M Phil Thesis, unpublished, Christ Church, Oxford.

Dell, Sidney, 1981, 'On Being Grandmotherly: The Evolution of IMF Conditionality', *Essays in International Finance*, no. 144, Princeton, NJ, Princeton University, International Finance Section, October.

Feldstein, Martin, 1998, 'Refocusing the IMF', in *Foreign Affairs*, March/April, vol.77, no. 2, pp. 20–33.

Goldstein, Morris, 2000, 'IMF Structural Programs', paper prepared for NBER Conference on Economic and Financial Crises in Emerging Markets, Woodstock, Vermont, 19–22 October, Revised December, Institute for International Economics, Washington, DC.

Guitian, Manuel, 1995, 'Past, Present, Future', *IMF Staff Papers 42*, no.4, pp. 792–835.

IMF 'Articles of Agreement', 1993, International Monetary Fund, April, Washington, DC.

——, 2001, 'Conditionality in Fund-supported Programs', Policy Issues SM/01/60, and Supplements 1 and 2, February, Washington, DC.

——, 2001, 'Conditionality in Fund-supported Programs, External Consultations', SM/01/219, Supplements 1 and 2, July, Washington, DC.

——, 2002, 'IMF Reviews its Approach to Conditionality, Emphasizes Country Ownership of Reforms', IMF Survey, September.

——, 2002, 'Guidelines on Conditionality; Principles, Modalities, Evaluation and Review', 25 September, IMF Website.

——, 2001, 'Strengthening Country Ownership of Fund-supported Programs', SM/01/340, 13 November, Washington, DC.

——, 2001, 'Streamlining Structural Conditionality Review of Experience', SM/01/219, 12 July, Washington, DC.

Kapur, Devesh and Webb, Richard, 2000, 'Governance-related Conditionalities of the International Financial Institutions', UNCTAD, *G-24 Discussion Paper Series*, no. 6, August.

Kapur, Devesh, Lewis, John P and Webb, Richard, 1997, 'The World Bank: Its First Half Century', The Brookings Institution, Washington, DC.

Khan, Mohsin S and Sharma, Sunil, 2001, 'IMF Conditionality and Country Ownership of Programs', IMF Working Paper 01/142, Washington, DC.

Killick, Tony, Gunalatika, Ramani and Marr, Ana, 1998, 'Aid and the Political Economy of Change', London, Routledge.

Krugman, Paul, 1979 'A Model of Balance of Payments Crises', *Journal of Money, Credit and Banking*, no. 11, August, pp. 311–25.

Moggridge, DE, ed., 1974, 'Keynes: Aspects of the Man and his Work', Macmillan Press, London.

Obstfeld, Maurice, 1986, 'Rational and Self-Fulfilling Balance of Payments Crisis', *American Economic Review*, 76, March, pp. 72–81.

——, 1995, 'The Logic of Currency Crises', 1995, in Barry Eichengreen, Jeffrey Frieden, Jurgen von Hagen, eds, 'Monetary and Fiscal Policy in an Integrated Europe', European and Transatlantic Studies, Heidelberg, New York and London, Springer, pp. 62–90.

Polak, J Jacques, 1993, 'The Changing Nature of IMF Conditionality', *Princeton Essays in International Finance*, no. 184, Princeton University, International Finance Section, October.

Rodrik, Dani, 1999, 'Governing the Global Economy: Does One Architectural Style Fit All?', at www.ksg.harvard.edu/rodrik/papers.html.

Schadler S, Bennett A, Carcovik M, et al., 1995, 'IMF Conditionality: Experience Under Stand-By and Extended Arrangements', Part I 'Key Issues and General Findings' and Part II 'Background Papers', IMF Occasional Papers nos 128 and 129, International Monetary Fund, Washington, DC, September.

4

ACHIEVING LONG-TERM DEBT SUSTAINABILITY IN HEAVILY INDEBTED POOR COUNTRIES (HIPCs)

Bernhard G Gunter

Abstract

This chapter builds on the emerging consensus in the development literature that the enhanced HIPC Initiative does not fully remove the debt overhang in many poor and highly indebted countries. It examines the six most crucial problems of the enhanced HIPC initiative: the use of inappropriate eligibility and debt sustainability criteria; the use of overly optimistic growth assumptions; insufficient provision of interim debt relief; the delivery of some HIPC debt relief through debt rescheduling; non-participation and financing shortfalls of creditors; and the use of currency-specific short-term discount rates to calculate the net present value (NPV) of outstanding debt. To address these shortcomings, the chapter suggests: revising the HIPC eligibility and debt sustainability indicators; using lower bounds of growth assumptions; providing deeper and broader interim debt relief; delivering HIPC debt relief only through debt cancellation; adjusting the current equal burden-sharing concept by releasing the HIPC Trust Fund resources immediately to finance-constrained small regional MDBs; exempting minor creditors from the provision of HIPC debt relief; and using a single fixed low discount rate for all NPV calculations. However, even with these changes, the long-term debt sustainability of HIPCs would remain fragile. The chapter argues that more aid coordination is urgently needed for HIPCs that have not yet reached their decision points; that it makes sense to substitute some loans with grants; that HIPC debt relief has thus far been neither frontloaded nor additional and that 100 per cent debt relief would be feasible as well as desirable for the poorest debtors, irrespective of what their debt levels are.

1. Introduction

Achieving long-term debt sustainability is a complex and challenging task that requires a combination of appropriate macroeconomic, structural, investment and debt management policies. In poor countries, long-term debt sustainability is also heavily influenced by such external factors as terms of trade, donor financing, and the provision of debt relief. Debt sustainability, however, can be defined in a variety of ways. As EURODAD, Northover and Sachs et al. illustrate, if debt sustainability is approached from a human and social development perspective,[1] most of the poorest countries have an unsustainable debt regardless of their debt levels. The rationale of such a definition of debt sustainability is that countries with large proportions of their populations living below the poverty line have a more urgent need to spend their resources on poverty reduction than on debt service.

For analytical purposes, a narrower definition of debt sustainability is whether a country can meet its current and future debt service obligations in full, without recourse to debt relief, rescheduling, or the accumulation of arrears. Most of the theoretical debt sustainability literature looks at the debt dynamics over an infinite horizon and then derives some kind of solvency conditions according to which debt sustainability can be determined. Given the practical limitations of such infinite horizon solvency conditions, however, practitioners have suggested a variety of more specific debt sustainability indicators. Recently, Gunter, Lopez, Ramadas and Wodon have developed a simulation tool, called SimSIP Debt, that can be used for the practical analysis of debt sustainability issues.[2]

This chapter concentrates on a review of the Heavily Indebted Poor Countries (HIPC) Initiative. After providing some historical and analytical background, it reviews some of the key problems of the HIPC Initiative and offer concrete suggestions on how to adjust the framework to overcome current implementation problems. Even after the adoption of such changes, however, the long-term debt sustainability of HIPCs would still remain fragile. The chapter thus addresses some of the key issues related to a new aid architecture and the structural transformation HIPCs must undergo to achieve long-term debt sustainability.

Figure 1. **Relationship between debt and GNP growth**

GNP growth

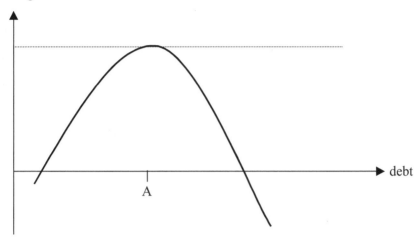

2. Background

Beginning in the early 1980s, more and more low-income countries became unable to pay their scheduled debt service and were thus repeatedly allowed to reschedule their debt at increasingly concessional terms. The Group of Seven (G7) summits in Toronto (1988), London (1991) and Naples (1994) concluded with agreements that constitute 'traditional' debt relief, providing, respectively, 33 per cent (Toronto terms), 50 per cent (London terms) and 67 per cent (Naples terms) debt relief in net present value (NPV) terms on eligible debt.[3]

The seminal contributions by Krugman and Sachs[4] show that debt relief is more efficient than the provision of new loans in cases where debt has accumulated beyond some critical level (point A in Figure 1). Debt accumulated beyond point A represents a debt overhang, which stifles private investment, growth and development. Starting in the early 1990s, a large empirical literature has confirmed the existence of a debt overhang in many low-income countries.

Based on these developments and the continuous failure of traditional debt relief to end the repeated process of debt rescheduling, the International Monetary Fund (IMF) and the World Bank adopted the Heavily Indebted Poor Country (HIPC) Initiative in the fall of 1996 (following the G7 summit in Lyon). The key goal of the HIPC Initiative has been to reduce the public and publicly guaranteed external debt of indebted poor countries to a level that would allow them to permanently exit the process of repeated debt rescheduling. Three years after launching the HIPC Initiative, it was clear that the original HIPC framework was not sufficient to provide HIPCs with a permanent exit from repeated debt rescheduling. Because of this, and public pressure (and the agreement reached at the G7 summit in Cologne), the IMF and World Bank formally agreed in September 1999 to enhance the HIPC framework.[5]

The enhancements provide broader, deeper and faster debt relief mainly by:

- lowering the NPV debt ratios considered by some to provide debt sustainability (together with a lowering of the minimum thresholds to qualify under the fiscal window);
- replacing the principally fixed three-year period between decision and completion points by the concept of a floating completion point; and
- providing interim debt relief from some creditors during the period between decision and completion points.

Another key enhancement was to link HIPC debt relief to the preparation of a country-owned Poverty Reduction Strategy Paper (PRSP).

The period since the adoption of the enhanced framework has been characterized by three developments:

1. Evidence has been mounting that the enhanced HIPC framework ('HIPC-2') is insufficient to provide even short-term debt sustainability for many of the poorest countries, of which some are considered to be HIPCs and others are excluded from the official group of HIPCs. While the many serious problems of HIPC-2 would more than justify further enhancements (that is, 'HIPC-3'), the fact that HIPC-2 continues to face severe financing problems have prevented the IMF and World Bank from suggesting any further enhancements in the HIPC framework. Related to the emerging consensus that the HIPC Initiative is unlikely to provide debt sustainability is the emerging view that domestic debt needs to be taken into account when analyzing debt sustainability.

2. The IMF and World Bank have begun to shift the task of achieving debt sustainability away from the HIPC Initiative toward the PRSP framework, 'within which the authorities should seek to maintain a sustainable debt burden.'[6] While this implies an important change in the key objective of the HIPC Initiative, it follows an April 2001 paper in which the IMF and the World Bank's International Development Association (IDA) recognized for the first time that the HIPC Initiative might not achieve long-term debt sustainability. In September 2002, the IMF and IDA

cemented the shift, stating that 'the HIPC Initiative is designed to deal with ... the existing stock of debt ... at a given point in time' and 'debt relief under the HIPC Initiative provides a basis, but no guarantee, for long-term debt sustainability in HIPCs.' While it is obvious that the HIPC Initiative cannot guarantee long-term debt sustainability, the stated goal of the Initiative was 'to achieve a sustainable debt situation'[7] in the eligible countries, at least in the short and medium term; a goal which the HIPC Initiative has clearly not achieved for at least some of the countries that have exited the HIPC process, especially Uganda.[8]

3. Related to recent debt problems in middle-income countries (such as Argentina and Brazil), the last two years have seen an increasing interest in the adoption of a much broader international debt workout mechanism. While the IMF has proposed a Sovereign Debt Restructuring Mechanism (SDRM), most international advocacy groups have called for a Fair and Transparent Arbitration Procedure (FTAP). It is not clear yet how the HIPC Initiative will be related to these broader proposals, though it is likely that HIPCs would be covered under such debt workout mechanisms if they continue to face debt service problems after having completed the HIPC process.

3. Key Problems of the Enhanced HIPC Initiative

The following six are likely the most crucial problems undermining the effectiveness of the HIPC Initiative:

- inappropriate eligibility criteria,
- unrealistic growth assumptions,
- insufficient provision of interim debt relief,
- delivering HIPC debt relief through debt rescheduling,
- lacks in creditor participation and financing problems, and
- currency-specific short-term discount rates.

Given that most of these problems are sufficiently addressed in the recent literature,[9] we concentrate here on the problems of inappropriate eligibility criteria and insufficient interim debt relief. The important point is, however, that the combination of these six problems makes it unlikely that HIPC-2 will remove the debt overhang, hence will not even provide short-term debt sustainability. There might be some advantages from shifting the goal achieving long-term debt sustainability from the HIPC Initiative to the PRSP process. But this is ultimately likely to prove inefficient and ineffective in cases where countries exit the HIPC process before they have reached debt sustainability. Although increased social expenditures may help to reduce poverty, private investors are unlikely to invest in a country as long as there are doubts that it has achieved debt sustainability. Consequently, the country will continue to grow far below its potential.

3.1 Inappropriate eligibility criteria

HIPC-2 defines a country as 'heavily indebted' if traditional debt relief mechanisms are unlikely to reduce its external debt to a sustainable level. The HIPC framework assumes that a country's external debt is sustainable if the NPV debt-to-export ratio is about 150 percent. In cases where a country has both an export-to-GDP ratio of at least 30 percent and a government revenue-to-GDP ratio of at least 15 percent, the HIPC framework considers also a fiscal window, whereby it is assumed that a country's debt is sustainable if the NPV debt-to-government revenue ratio is about 250 percent. The criterion for being 'poor' is to be an 'IDA-only' country, which is defined as a country that relies on highly concessional financing from the World Bank's concessional lending-arm (the IDA). Hence, the HIPC Initiative was not intended to solve the debt problems of all countries; but rather to assist the poorest and most heavily indebted countries. While questions may be raised about the logic of solving the debt problem of only the poorest countries, this is not the key criticism related to the HIPC eligibility criteria. The key criticism is that the current eligibility criteria are neither based on a comprehensive measure of poverty nor on a comprehensive measure of indebtedness.

The HIPC framework's poverty criterion (the largely income per capita-determined 'IDA-only' criterion) completely neglects that poverty is a multi-dimensional phenomenon. Even worse, since the 'IDA-only' criterion is based mainly on nominal GDP per capita, the HIPC framework's poverty criterion does not even allow for differences in purchasing power. Furthermore, the reclassification of Nigeria (poor and heavily indebted by any standard) from an 'IDA-only' country to a so-called blend country has shown that political and cost factors also played a significant role in the determination of HIPC eligibility.

The HIPC Initiative is widely criticized for using inappropriate debt sustainability criteria. For example, Sachs maintains that the HIPC sustain-ability criteria have nothing to do with debt sustainability in any real sense.[10] Others have stressed that 'the ratios of debt and debt service to exports … are hard to justify on theoretical grounds' and that 'at the very least, indicators relative to GDP should be taken as seriously as indicators relative to exports.'[11] While completely ignored in the HIPC framework, the NPV debt-to-GNP ratio is a good overall indicator of a country's indebtedness. It is also less volatile than the NPV debt-to-exports indicator and more easily available than the NPV debt-to-government revenue indicator.

In any case, the required thresholds for the fiscal window (the NPV debt-to-revenue ratio) are far too restrictive, and the history behind this – also called the 'Côte d'Ivoire' criterion[12] – shows that the HIPC framework's debt sustainability criteria were heavily influenced by political considerations. While more than half of the eligible HIPCs have a NPV debt-to-revenue ratio of more than 250 per cent, most do not qualify for HIPC debt relief under the fiscal window owing to the threshold requirements. While most of these fiscally unsustainable HIPCs still qualify for HIPC debt relief under the export criterion, the debt relief provided is usually far below what would be needed to obtain fiscal debt sustainability. As a World Bank report shows, at least four countries will continue to pay more than 20 per cent of government revenues as external debt service after HIPC-2 debt relief.[13]

The following remarks show how inappropriate the NPV debt-to-export ratio is for determining the debt sustainability of low-income countries, and especially of such import- and aid-dependent economies as HIPCs. As is well known, the debt-to-export ratio has been used for mostly middle-income Latin American countries in the aftermath of the 1982 debt crisis. But the situation there was different. First, a substantial part of Latin American debt was private, and second, exchange rate devaluations following the outbreak of the crisis led to substantial trade surpluses with which the subsequent negative net resource flow was financed. This obviously cannot be the solution for HIPCs, and even if HIPCs would be forced to cut their imports and increase their exports, such a strategy would not work for HIPCs, as their governments usually capture only a small proportion of export revenues. In same cases, exports of HIPCs reflect a large degree of re-exports (the exports simply pass through the country and no foreign exchange is earned by anybody). Finally, the way the NPV debt-to-export criterion is currently used in the HIPC framework discourages an export-led growth strategy, especially in HIPCs where decision and/or completion points are some time in the future. In conclusion, while the debt-to-export ratio may have some justification for determining an upper limit of a country's debt sustainability, it says very little about a government's ability to repay its external (as well as domestic) public debt.

Using more comprehensive measures of poverty and indebtedness would give us a considerably different group of HIPCs. For example, using the UNDP's human poverty index for developing countries (HPI-1)[14] and the NPV external debt-to-GNP ratio[15] as reference criteria for poverty and overall external indebtedness, more than 20 non-HIPC-eligible countries are both poorer and more indebted than the two highest-ranking eligible HIPCs.[16]

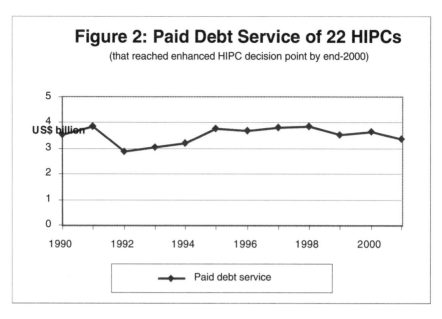

Figure 2: Paid Debt Service of 22 HIPCs
(that reached enhanced HIPC decision point by end-2000)

Source: World Bank, *Global Development Finance*, 2003.

3.2 Insufficient provision of interim debt relief

The enhancements of the HIPC Initiative of fall 1999 recommended the provision of interim debt relief (HIPC debt relief provided during the interim period, that is, the period between reaching decision and completion points). While it was anticipated that interim debt relief would provide substantial reduction in actual debt-service payments in order to support the ambitious poverty reduction strategies necessary to reach the completion point, the experience so far has not confirmed this anticipation.

Figure 2 shows that the actual 2001 debt service payments of the 22 HIPCs that reached their enhanced decision point by the end of 2000 is less than 10 percent lower than the 1998–2000 average. When comparing these actual payments, we should keep in mind that most HIPCs had increased their actual debt-service payments since the adoption of the HIPC Initiative, as prospective HIPCs were not allowed to accrue arrears. Hence, the actual 2001 debt service payments for these 22 HIPCs ($3.4 billion) have been higher than the average actual debt-service payments of these 22 HIPCs just before the adoption of the HIPC Initiative, 1993–5 ($3.3 billion). These comparisons of actual debt-service payments show clearly how marginal interim debt relief has been thus far, especially if we consider that by 2001 some HIPCs had already reached their completion points.

Finally, while the amount of interim debt relief was already too little before the recent slowdown of the world economy, it is clearly inadequate in the current economic situation. As a result, many HIPCs are having considerable difficulties in reaching their completion points. As of the end of February 2003, more than three years after the adoption of the enhanced framework (which was supposed to shorten the time to reach the completion point), only six HIPCs have reached their enhanced completion points.

4. Suggested changes in the HIPC Initiative framework

Following the six key problems with the enhanced HIPC Initiative, we suggest specific changes in six areas:

- revisions of HIPC eligibility and debt sustainability indicators,
- the appropriate use of growth projections,
- the provision of interim debt relief,
- the delivery of HIPC debt relief,
- adjustments in the burden-sharing concept, and
- the appropriate use of discount rates for the NPV calculation.

4.1 Revision of HIPC eligibility and debt sustainability indicators

The replacement of the current eligibility criteria with more poverty-focused and more fiscal sustainability-based eligibility criteria would imply an improvement, particularly if HIPC debt relief is linked more closely to the achievement of the Millennium Development Goals (MDGs). This could be achieved through the following six changes:

1. Replace the theoretically inappropriate and politically charged 'IDA-only' criterion with a more poverty-focused poverty criterion, such as, for example, the UNDP's Human Poverty Index for developing countries (HPI-1). We do not suggest extending HIPC debt relief to all low-income countries as the low-income criterion (purely based on nominal GDP per capita) does not really target debt relief at poor countries.
2. Eliminate the two threshold ratios for the applicability of the fiscal window (that is, the requirements of having an export-to-GDP ratio of at least 30 per cent and a government revenue-to-GDP ratio of at least 15 per cent).[17]
3. Abolish the inappropriate NPV debt-to-export criterion and concentrate instead on fiscal debt-sustainability criteria. The appropriate combination of a NPV debt-to-GDP indicator[18] and a NPV debt-to-government revenue indicator could – together with poverty levels and vulnerability

factors – be used to assess a HIPC's long-term debt sustainability, upon which the cumulative amount of debt relief could be determined. An appropriately defined debt service-to-government revenue indicator could – together with criteria for necessary investments of anti-poverty programs – be used to determine the maximum annual debt service payments each specific HIPC can bear.[19]

4. Instead of calculating government revenues based on current or a three-year backward-looking average ending with the year previous to the decision/completion point, it would make more sense to use a much longer backward-looking average ending with the year before the initiative is adopted. Using a backward-looking average that ends with the year previous to the decision/completion point gives HIPCs incentives to keep revenues low, as higher revenues imply lower HIPC debt relief. There is no such incentive if government revenues are fixed at a predetermined level. Hence, there are easy ways to make use of the fiscal criteria without giving countries incentives to reduce fiscal revenues.

5. Debt relief for the poorest countries must be deepened, and therefore the NPV debt-to-revenue ratio should be reduced. While some critics have argued that HIPC debt relief should not be deepened – maintaining that the majority of the world's poor people live in countries that are not eligible for HIPC debt relief – the fact that most of the world's poor live in countries not eligible for HIPC debt relief simply reflects inappropriate eligibility criteria; it does not constitute an argument against deeper debt relief. The fact that such IDA-only countries as Bangladesh, Cambodia, Haiti, Nepal, and Tajikistan have a GDP-per-capita of less than one dollar a day, makes it obvious that these countries do not have their own resources to repay their external debt, either now or in the foreseeable future. The only reason these countries can service their external debt at present is that they currently receive new loans that are more than sufficient to refinance old debt. This continuous refinancing of old debt with new debt, however, cannot be seen as constituting debt sustainability.

6. Finally, it might also make sense to take other vulnerability factors into account, such as, for example, export concentration and export price volatility (especially as these factors usually have considerable fiscal implications). Vulnerability factors were actually taken into account in the original HIPC Initiative, but have been dropped in the enhanced framework, as Bank and Fund staffs usually disagreed on how much more debt relief should be provided owing to these country-specific vulnerabilities. Obviously, the official explanation for disregarding vulnerability factors was related to simplifying the HIPC framework.

4.2 Using lower bounds of realistic growth assumptions

While the World Bank and the IMF have recognized that they have used overly optimistic growth rates in the past, a review of the most recent HIPC Status Report[20] indicates continuing problems, given the excessive use of past trends to extrapolate future growth rates. Obviously, historical data can provide some indications for the future but there are better ways to project growth rates. For example, when making projections on future growth rates of exports, one should analyze the impact of export price volatility, the diversification of exports, and a variety of other structural aspects. Furthermore, given that the amount of debt relief to be provided will need to be sufficient to convince skeptical private investors that a country is likely to remain debt sustainable for the foreseeable future, the framework should use the lower bounds of realistic growth projections. This would be better than using point estimates of growth projections and stressing that the inherent volatility in growth rates provides challenges when making projections of economic growth.

4.3 Provision of deeper and broader interim debt relief

Given that more than half of the 20 countries in the interim period are expected to show debt ratios in excess of the HIPC sustainability thresholds at the time of their completion points,[21] the provision of interim debt relief should be stepped up considerably. A common misunderstanding is that this would increase the costs of the HIPC Initiative. This is not the case, however, as the total amount of HIPC debt relief is fixed in net present value terms. Thus, the point in time at which HIPC debt relief is provided is not important for the creditor. Furthermore, when determining the amount of interim debt relief, creditors should also look at the amount of domestic debt servicing. Most of HIPC countries' domestic debt is short-term debt, which implies a high fiscal burden, especially during the interim period.

4.4 Delivery of HIPC debt relief

Following our discussion above, showing that the delivery of HIPC debt relief through a rescheduling at concessional interest rate does not contribute to achieving long-term debt sustainability, it is obvious that HIPC debt relief should only be delivered through debt or debt service cancellation. To the degree that this may have negative short-term effects,[22] additional changes in the front-loading of debt service reduction and/or improved interim debt relief may be required.

4.5 Adjustments in burden-sharing

The HIPC Initiative's burden-sharing concept is – compared with earlier debt initiatives – in principle a major step forward, as all creditors are supposed to share the costs of the Initiative based on each creditor's NPV share in outstanding debt. However, we have seen that the theoretically optimal burden-sharing concept has run into serious implementation problems. When looking for a better functioning burden-sharing concept, we should keep in mind that most of the multilateral debt relief (excluding that of the IMF) is actually financed by bilateral donors, partly through bilateral contributions to the HIPC Trust Fund and partly through direct contributions to multilateral development banks (MDBs) in the form of replenishments (such as IDA). Given this background, we offer the following suggestions to make the HIPC burden-sharing practice more efficient:

- Given that financing constraints are the most severe for small regional MDBs from the South, whose debt relief will most likely be financed through the HIPC Trust Fund, these Trust Fund resources should be released immediately and thus allow the full participation of the currently non-participating MDBs. According to the latest HIPC status report, the total costs to all non-participating MDBs together would amount to $46 million in NPV terms, which is marginal compared with the $1.7 billion bilateral donors have thus far paid in.[23]
- There are two options for dealing with HIPC creditors. One option would have been to exclude HIPC creditors from the provision of HIPC debt relief. Besides the disadvantage of deviating from the equal burden-sharing concept, the problem with this option is that it implies a reduction in debt relief to the HIPC debtor. The second option would have been to allocate the amount of debt relief a HIPC creditor is supposed to provide into a Trust Fund, financed from the amount of debt relief the HIPC creditor is supposed to receive from its creditors. Note that the financial impact of this second option is exactly the same for all creditors and debtors as that of the current burden-sharing concept; however, it would have avoided the costly negotiations and litigations of HIPCs against HIPCs.
- Consistent with existing Paris Club regulations, the HIPC Initiative should have adopted a 'de minimus' clause, which would have exempted minor creditors from the provision of HIPC debt relief.
- Centralized consultations – possibly through the United Nations – may have been undertaken (and can still be undertaken) with bilateral creditors that are not members of the IMF and World Bank bilateral creditors that had a history of not participating in traditional debt relief,

and all commercial creditors. While such negotiations might not have led to the full provision of HIPC debt relief, it is likely that these creditors would have provided more debt relief than under the current situation in which HIPCs were advised to stop payments to non-participating creditors and now face costly litigations.

In sum, given the costs HIPCs face from creditor litigations, these four changes in the burden-sharing concept would have been more effective than the strict insistence on equal burden-sharing.

4.6 Using one fixed low discount rate for the NPV calculation

The use of currency-specific discount rates would make sense if we wish to know the future interest rate differentials of currencies for the remaining repayment periods, and if these future interest rate differentials would appropriately reflect differences in future currency values (as the theory of interest rate parity suggests). Given that both assumptions are inaccurate, however, it does not make sense to use currency-specific interest rates for the NPV calculation. There is some belief that currencies of developing countries are less stable than OECD currencies. But there is no objective way to quantify such differences and therefore it would make more sense to use one fixed discount rate for the NPV calculation of all debt, independent on what currency the debt is nominated in.

5. Key issues related to a new aid architecture

When the size of debt relief is compared with the size of aid, it is clear that debt relief plays a minor role. Overall debt relief (including traditional debt relief) to HIPCs currently amounts to about $1.5 billion a year; gross disbursements from bilateral and multilateral donors totals about $15 billion a year.[24] Hence, were it not necessary to remove the debt overhang, we could easily ignore the whole issue of debt relief and concentrate instead on the financing of poverty reduction policies. While important steps have been taken to better coordinate aid, a large problem of coordinating aid with debt relief remains. Linking debt relief to a new aid architecture, Birdsall and Williamson point out that further debt relief will need to be complemented by a larger reinvention of the international aid architecture. We limit our arguments here to four related aspects: the aid coordination for HIPCs that have not yet reached their HIPC decision points; the debate on whether loans should be replaced by grants; the issue of additionality; and the feasibility and desirability of 100 per cent debt reduction.

5.1 Aid coordination for HIPCs that have not reached their decision points

Given that the amount of HIPC debt relief to be provided by each creditor is calculated based on each creditor's share in the total NPV debt at the year previous to the HIPC decision point, no creditor currently has any incentive to provide new loans to HIPCs that have not yet reached their decision point. To overcome this large disincentive, it is either necessary to coordinate all new disbursements (which is very difficult) or to simply change the reference date for the allocation of costs of HIPC debt relief.

5.2 Grants versus loans?

If the objective of the current development agenda is to secure long-term debt sustainability, there can be no doubt that some loans should be replaced by grants. One of the key questions related to switching toward grants, however, is how they can be financed. Grant financing should not lead to a long-term reduction in the overall availability of financial assistance to the poorest countries, as will be the case if IDA is not properly replenished. Obviously, most of this problem would be solved if all OECD countries would raise their aid flows to the long recommended level of 0.7 per cent of GNP, and/or if the international community were to adopt global taxes to finance development (such as the Tobin tax). In any case, as the US government's GAO (2002) report shows, even after the full implementation of the suggested switching from loans to grants, HIPCs would continue to face unsustainable debt, and thus more debt relief is needed.

5.3 The issue of additionality

There is broad agreement (including by the World Bank and the IMF) that HIPC debt relief needs to be additional to conventional aid in order to effectively reduce poverty. We have shown in Figure 2 above that, thus far, the HIPC Initiative has not achieved the desired reduction in actual debt-service payments for the 22 HIPCs that reached their enhanced decision points by end-2000. Indeed, Figure 3 shows that official net resource flows to these 22 HIPCs had been declining for most of the 1990s, amounting currently to $6.9 billion a year (1999–2001 average). Hence, current official net resource flows to the 22 early HIPCs are 22 per cent less than what official net resource flows were to these 22 countries in the early 1990s (amounting to an average $8.9 billion). The picture is even worse in Sub-Saharan Africa, where official net resource flows have declined from an average of $16 billion during the early

Figure 3. **Official net resource flows 1990–2001**

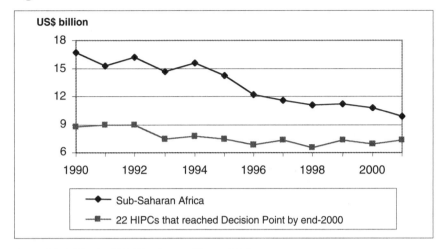

Source: World Bank, *Global Development Finance*, 2003.

1990s to less than $10 billion in 2001. These are alarming trends, especially when taking into account the large amount of resources needed to combat the HIV/AIDS epidemic.[25]

5.4 Is 100 per cent debt relief feasible and desirable?

Given that debt relief is only a small portion of overall aid and is not additional to conventional aid (at least not until now, and unlikely to ever be in the future), it is obvious that 100 per cent debt relief is feasible only by simply switching from the provision of conventional aid to debt relief. The remaining question is thus if 100 per cent debt relief is desirable. Looking at the desirability of this, we will differentiate between multilateral and bilateral debt relief, arguing that 100 per cent debt relief is desirable on bilateral debt though not necessarily on multilateral debt. In addition to differences in financing constraints and debt structures (maturity and concessionality) between bilateral and multilateral debt, we argue that the following points support 100 per cent bilateral debt relief for a selected group of extremely poor countries:

- First, limiting 100 per cent debt relief to bilateral debt minimizes the equity problem of 100 per cent debt relief. A 100 per cent debt relief on multilateral debt would have serious consequences for the availability of funds for less indebted though equally poor countries (for example, Bangladesh), although there would be options to reduce the equity effect by extending multilateral debt relief to all countries with the same level of poverty.

- Second, HIPC debt relief is supposed to provide approximately 90 percent debt relief in NPV terms on eligible bilateral debt. Hence, only about 10 percent of eligible bilateral debt in NPV terms, post-cut-off-date debt, and official development assistance (ODA) debt would need to be canceled – together amounting to only a small portion of overall bilateral aid.
- Third, to the degree that debt relief constitutes actual reductions on debt-service payments, it must be spent fully on poverty reduction measures.

Looking at the desirability of 100 per cent debt relief on bilateral debt under these circumstances, it is difficult to find compelling arguments against its providing to a selected group of extremely poor countries. Indeed, some bilateral creditors have recently promised to provide 100 per cent debt relief to HIPCs as well as to other equally poor countries. Furthermore, some donor countries have already provided 100 per cent debt relief many years ago when they cancelled their ODA debts and moved to 100 per cent grant financing.

6. Necessary structural changes

Geda poses the question: Would the debt problem be over for African HIPCs if the HIPC Initiative wrote off all debt owed by African HIPCs?[26]

Figure 4. **Stuctural Transformation of 42 HIPCs, 1990–2001**

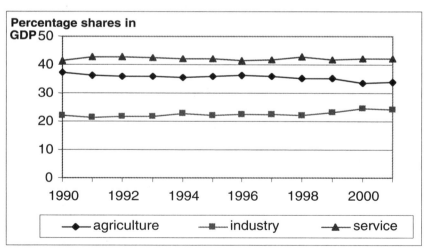

Source: World Bank, *World Development Indicators* (central database, February 2003).

Figure 5. **Structural Transformation (Share of Manufacturing of 42 HIPCs, 1990–2001)**

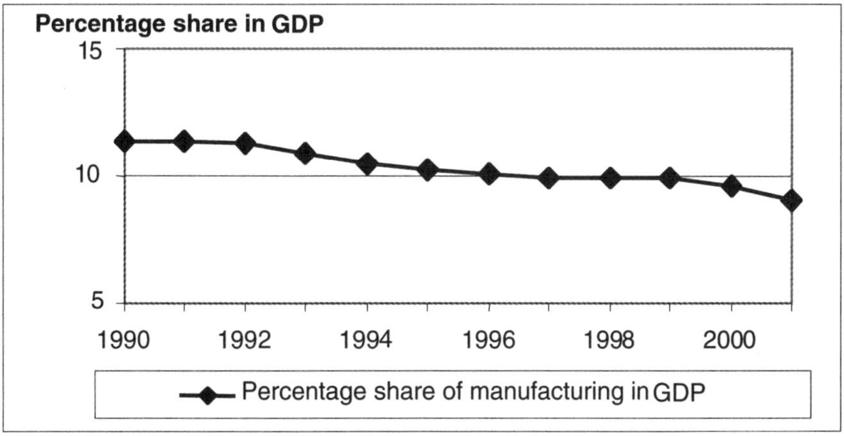

Source: World Bank, *World Development Indicators* (central database, February 2003).

Geda answers the question with a clear no, pointing to the historical origins of the African debt crisis and the structural problems the continent confronts. Similarly, Birdsall and Williamson point out that "debt reduction alone is not enough to get development in the poorest countries back on the rails."[27] Indeed, excluding the option of 100 per cent debt relief followed by 100 per cent grant financing, there is broad consensus that no debt relief package would provide long-term debt sustainability as long as countries fail to pursue sound economic, social and structural policies that stimulate economic growth and help attract increased investment, especially from private sources. Given the existing emphasis on governance, institutions and social policies, we concentrate here on the missing structural transformation in HIPCs. We look specifically at sectoral shares of GDP, long-term trends in savings and investment, and some of the key issues related to high-export concentration and high-export price volatility.

6.1 Sectoral shares of GDP

As Figures 4 and 5 show, HIPCs have not experienced any significant structural transformation of their economies. While the last two years seem to indicate a decreasing share of agriculture and an increasing share of industry, Figure 5 shows clearly that the increase in the share of industry is not due to an increase in the share of manufacturing, as would have been desirable. Instead the downward trend in manufacturing seems to have accelerated during the last two years (2000–01). The continuing downward trend in the share

Figure 6. **Percentage Shares of Investment and Savings in GDP, 1990–2001**

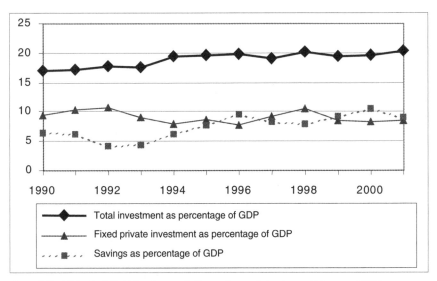

Source: World Bank, *World Development Indicators* (central database, February 2003).

of manufacturing shows that HIPCs are not undergoing the structural trans-formation needed to achieve long-term growth and debt sustainability.

6.2 Long-term trends in domestic savings and domestic investment

Figure 6 shows the structural transformation of HIPC economies in terms of domestic savings and investment from 1990 to 2001. While the dotted line in Figure 6 shows an overall positive trend in domestic savings, the share of domestic savings shows a drop from 10.5 percent in 2000 to 9.0 percent in 2001. The shares of total investment also show a positive long-term trend, and without having experienced a recent decline. While these long-term trends in domestic savings and total domestic investment are promising, it is trouble-some that the shares of fixed private investment show a declining trend, with a relative sharp drop of more than 2 percentage points from 1998 (10.4 percent) to 1999 (8.3 percent). This clearly indicates that private domestic investors have not been convinced about the long-term prospects of HIPCs.

6.3 Long-term trends in foreign investment

Figure 7 shows the recent trends in foreign direct investment and Figure 8 shows the trends in portfolio direct investment. Each chart shows two curves,

Figure 7. Trends in Foreign Direct Investment (FDI) of 42 HIPCs, 1990–2001

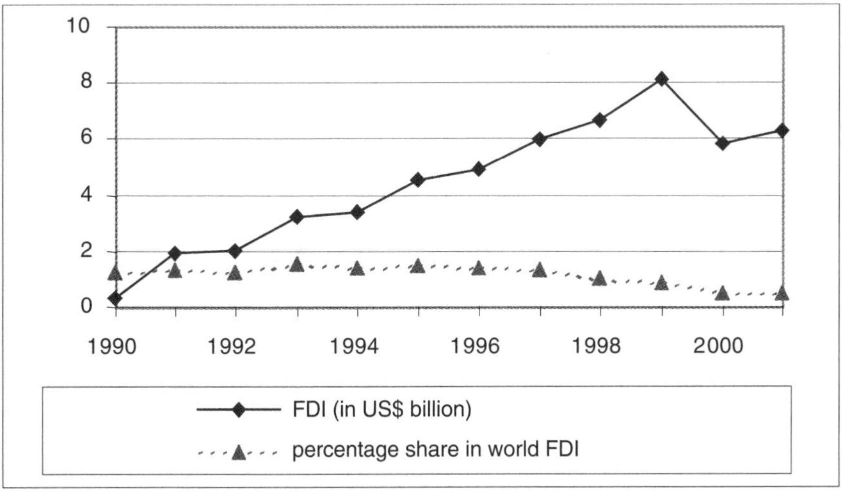

Source: World Bank, *Global Development Finance*, 2003; and IMF, *International Financial Statistics*, 2003.

the continuous lines show the nominal amounts of foreign direct investment (FDI) and portfolio direct investment, the dotted lines show the relative shares of the 42 HIPCs relative to world levels of FDI and portfolio direct investment.

6.3.1 Long-term trends in flows on FDI to HIPCs

Looking at the nominal amounts of FDI to the 42 HIPCs (the continuous line in Figure 7), we see that FDI flows to the 42 HIPCs have increased in nominal terms through most of the period (though they experienced a seemingly temporary shock in 2000). While this is a positive development, the share of the 42 HIPCs in world FDI flows (the dotted line in Figure 7) shows a continuous decrease since 1995, reaching a marginal share of less than half per cent in 2001. Hence, similar to the experience of most other low-income countries, HIPCs are increasingly marginalized in an increasingly globalized world. Furthermore, most of the FDI flows to HIPCs are related to the extraction of natural resources (which are usually exclaves to the real economy).

Figure 8. **Trends in Portfolio Direct Investment of 42 HIPCs, 1999–2001**

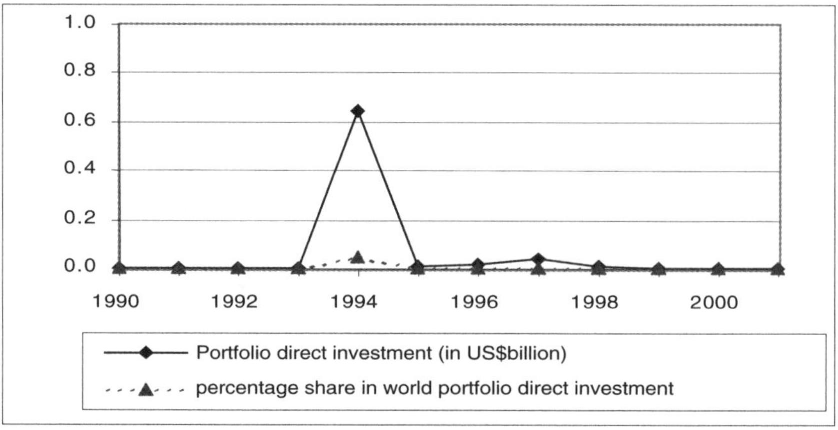

Source: World Bank, *Global Development Finance,* 2003; and IMF, *International Financial Statistics,* 2003.

6.3.2 Long-term trends in flows of Portfolio Direct Investment to HIPCs

Looking at portfolio direct investment flows to the 42 HIPCs (Figure 8), we notice that both the nominal amounts as well as the relative shares of portfolio direct investment to the 42 HIPCs are basically non-existent; nominal amounts averaged about $65 million during 1990–2001 – representing about 0.002 percent of average world flows of portfolio direct investment during 1990–2001. The only periods in which the group of 42 HIPCs experienced some significant inflows of portfolio direct investment were in 1994 and in 1997 (it is not even sure if these two exceptional peaks are data errors). Nonetheless, it is clear that HIPCs are largely excluded from the world flow of portfolio direct investment (amounting to about $5 trillion a year), which is largely consistent with the experience of other low-income countries.

Considering the HIPCs' weak regulatory framework to deal effectively with increasingly volatile international capital flows, it could be considered an advantage that HIPCs do not receive large amounts of short-term capital. However, there are obviously some costs to HIPCs from being increasingly marginalized in terms of world capital flows. In any case, as was the case for domestic investors, there is some indication that foreign investors are not yet convinced that HIPCs are likely to achieve debt sustainability.

Figure 9. **Terms of Trade, 1999–2001**

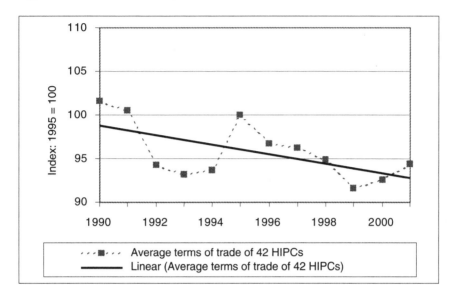

Source: World Bank, *World Development Indicators* (central database, February 2003).

6.4 Export concentration, export price volatility and contingent facility

HIPCs are well known to have a high degree of export concentration, which makes them highly vulnerable to export price volatility. Based on 2001 data provided by IMF and IDA (2002), the commodity export dependency (defined as the ratio of the three main commodities in total exports) averages about 60 percent, the average change in export price changes is 6.5 per cent and the average change in the terms of trade is 7.3 per cent.

While some recent research has made valuable contributions to the analysis of developing countries' vulnerability based on developing countries' high export concentration and high commodity price volatility,[28] it is somehow overlooked that most developing countries, especially HIPCs, continue to experience considerable deteriorations in their terms of trade (see Figure 9, in which the straight line represents the linear trend). Woodward suggests a link between deteriorating terms of trade for low-income countries and their high export concentration.[29] Gunter shows that a high export concentration is highly correlated with macroeconomic uncertainty and low investment. At the same time, it is well known that developing countries' exports in agricultural products face significant trade barriers, which has led to the call for a 'development round' of trade negotiations.[30]

Figure 10. **Exports of 42 HIPCs, 1990–2001**

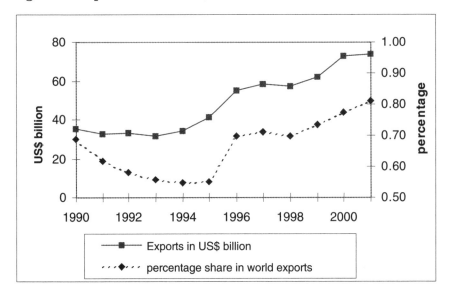

Source: World Bank, *Global Development Finance*, 2003; and IMF, *International Financial Statistics*, 2003.

Taking all these negative aspects into account, it is actually surprising that the HIPCs managed to increase their exports from $35 billion in 1990 to over $73 billion in 2001 (see the left scale of Figure 10). Furthermore, looking at the right-hand scale of Figure 10, we can see that the HIPCs' share in world exports declined from 0.69 percent in 1990 to 0.55 percent in 1995, but it rose sharply from 1995 to 1997 and again from 1998 to 2001, amounting to 0.81 percent in 2001. While the HIPCs' share in world exports remains marginal, the recent trend is impressive. Yet observers question how much this increase in exports has truly benefited HIPCs. Looking at the missing structural trans-formation of HIPCs, there is some indication that the increase in HIPCs' exports is due largely to the extraction of natural resources, which is unlikely to provide the urgently needed forward and backward linkages to achieve long-term growth and sustainable development.

While more research on structural relationships is needed, the HIPCs' high indebtedness is clearly due at least partly to economic structures. Further-more, suggestions to stabilize world commodity prices and to create a contin-gency fund to compensate HIPCs for events beyond their control are also welcome, especially over the medium term; they are, however, unlikely to constitute a sustainable long-term solution.[31] Therefore, HIPCs must find market niches in the industrial and service sectors that will make them less dependent on world commodity prices and the industrial countries' demand for agricultural goods.

7. Conclusion

In contrast to the conclusions drawn in the official HIPC documents, we have shown that key shortcomings in HIPC-2 are unlikely to remove the debt overhang. Only if the debt overhang is removed is it likely that increased social expenditures will be complemented by increased long-term private investments, which is needed to facilitate a structural transformation. Without long-term private investment, it is unlikely that an economy will undergo the necessary structural transformation (including a diversification of its exports). Thus, the vicious circle of low levels of private investment, low degrees of export diversification, high vulnerability, low growth, and high debt ratios is likely to prevail.

Though most of these problems have been recognized, there is real fear that the international community will not address them appropriately, but will muddle through by shifting the debt sustainability agenda to the PRSP process and possibly wait for an international debt workout mechanism. This ineffective approach might ultimately fail. It is then likely that at some time in the future, the HIPCs will be blamed for not having achieved debt sustainability. Obviously, sustained economic growth and a diversification of exports are crucial, but sound economic management and improved governance will not be sufficient for this to happen.

The agenda for achieving long-term debt sustainability must focus more on a long-term development strategy that fosters the necessary structural transformation of HIPCs. The HIPCs are not likely to undergo the necessary structural transformation without targeted policy interventions. More specifically, this calls for a combination of industrial investments, supporting competition policies, and strategic trade policies that go beyond the existing (though blocked) comparative advantages in agriculture. An appropriate mix of such policies could lead to the development of selected industrial bases and service centers that can – at least in the long term – compete with those of industrial countries.

While much of the preceding analysis may give rise to pessimism, HIPC-2 is likely to provide debt sustainability for some countries, especially if future lending is more concessional than in the past and supported by increased grant financing. While the additionality of debt relief would be desired to reduce poverty more effectively, it is not a necessary condition for removing the remaining debt overhang. Thus, the additional costs of a HIPC-3 outlined above could be marginal if compared with overall aid budgets. Moreover, much more can be done in developing countries, especially in shifting the few resources they have toward a national development strategy and away from highly unproductive expenditures.

Notes

1 EURODAD 2002; Northover 2001; Sachs et al. 1999. The human development approach to debt relief has originally been suggested by Northover, Joyner, and Woodward at CAFOD in 1998; see http://www.cafod.org.uk/policy/acaf1.shtml for more details.
2 Gunter, Lopez, Ramadas, and Wodon 2002.
3 The net present value (NPV) is the sum of all future debt service discounted by currency specific discount rates. Eligible debt was defined as pre-cutoff-date, non-ODA (official development assistance) bilateral debt. The cutoff date refers to the date a debtor country approached the Paris Club for the first time for a debt rescheduling.
4 Krugman 1988 and Sachs 1989.
5 For a brief description of the enhanced HIPC Initiative, see the IMF website (www.imf.org/external/np/exp/fact/hipc.htm).
6 See IMF and IDA 2002, p. 39.
7 See World Bank 2003, referring to the original HIPC concept paper of August 1996: *The HIPC Debt Initiative—Elaboration of Key Features and Possible Procedural Steps.*
8 The most recent HIPC DSA of July 2002 has shown that because of the unanticipated decline in world coffee prices, Uganda's NPV debt to export ratio will remain considerably over the 150 per cent level for at least the next 10 years, for some years even above 200 percent. Also, the official HIPC DSA has not even taken into account that 13 of Uganda's creditors have not yet agreed to provide HIPC debt relief; see IMF and World Bank 2002, p. 68.
9 See, for example, Birdsall and Williamson 2002, various reports of the United States General Accounting Office (GAO), Gunter 2002, and the most recent Operation Evaluation Department (OED) review: World Bank 2003.
10 Sachs 2000.
11 See IMF, Report of the Group of Independent Persons Appointed to Conduct an Evaluation of Certain Aspects of the Enhanced Structural Adjustment Facility, June 1998, pp. 39–40, on IMF website.
12 See Martin 2002, p. 3, reporting that the NPV debt-to-revenue ratio 'was set at a level just low enough to include Côte d'Ivoire in HIPC (under pressure from France which was threatening to vote against the eligibility of other HIPCs), but was accompanied by empirically unjustified sub-criteria which exclude many other HIPCs.'
13 World Bank 2001.
14 The HPI-1 has been designed to address the now well-accepted notion that poverty is multi-dimensional and certainly goes far beyond income-poverty; the data have been taken for two consecutive years of the *Human Development Report* 2001 and 2002.
15 The data for the NPV debt to GNP ratios have been taken for two consecutive years of the World Bank's *Global Development Finance* (GDF) 2001 and 2002.
16 In terms of poverty, the two highest-ranking (least-poor) eligible HIPCs are Bolivia and Guyana; in terms of indebtedness, the two highest-ranking (least-indebted in terms of NPV debt-to-GNP) eligible HIPCs are Burkina Faso and Mozambique.

17 While it has been argued that the thresholds are justified to provide some incentives for countries to increase their exports-to-GDP and revenue-to-GDP ratios, ratios below the thresholds usually reflect structural problems, which are unlikely to be overcome in the short term. Furthermore, given that countries are required to have undergone at least three years of 'successful' adjustment supported by the Bank and the Fund before reaching the HIPC decision point, is difficult to argue that further incentives are needed to determine HIPC eligibility, and/or that without these thresholds, the HIPC Initiative would reward inefficient countries.

18 As Birdsall and Williamson 2002 point out, debt criteria based on GDP would avoid rewarding countries for having failed to collect taxes. These need not, however, be the only criteria.

19 This builds on a recent suggestion by EURODAD 2002, calling for a country-by-country analysis of how much debt each country can afford to carry without preempting resources available for spending on a basic level of social service delivery.

20 IMF and IDA 2002.

21 See IMF and IDA 2002, p. 28.

22 Negative short-term effects are especially possible where reschedulings involve a grace period.

23 Alternatively, given that some bilateral donors have made higher pledges to the HIPC Trust Fund than they have yet paid-in, it would be sufficient if one bilateral donor would pay in $46 million and earmark the amount for the immediate release to non-participating MDBs.

24 See Birdsall and Williamson 2002, p. 70.

25 See Oxfam 2002 for linking debt relief to the HIV/AIDS epidemic. Culpeper 2001 presents a detailed analysis of long-term financing for the poorest countries.

26 Geda 2002.

27 Birdsall and Williamson 2002, p. 5.

28 See Berthélemy and Söderling 2001, Collier 2002, and Combes and Guillaumont 2002.

29 Woodward 1996.

30 Gunter 1998. See Birdsall and Hamoudi 2002, as well as World Bank 2002.

31 See Birdsall and Williamson 2002 for more detailed suggestions on a contingency fund. An even more comprehensive report has recently been issued by the International Task Force (ITF) on Commodity Risk Management 2002. For a more critical assessment on the viability of price stabilization schemes, see Cashin, Liang and McDermott 2000.

Bibliography

Addison, Tony, Henrik Hansen, and Finn Tarp, eds, *Debt Relief*, New York: Oxford University Press for UNU/WIDER (forthcoming).

Berthélemy, Jean-Claude and Ludvig Söderling, 2001, 'The Role of Capital Accumulation, Adjustment and Structural Change for Economic Take-Off: Empirical Evidence from African Growth Episodes', *World Development*, vol. 29, no. 2, February, pp. 323–43.

Birdsall, Nancy and Amar Hamoudi, 2002, *It's Not about Trade Policy! Commodity Dependence, Trade, Growth, and Poverty*, Washington, DC: Center for Global Development, Working Paper no. 3.

Birdsall, Nancy and John Williamson with Brian Deese, 2002, *Delivering on Debt Relief: From IMF Gold to a New Aid Architecture*, Washington, DC: Center for Global Development and Institute for International Economics.

Cashin, Paul, Hong Liang, and C John McDermott, 2000, 'How Persistence are Shocks to World Commodity Prices?' *IMF Staff Papers*, vol. 47, no. 2.

Collier, Paul, 2002, 'The Macroeconomic Repercussions of Agricultural Shocks and their Implications for Insurance', United Nations University/World Institute for Development Economics Research (UNU/WIDER) Discussion Paper no. 2002/46.*

Combes, Jean-Luis, and Patrick Guillaumont, 2002, 'Commodity Price Volatility, Vulnerability and Development', *Policy Development Review*, vol. 20, no. 1, March, pp. 25–39.

Culpeper, Roy, 2001, *Capital Volatility and Long-Term Financing for the Poorest Countries*, London: International Development Committee (IDC); also available on the Internet: www.adb2001.org/annualmeeting/Seminars/culpeper_paper.pdf.

European Network on Debt and Development (EURODAD), 2001, 'Debt Reduction for Poverty Eradication in the Least Developed Countries: Analysis and Recommendations on LDC Debt', United Nations University/World Institute for Development Economics Research (UNU/WIDER) Discussion Paper no. 2001/110.*

European Network on Development and Debt (EURODAD), 2002, 'Putting Sustainable Development First', Brussels: EURODAD; available on the EURODAD website: www.eurodad.org/.

Geda, Alemayehu, 2002, 'Debt Issues in Africa: Thinking beyond the HIPC Initiative to Solving Structural Problems', United Nations University/World Institute for Development Economics Research (UNU/WIDER) Discussion Paper no. 2002/35.*

Gunter, Bernhard G, 1998, *Economic Structure and Investment Under Uncertainty*, unpublished dissertation, Washington, DC: American University, Department of Economics, May.

Gunter, Bernhard G, 2001, 'Does the HIPC Initiative Achieve its Goal of Debt Sustainability?', United Nations University/World Institute for Development Economics Research (UNU/WIDER) Discussion Paper no. 2001/100 (September); forthcoming in Addison, Hansen, and Tarp eds., *Debt Relief*, Oxford University Press.

Gunter, Bernhard G, 2002, 'What's Wrong With the HIPC Initiative and What's Next?', *Policy Development Review*, vol. 20, no. 1, March, pp. 5–24.

Gunter, Bernhard G, Humberto Lopez, Krishnan Ramadas and Quentin Wodon, 2002, *SimSIP Debt: A Simulation Tool for Analyzing Debt Sustainability*, Washington, DC, World Bank, July; available on the Internet: http://www.worldbank.org/simsip.

International Monetary Fund (IMF), *International Financial Statistics*, Washington, DC: IMF (various years).

International Monetary Fund (IMF) and International Development Association (IDA), 2002, *The Enhanced Initiative for Heavily Indebted Poor Countries – Review of Implementation*, Washington, DC, IMF and World Bank. September.**

International Monetary Fund (IMF) and International Development Association (IDA), 2001, *The Challenge of Maintaining Long-Term Debt Sustainability*, Progress Report presented to the Development Committee and the International Monetary and Financial Committee (IMFC), Washington, DC, IMF and World Bank, April.**

International Monetary Fund (IMF) and International Development Association (IDA), 2002, *Heavily Indebted Poor Countries (HIPC) Initiative: Status of Implementation*, Progress Report presented to the Development Committee and the International Monetary and Financial Committee (IMFC), Washington, DC, IMF and World Bank, September.**

International Task Force (ITF) on Commodity Risk Management, 2002, *Report on Commodity Price Volatility and Developing Countries*, Washington, DC, ITF, available on the Internet: http://www.itf-commrisk.org/documents/discussionpaper.pdf.

Krugman, Paul, 1988, 'Financing vs. Forgiving a Debt Overhang', *Journal of Development Economics*, vol. 29, no. 3, November, pp. 253–68.

Martin, Matthew, 2002, *Debt Relief and Poverty Reduction: Do We Need a HIPC III?*, Paper presented to the North-South Institute, Global Finance Governance Initiative Workshop, May 1–2; available on the Internet: http://www.nsiins.ca/download/Martin.pdf.

Northover, Henry, 2001, 'A Human Development Approach to Debt Relief for the World's Poor' (Update on the 1998 Working Paper by Northover, Joyner, Woodward), London, CAFOD, December; available on the Internet: http://www.cafod.org.uk/policy/acafl.shtml.

Oxfam International, 2002, 'Debt Relief and the HIV/AIDS Crisis in Africa: Does the Heavily Indebted Poor Countries Initiative Go Far Enough?' Oxfam Briefing Paper, no. 25, June; available on the Internet: http://www.oxfam.org/eng/pdfs/pp0206_no25_debt_relief_and_the_HIV_crisis.pdf.

Sachs, Jeffrey, 1989, 'The Debt Overhang of Developing Countries', in Jorge de Macedo and Ronald Findlay, eds, *Debt, Growth and Stabilisation: Essays in Memory of Carlos Dias Alejandro*, Oxford, Blackwell, pp. 80–102.

Sachs, Jeffrey, 2000, 'The Charade of Debt Sustainability', *Financial Times*, September, p. 17.

Sachs, Jeffrey, Kwesi Botchwey, Maciej Cuchra, and Sara Sievers, 1999, 'Implementing Debt Relief for the HIPCs', Cambridge, Center for International Development, Harvard University, August; available on the Internet: www.cid.harvard.edu/.

Serieux, John E, 2001, 'The Enhanced HIPC Initiative and Poor Countries: Prospects for a Permanent Exit', *Canadian Journal of Development Studies*, vol. 22, no. 2, pp. 527–48.

United Nations Development Program (UNDP), *Human Development Report 2001*, and *Human Development Report 2002*, New York, Oxford University Press.

Woodward, David, 1996, 'Effects of Globalization and Liberalization on Poverty: Concepts and Issues' in UNCTAD, *Globalization and Liberalization: Effects of International Economic Relations on Poverty*, New York, UNCTAD, pp. 25–128.

World Bank, *Global Development Finance*, Washington, DC, World Bank (various years).

World Bank, *World Development Indicators*, Washington, DC, World Bank (various years).

World Bank, 2002, *Globalization, Growth, and Poverty: Building an Inclusive World Economy*, New York, Oxford University Press.

World Bank, 2003, *The Heavily Indebted Poor Countries (HIPC) Debt Initiative: An OED Review*, Washington, DC, World Bank, Operations Evaluation Department (OED), February; also available on the OED website: http://www.worldbank.org/oed/.

* Available on the WIDER website: http://www.wider.unu.edu/
** Available on the HIPC website: www.worldbank.org/hipc/

5

THE POVERTY REDUCTION STRATEGY PAPER APPROACH: GOOD MARKETING OR GOOD POLICY?[1][*]

Jim Levinsohn

Abstract

I begin by posing a key question: Has the Poverty Reduction Strategy Paper (PRSP) process yielded benefits that exceed its considerable administrative costs? I first review the PRSP process and then examine some of the existing reviews, explain why these reviews tend to fall short of their goals, and finally try to answer the question stated above. I find that the first round of reviews of the PRSP approach have been dominated by little careful quantitative analysis, and instead by anecdotes and stories. I recommend that the future reviews of the PRSP process, from all sides, confront the difficult task of determining the marginal impact of the PRSP approach. I also present a detailed list of the types of household data that are needed for a successful PRSP implementation. I conclude with a specific suggestion: The Bank and the Fund or an NGO should undertake one careful, detailed and rigorous analysis of a specific PRSP process based on a multiple waves of a household survey, which can then serve as a model for future reviews and analyses.

1. Introduction

In 1999, the World Bank and the International Monetary Fund (IMF) adopted a new set of policies to guide lending to some of the world's poorest

---

[*] This Paper is also published by UNCTAD as G24 Discussion Paper no. 21, United Nations, New York and Geneva (forthcoming).

countries. Amid the blizzard of acronyms explaining the new policies, the Bank and the IMF laid out a framework to be followed by poor countries wishing to make use of various concessionary (low-cost) lending facilities. About two and a half years later, in the spring of 2002, the Bank and the IMF concluded a review of these policies. Contributors to this review included dozens of non-governmental organizations (NGOs) as well as the Bank and the IMF themselves. The Bank and the Fund, while acknowledging that the process could be improved, concluded that it worked pretty well based on the preliminary evidence so far available. The NGOs were, on the whole, less enthusiastic.

My reading of the record is that neither the Bank nor the outside commentators are asking the hard questions. The right question to ask is the following:

Relative to what would have happened absent the adoption of the Poverty Reduction Strategy Paper (PRSP) framework, has the implementation of the PRSP process yielded benefits that exceed its often considerable administrative costs?

Instead of tackling this difficult question, the Bank and the Fund have basically evaluated the PRSP process, noting that some potentially replicable good practices have emerged and that the inclusivity that the PRSP process promotes is helpful. In particular, the process is better than one that ignores the poor, never solicits outside opinion, imposes solutions with no reference to the particulars of the recipient country and involves consultation with the recipient country. Compared with such an international lending hell, the PRSP process fares quite well indeed. Many of the NGOs, on the other hand, seem not to be evaluating the PRSP process but rather to be asking whether the Bank has achieved its stated mission of a 'World without poverty'. By this criterion, the process falls rather short.

Before trying to answer whether the PRSP has been a good thing, I first review just what the process is meant to be. I go on to examine some of the existing reviews of the PRSP approach, try to explain why these tend to fall short of their goal and finally try to answer the question formulated above. Knowing whether the PRSP process is addressing the concerns of the poor means being able to identify the poor and to measure *changes* in their wellbeing. This is hard enough, but to really answer the question at hand, one also needs to examine whether the changes in the welfare of the poor are in fact the result of changes in policy associated with the PRSP approach. This is a tall order, but in a surprisingly large number of countries it is, at least in principle, doable. The first round of reviews of the PRSP approach have been dominated by precious little careful quantitative analysis and, instead, a lot of stories, which are not the way to guide policy. Future reviews of the PRSP process, from all sides, should honestly confront the challenge of determining the marginal impact of the PRSP approach and refrain from reaching conclusions based on pre-existing notions of whether the process is working or not.

2. The PRSP process

Poverty reduction strategy papers are not a trivial bureaucratic hoop through which countries have to jump. Rather, they constitute a major effort. How did it come to pass that countries from Albania to Zambia have, in the last couple years, written papers averaging some one hundred pages on how these countries plan to reduce poverty? Before presenting a critical analysis of the PRSP process, I begin with a discussion of how the process is, on paper, supposed to work.

2.1 How the process is supposed to work

At their September 1999 annual meetings, the Bank and IMF lined up behind a proposal that 'country-owned' poverty reduction strategies should form the basis for all Bank and Fund concessional lending. These strategies would be embodied in Poverty Reduction Strategy Papers. Thus was born the PRSP process. The process was essentially a way to implement a set of principles the Bank had earlier adopted. These principles were called the Comprehensive Development Framework. The relationship between the Comprehensive Development Framework and the PRSP process is confusing, but it is probably easiest to think of the Framework as the destination and the PRSP as the route selected.

In time, the plan is that every country receiving debt relief under the Initiative for Heavily Indebted Poor Countries (HIPCs), and all countries making use of the IMF's Poverty Reduction and Growth Facility (PRGF), will need to author a full PRSP that must be approved by the Executive Boards of the Bank and Fund. The expectation is that eventually about 70 low-income countries will be expected to prepare PRSPs. Clearly, the process is going to be pervasive and will not be restricted to only the most troubled or very poorest economies.

The Bank and the Fund have taken pains to emphasize that there is no single template for a PRSP. Rather, each nation's PRSP is expected to be based on five principles. In the language of the PRSP Sourcebook, PRSPs should be:

- country-driven and owned, based on broad-based participatory processes for formulation, implementation and outcome-based monitoring
- results-oriented, focusing on outcomes that would benefit the poor

- comprehensive in scope, recognizing the multidimensional nature of the causes of poverty and measures to attack it
- partnership-oriented, providing a basis for the active, coordinated participation of development partners (bilateral, multilateral, non-governmental) in supporting country strategies
- based on a medium and long-term perspective for poverty reduction, recognizing that sustained poverty reduction cannot be achieved overnight.

Because I want to focus on what I see as the marginal changes brought about by the PRSP process, I consider which of the above represents a change from the Bank and IMF's usual way of doing business. This is an analysis of intent, not necessarily one of outcomes. I emphasize five points:

1. The notion that a country's plan of action should come first and foremost from the recipient country and not from the Bank and IMF is a fine idea and is, if not new, at least more apparent than in the past. In the end, the plan will be a collaborative effort between the poor country and the Bank and Fund. Under the PRSP process, it is now clear that the first hand played is that of the country, with the lending agencies then responding. One of the real changes highlighted in this first principle is the inclusion of all the groups that comprise 'broad based participatory processes'. The phrase 'country owner-ship' has come to mean more than just that the finance ministry of a borrow-ing country has to sign off on the plan. Rather, it is expected that country ownership will come about through:

- the participation of many ministries, parliament and provincial or state governments
- the inclusion of other 'stakeholder groups'. This list includes 'civil society groups, women's groups, ethnic minorities, policy research institutes and academics, private sector, trade unions [and] representatives from different regions of the country'
- the participation of other external aid providers
- the inclusion of mechanisms used to consult the poor and their representatives'.

Some of these really are changes from the usual way of doing business. In par-ticular, the explicit inclusion of multiple branches and layers of government, and the inclusion of civil society groups is new. Readers from developed countries that tend to have less geographic and ethnic divisions, a better com-munication infrastructure and more established governmental institutions can imagine how difficult it would be to get all of the above stakeholder groups to agree on a strategy to alleviate poverty in their own country. Still, in principle, it is a good idea to at least ask for everyone's involvement, and explicit inclusion of the poor in the consultative process is a new thing. How this is actually done is again tricky, and whether it is effective is a separate matter. Finally, the idea that the first draft of the document be initially prepared by the recipient country and not by the Bank or IMF also represents a genuine change from the past.

2. The focus on a 'results-oriented' process is, one hopes, not new. I am not completely sure what the alternative is, but few seem to have advocated a process-oriented strategy without reference to results prior to 1999. On the other hand, the focus on how the results affect the poor is a marginal (in the positive sense) change in emphasis if not content. This is a very good idea in principle. In practice, however, it is often hard to analyse in a rigorous way the distributional impact of government expenditures and other policies, but the intent is right on target. There is a danger that the parties involved will shy away from the difficult question of just how a policy affects the poor and instead take the much easier route of suggesting that any policy that promotes economic growth is good for the poor since in general growth is good for the poor.

3. The PRSP process should acknowledge the many dimensions of poverty. One way in which Bank thinking about poverty today really does seem different from that of 10 or 20 years ago is its increased emphasis on dimensions of poverty beyond income-based measures. This does then seem like a change in Bank and IMF policy. This change is not always for the better, however, and there are some pretty good reasons for sticking with income 23-based (or consumption-based) measures of poverty. Still, it is a change.

4. The PRSP process should include participation by other aid providers, or, to use the language of the PRSP Sourcebook, 'development partners'. The idea here is that the PRSP process should be such that all the aid providers come together to support the poverty reduction plan. The plan is, in principle, the work of the country and not the Bank – this means aid providers should be supporting the country's own plan. This seems ingenious. Because at the end of the day the Bank and Fund have to approve the PRSP, this point could appear to be a strategy for getting other aid providers to buy into a Bank/Fund development strategy. But if the PRSP strategy is a good one and if this results in other aid givers also focusing on the poor, this is a laudable goal. Whether this point represents a marginal change is unclear. The fact that PRSPs need Bank/Fund approval still gives the Bank and Fund the final say on the policy environment required to obtain concessional lending. This has been and continues to be the case. Whether the Bank and Fund have in the past tried to get other bilateral, multilateral and non-governmental parties to support the Bank and Fund's policy prescriptions varies by instance.

5. The last point is a concession to reality. Because poverty reduction is a long-term challenge, PRSPs should adopt a medium and long-term perspective. This does not seem to represent much of a change from the past.

These are the goals of the PRSP process. Devising the plan to implement these goals has proven to be a time-consuming task. Because PRSPs are 'country-owned', the burden falls on the country to develop the plans. This is costly for the country as it can easily take about two years to develop a PRSP, and in many of the very poorest countries, there is a dearth of qualified talent to draft a good PRSP. Still, the alternative is for the Bank and Fund to develop the PRSP itself. A middle ground, and one that has in practice been adopted in several countries, is for the Bank and Fund to provide assistance when needed but to leave the main responsibility for writing the plan to the country.

2.2 What should a PRSP include?

A good PRSP should lay out a plan to reduce poverty and increase sustainable economic growth. Of course, if this was easy, the Bank, with its thousands of PhD-trained professionals and billions of dollars of resources, would have solved the issue a long time ago. Still, it is important to specify the goals of the PRSP. The PRSP Sourcebook focuses on four key elements of a good PRSP. These are:

- macroeconomic and structural policies that support sustainable growth in which the poor countries participate
- policies to improve governance – including public sector financial management
- appropriate sectoral policies and programs
- realistic costing and appropriate levels of funding for the major programs.

The guidelines outlining what countries should include in their PRSPs also highlight the importance of prioritizing. Finally, there is the need to discuss 'appropriate sequencing' of policy actions. This last point is especially important and too frequently ignored. In the critical analysis in the last section, I discussed the importance of the sequencing of policy actions (which may be very different from the priority of policy actions).

Each of the above four elements certainly belong in a PRSP. Indeed, given this list, it is not clear what area of development-related government policy does *not* belong. I will discuss each area in turn.

2.2.1 Macroeconomic and structural policies

The first area speaks of the importance of macroeconomic policy as well as regulatory policy. The macroeconomic focus results from the belief (which is empirically pretty well-founded) that sound macroeconomic policies and growth are good for the poor. This part of the PRSP is intended to address some of the concerns traditionally in the IMF's domain – for example, inflation and exchange rate policy. Alas, while the evidence strongly supports the idea that growth is good for the poor, the record on just what promotes economic growth is much less clear. The PRSP Sourcebook is apparently less ambivalent as to what makes an economy grow or not. For example, it explicitly mentions such constraints on growth as exchange rate controls (tell that to Malaysia) and trade barriers (someone inform China). The Sourcebook also mentions specifically labor-market policy as well as other regulatory and market controls. The broad prescription seems to be one in which macroeconomic reform should be planned out according to the mostly standard Fund prescriptions but with concern for how the policies will affect the poor. There is specific mention of the possible need 'to strengthen social safety net programs prior to embarking on the reform program'. This is right, but many – probably most – of the countries writing PRSPs do not have much in the way of social safety nets to start with. To ask a country such as Mauritania or Burkina Faso to be sure to implement policies (that is, expend funds) to protect the poor from the adverse impacts of contractionary monetary policy while keeping an eye on the government budget deficit is too much to expect.

The discussion of labor-market policy in the PRSP Sourcebook is also ambitious. The PRSP should address such issues as 'minimum wages; payroll taxes; rules governing hiring/firing of workers; labor standards' and other labor-market regulations and how these regulations affect the poor. Really? Doing this for a country like the USA for which there is an astounding wealth of high-quality labor-market panel data would be a real contribution to the state of the art of economic policy analysis. Doing this in a convincing way for Chad (which acknowledges in its interim PRSP that it does not have a lot in the way of data) would be inspirational in its ambition.

Overall, some parts of the discussion of the macroeconomic content of PRSPs strike me as extraordinarily hopeful. It might seem like there is little downside to asking for countries to at least try to address these important macroeconomic concerns *and* the linkage of these concerns to poverty. That might be right, but an alternative view is that when one asks for a policy plan for which there is no hope of careful analytic support, one just gets platitudes and, if the country is gaming the situation, a discussion of what the country thinks the Bank and Fund want to hear.

2.2.2 Improving governance

The second area of content for PRSPs is its plan to improve governance. The inclusion of governance in the PRSP process speaks to the growing awareness that the quality of institutions matters for economic progress. There is little doubt of what the Bank and Fund are looking for here. The countries are expected to address such issues as the accountability and transparency of governmental expenditures as well as the poor functioning of the civil service. World Bank and IMF documentation regarding the link between this aspect of the PRSP and poverty is somewhat nuanced, but the basic idea is straightforward and seemingly correct. If the government is corrupt, the poor are going to have less influence on government policy and more difficult access to government services, for the simple reason that they are less able to afford the access and services.

2.2.3 Appropriate sector policies

The PRSP Sourcebook includes chapters on several specific areas of sectoral policies and programs. These include education, health, environment, mining and 'social protection', among others. Although suggested policy prescriptions differ by country and by sector of policy, the general approach suggested for PRSPs is that countries ascertain what makes poor households poor and use policies to mitigate the resulting poverty.

There seem to be two broad approaches. First, countries should examine the roles that lack of access to health care, education, credit, sanitation and the like play in determining poverty. Countries should then direct policy appropriately in keeping within their budget constraints. The PRSP Sourcebook makes clear that 'policy and program priorities will not be implemented unless countries ensure that they can afford the public expenditures they plan'. Second, countries should analyse the distributional impact of the expenditures they plan to make. These distributional impacts can vary by geographic region, income group, gender and religious or tribal group. The PRSP guidelines make clear that countries should analyse these distributional impacts of proposed policies. Furthermore, the prioritization and sequencing of the different policy options should take into account the impact on the poor. While these are also ambitious goals, economists know how to undertake these tasks if the data permit. Conversely, the data requirements are not trivial and requiring information on the distributional impact of policies when the data does not now exist, and will not exist in the foreseeable future, encourages hollow and unsubstantiated claims that only sound good on paper.

2.2.4 Realistic costing and funding

The last area that PRSPs should address is just how much all the grand plans are going to cost, and to propose a budget. This requirement of the PRSP ties in closely with the first requirement, macroeconomic stability. The budgetary implications for PRSPs must take account of the possibility of shifting existing expenditures, raising new government revenues and external assistance. Because the Bank and Fund are the ones approving (or not) the PRSP, they are presumably best able to judge the likelihood of external assistance. The request for realistic budget information is both necessary and appropriate.

I devote the rest of this chapter to trying to analyse the effectiveness of the PRSP process. That is, how well has it worked and what lessons are emerging after more than three years of experience? Simply, the volume of work product stemming from the PRSP process is overwhelming. There are tens of thousands of pages of PRSPs, interim PRSPs, Bank and Fund joint staff assessments of the PRSPs, progress reports, status reports, policy papers and notes to guide Bank and Fund staff, as well as the PRSP Sourcebook, to guide nations in preparing PRSPs. Even if one restricted one's attention to just PRSPs (final and interim) themselves, there are about four dozen countries with quite varying experiences. In light of the tremendous quantity of material that could be evaluated, I have elected to begin by assessing the existing evaluations. I provide a critical look at what those inside the process (the Bank and Fund) as well as those outside the process (mostly NGOs) think of the PRSP approach. I begin with the Bank and Fund review and then turn to the outside reviews. I conclude with yet another review – my own.

2.3 Evaluation from the inside

As I noted at the outset of this paper, in the summer of 2001 the Bank and Fund undertook an extensive review of the PRSP process, which was completed in March 2002. The results of this review, in keeping with the spirit of inclusion, are available on the web. The Bank and Fund findings are presented in both an executive summary and a lengthy detailed report. My summary of this internal review is taken from the latter – 'Review of the Poverty Reduction Strategy Paper (PRSP) Approach: Early Experience with Interim PRSPs and Full PRSPs', dated 26 March 2002.

One can take two broad approaches in evaluating the PRSP process. The first is to examine the multitude of experiences and then highlight best practices. The second is to step back and ask if the process is working and, relative to what probably would have happened without it, whether it is truly beneficial to the poor. It is possible to do the former and never really tackle the latter. The Bank and Fund's internal review illustrates the point.

Highlighting best practices is, for sure, useful. Over time, dozens of countries will move from their interim PRSPs to preparing the full paper. Learning from the experiences of those who have come before makes perfect sense. But this is not the same as asking whether the entire approach is working. This criticism of the internal review, though, is admittedly rather too harsh. The internal review concludes that it is simply too early to know if the process is affecting poverty. Instead, since many countries are in the process of either writing an interim PRSP or moving from an interim to a full PRSP, it is more useful to simply highlight best practices. I agree that it is probably too early to make firm judgments about how the process is affecting poverty. It is not, however, too early to ask whether we will *ever* be able to answer this question. The Bank and Fund are optimistic as they predict that a 'rich information base should be available from a range of countries during the next three years to allow these questions (concerning poverty outcomes) to be posed more precisely'. My more cautious conclusion is that time-series data on income or expenditure-based poverty outcomes is currently scarce in most countries writing PRSPs. Countries are being urged to collect the needed data, but it remains to be seen whether this will in fact happen. While some data on variables such as primary school completion rates and changes in government expenditure patterns are likely to be available, data on changes in poverty outcomes over time are less available.

The internal review of what has happened so far, though, focuses on high-lighting best practices. Those countries that have completed full PRSPs have often built upon existing data and analyses as well as on prior strategies. That is, many of the countries that did full PRSPs already had poverty reduction programs in the works before the PRSP process was announced. One of the countries often mentioned as doing a pretty good job is Uganda. Uganda, though, put together its 'Poverty Eradication Action Plan' in 1997 so it was ready to go when the PRSP approach was announced in 1999. This accentuates the *marginal* impact of the PRSP approach. In the case of Uganda, much of what showed up in its PRSP was going to happen anyway. The organization of the plan, and perhaps the increased emphasis on inclusivity, were affected by the PRSP process, but the overall plan was already well underway. Similarly, in Mozambique, the PRSP built upon the government's 1999 poverty reduction plan. In Mauritania and Burkina Faso, the governments set up plans to attack poverty in 1998, while Bolivia did so in 1997 and Honduras and Nicaragua put together anti-poverty strategies following Hurricane Mitch in 1999. Hence, if one were to look only at those countries that either have already or have almost completed full PRSPs, many are articulating plans that predated the PRSP approach. In these cases, the marginal impact of the PRSP approach is diminished.

The Bank and Fund internal review does suggest that the PRSP approach has yielded some changes in process. For example:

1. PRSPs have led to wider governmental involvement. Before the PRSP process, it was common for Bank and Fund borrowing issues to be handled almost entirely by the finance ministry. The new process has led to ministerial-level involvement by several ministries. The 'core' ministries (for example, planning or finance) remain more involved than sectoral ministries, but the change is in the right direction.

2. PRSPs have led to greater involvement by civil-society organizations. These organizations frequently had no opportunity to offer meaningful input prior to the PRSP approach. This is a two-edged sword. On the positive side, it means that more segments of society have an opportunity to weigh in with opinions and concerns. On the negative side, the additional participation tends to 'compound rather than resolve the problem of prioritization'.

3. The PRSP approach has highlighted the need for decent data to implement careful poverty diagnostics. The internal review notes that the PRSP process has 'been marked by useful steps toward better poverty data and diagnostics'. So far, every one of the completed full-PRSPs has drawn upon 'nationally representative household surveys from which income/consumption poverty estimates were derived'. While some of these surveys were almost a decade out of date, it is nonetheless impressive that all the countries even had a national household income/consumption survey on which to draw. There is a concern, though, that those countries that have completed their full PRSPs are not representative of poor countries in terms of data. Rather, those that had the necessary data were, not surprisingly, the first to get their PRSPs completed. It might seem overly obvious that careful poverty measurement and diagnostics will require a national-level household survey, but the point is an important one. Simply focusing on the need for this sort of data, all by itself, represents a contribution of the PRSP process.

4. Finally, the PRSP process has highlighted the importance of better understanding and analysis of the distributional consequences of government expenditure. While such issues as efficient public administration, honest and transparent government-expenditure systems and the distributional aspects of revenue collection are part of the PRSP approach, none of these are really new. An explicit focus on the distributional aspects of the expenditure side of the budget is, if not new, at least more prominent. This is a great idea, but the data requirements necessary to implement this analysis are substantial. Conducting this analysis correctly and informatively means

analysing whoever benefits from government expenditure. Good analysis probably requires more than just examining the fraction of the government budget devoted to, say, health and education (which is what is presented in the internal review). By presenting 'evidence' in their own report that doesn't even approach the level of care and detail that the PRSP Sourcebook suggests, the internal review sets a pretty bad example.

2.4 Evaluation from the outside

As befits an inclusive process, the review of the PRSP approach solicited opinions from those outside the Bank and Fund. In an admirable display of non-censorship, these reviews are posted on the PRSP review website. Most of the reviews submitted by nongovernmental organizations (NGOs) do not focus on whether the poor are or are not benefiting under the PRSP approach. Rather, most of the NGO reviews focus on the NGOs. Many of these reviews, for example, ask whether the NGOs are having the sort of input to the process that the Bank and Fund seemed to be promising. (Equating input with perceived influence on output, their answer seems to be 'No'.)

The occasional review that does focus on poverty alleviation concludes that poverty is not being alleviated. While my review was necessarily limited, it was not selective. I did not find a single NGO review that provided careful data analysis to back up its conclusions. Lack of data, though, did not stop some NGOs from concluding that the PRSP approach was essentially a fraud. One of the most negative of the reviews was jointly submitted by 'Jubilee South, Focus on the Global South, AWEPON, and the Centor do Estudios Internacionales with the support of the World Council of Churches'. Entitled, 'The World Bank and the PRSP: Flawed Thinking and Failing Experiences', the review is mostly as advertised. It concludes that 'Fighting poverty becomes the newest justification for the aging prescriptions geared to increasing the overall opening of the "host country" to external economic actors and free market rules'. While one can argue about whether open trade is good for poverty alleviation (and I do so below), this review makes no reference to any studies and cites precious little evidence of any sort in its broad-brushed conclusions. This review is a study in how *not* to do program evaluation, but it is not a bad case study for Manifesto Writing 101.

Several of the NGO reviews argue that the focus on income-based measures of poverty is too narrow. In an especially well-exposited review, for example, the Catholic Relief Services notes that while income-based measures are necessary, they are not sufficient: 'Too often, PRSPs fail to reflect a broader approach to poverty reduction that fully addresses dimensions related to security or empowerment as essential ingredients for poverty reduction'. This message is echoed by many other groups. None, though, offers suggestions of how one might measure these other 'ingredients' so as to be able to ascertain whether PRSPs are actually addressing these dimensions of poverty.

Another theme that permeates many of the NGO reviews is a sense of frustration that their input is not taken as seriously as, say, the input of the Bank and Fund. Some NGOs say that, while they are grateful for the opportunity to weigh in, their voices are not having much impact. While some NGOs remark that the PRSP approach has given civil society more scope for input than the old process, there seems to be a congruence of complaints that civil society is not having much impact in the design of economic policy programs. In particular, NGOs often complain that they have little influence when it comes to planning macroeconomic structural adjustment and other poverty- reducing economic policies. Catholic Relief Services states, in its review, that 'Despite some positive and real openings for dialogue between government and civil society, there has been little noticeable impact on the content of the PRSPs'. Save the Children UK writes that '[T]he experience to date is that there seems to have been little difference between policies outlined in the I-PRSP, describing current arrangements under the IMF Poverty Reduction and Growth Facility and the final or draft PRSPs, supposedly written after a participatory process has taken place'.[2] The European Network on Debt and Development (EURODAD) raises similar concerns.[3]

Taking as correct for the moment the assumption that civil society is not having much impact on the economic policy content of the PRSP approach, at least two explanations can be given. First, it is possible that civil society is simply being allowed a voice at the table and, no matter what it says, is preordained to be marginalized. Second, it may be that civil society is just not sufficiently informed or well trained to take on the tricky and complex task of designing well-targeted poverty reduction policies under the budget constraints that are a crucial aspect of the economic plight of poor countries.

Some reviews are more nuanced than others, but the depressing message of many of the NGO reviews is that these organizations are woefully underprepared when it comes to carefully evaluating the PRSP approach. Many of the NGOs that offer well-developed critiques of the PRSP process do an amazing amount of good on the ground in poor countries. Examples include Oxfam, Save the Children, Catholic Relief Services and World Vision. These organizations know how to run projects and, on a very personal level, enhance the quality of life of the world's poor. The knowledge gained in the field is invaluable, and these organizations contribute to the PRSP process by commenting on the PRSP approach. At the end of the day, though, they typically do not seem to have the capacity to offer compelling guidance when it comes to formulating economic policy and rigorously evaluating the distributional implications of that policy.

The PRSP process has also been reviewed by other multilateral institutions. One of the most sensible reviews comes from the Inter-American Development Bank (IDB.) The IDB notes that 'Making PRSPs a condition for debt relief imposes a timetable that is technically and politically sub-optimal; it undermines the quality of the document and compromises the social marketing of its content'. The IDB points out that while asking for input from many is, in principle, a good idea, it has led to PRSPs that are essentially a 'shopping list of problems'.[4] The IDB also notes that the process itself is simply too time-consuming and too expensive. In an understated summary, the IDB suggests that '[p]erhaps, less time could be spent in preparing diagnoses and more time in designing appropriate responses to the country's most pressing problems'.

3. Conclusion

Both the process and the content of the PRSPs are especially sensitive to the plight of the very poor. This raises the question of why the Bank and Fund have elected to highlight the link between their lending programs and poverty in the late 1990s. Part of the answer is probably what a for-profit business would call marketing. A quick read of issues of the Bank's *World Development Report* of around 20 years ago reveals consistent references to poverty reduction, most usually in the context of rural development. The advent of the inclusive PRSP process coincides with a heightened awareness of the Bank in civil (and sometimes not-so-civil) society. Recent anti-globalization demonstrations have put the Bank in the position of having to restate and better market its mission. The coincidental timing of the adoption of the PRSP process and the Bank's need to better explain what it does, leads some to wonder whether the PRSP process is but window dressing. That is, is the PRSP process simply good marketing? I believe the answer is clearly 'no'.

While the PRSP approach with its emphasis on inclusion and focus on poverty alleviation is undoubtedly good marketing, it is not *just* marketing. There is content. Content alone, though, does not mean that the PRSP approach embodies real change. The right question to ask is whether the content and results are really different from what would have happened anyway. This concern speaks to the need to address the question I have posed at the outset, namely, what are the marginal costs and benefits of the PRSP framework. Precisely because the more cynical observers may believe that the PRSP process is simply good marketing in response to the Bank and Fund's increased visibility, it is important to keep the spotlight on the marginal changes resulting from the PRSP process. This focus on what I refer to as marginal changes – changes apart from what would have happened anyway – matters because not all changes are marginal.

The inclusive aspect of the PRSP approach, if not new, at least receives more prominent billing. The same can be said for the explicit focus on how outcomes are likely to affect the very poor. The increased attention given to definitions of poverty that extend beyond those measured by income or expenditure is new, as, following from this, are the increased use of qualitative or narrative approaches to poverty research. The notion that the borrowing country should initially draft the poverty alleviation plan is, in many cases, new. Claims that the PRSP process is simply a relabeling of the existing process simply do not stand up to scrutiny. Not everything, though, is new. The emphasis on pro-growth macroeconomic policies, fiscal responsibility and the importance of both good policy and good government has been around for a while.

Moreover, not all that is new is good. Some of the innovations embodied in the PRSP approach seem flawed in practice. I consider these to be weaknesses of the approach. Some of the flawed parts of previous approaches have survived to see another day in the PRSP approach. These too I consider weaknesses. There are also some very good parts of the process that are mostly new. These are strengths of the new approach. I now turn to a more detailed discussion of the weaknesses and strengths of the approach. For those interested in counting, the strengths outweigh the weaknesses: it's not even close. First, though, some quibbles.

The current PRSP approach does not place sufficient heed to the importance of policy sequencing and instead highlights the need to prioritize policy decisions. These are not one and the same, and the distinction seems especially important when it comes to government spending and poverty alleviation. While sequencing is mentioned a couple times in the voluminous PRSP background material, it is hardly highlighted. The PRSP approach forces the country to explicitly state how poverty is to be addressed. Adding an increased emphasis on the tricky issue of policy sequencing would be a good idea.

The PRSP process discusses the role of trade policy in poverty alleviation with too much assuredness. (See, for example, the PRSP Sourcebook chapter on trade policy.) While links between trade and poverty are nicely highlighted in background documents (cited, but not well represented, in the Sourcebook) by Alan Winters, the trade policy guidance in the PRSP process does not adequately reflect the lack of evidence on the links between trade and poverty. While the focus on knowing what the poor consume and how they earn their livelihoods is right on target, the suggestion that more open trade is good for the poor is based more on faith than evidence. Although the PRSP documents are peppered with references to tailoring the particulars of a poverty alleviation program to the details of the country, the discussion of trade policy as well as some of the macroeconomic prescriptions seem to reflect a one-size-fits-all mentality.

The PRSP process also stresses the need to hear from the poor so as to be able to better address their concerns. To a degree, this is a great idea, but when anecdotal and qualitative approaches begin to guide policymaking, it is time to step back and re-evaluate. This approach is evidenced by the much-heralded 'Voices of the Poor' project in the Bank. (This project is not part of the PRSP program, but is clearly related.) The advantage of a project like this is that it gives a human face to an issue that might otherwise be obscured by facts and figures. That project also brings to the fore the sense of hopelessness that comes from simply not having a voice due to the way that poverty interacts with the politics of decision-making at the village, provincial and federal levels. The project also highlights gender-related aspects of poverty. It makes for engrossing and sad reading.

This sort of work is a useful complement to more rigorous quantitative work, but it is not a substitute. The qualitative work suggests some alternatives to income- or expenditure-based measures of poverty. The problem with measures such as, for example, disenfranchisement or opportunities-based measures of poverty is that they are very hard to quantify. If one cannot measure these aspects of poverty, it is hard to know whether they are being alleviated. Where there is absent data, it is all too easy for advocates or skeptics of one stance or another to simply assert the alleged effectiveness of their preferred poverty-alleviation policies. While income- and expenditure-based measures of poverty have their drawbacks (they do not address the issue of voicelessness to the extent that it is unrelated to income or expenditure), they also have their advantages. De-emphasizing these traditional measures seems a bad idea. Supplementing them with capabilities-related measures of poverty, many of which *can* be measured (for example, health, education, nutrition or even some self-reported measures of wellbeing) seems like a good idea. Adding to the mix metrics that cannot be measured is more problematic. It should be noted that the PRSP Sourcebook chapter on 'Well-Being Measurement and Analysis' does the job correctly, with the focus solely on measurable poverty indicators.

Many innovations in the PRSP approach count as strengths. These include the inclusivity of the approach, the principle that the country (and not the Bank or Fund) prepare the first draft of the plan, and, most of all, the focus on the need for data to evaluate the effectiveness of the PRSP process.

On the whole, the inclusivity of the PRSP approach is a good thing and a welcome change. This inclusivity extends most obviously to civil society but also to more broad branches of government than just the finance and planning ministry (this part is less obvious). It is the latter that will probably yield the greatest benefits. By at least trying to get multiple ministries and, in many cases, multiple levels of government involved in the development of a poverty reduction strategy, the likelihood of success of the strategy is enhanced. This seems to be one aspect of inclusivity that is working. The inclusivity of the PRSP approach, however, is a double-edged sword. When everyone's input is requested, the list of issues to be addressed starts to look like a shopping list, and many of those weighing in on the process are ill-trained to do so, as discussed earlier. The alternative is to proceed without soliciting the input of civil society, but this seems even more problematic. The uncomfortable truth is that the Bank and the Fund, and the recipient government, are still free to ignore what they perceive as bad advice. The problem arises when, for political reasons or otherwise, silly ideas get equal billing with good ones.

As noted earlier, the PRSP process is in principle structured so that the first draft of the poverty alleviation plan is written by the country and not the Bank or Fund. In reality, however, it does not always work this way since some countries lack sufficient capacity. Still, when there is capacity, this ordering of matters is an improvement and, in the absence of capacity, the process is no worse than before. It is however too early to know whether this move to enfranchise the country is working. The idea is that by instilling a greater sense of ownership, the country will feel more committed to implementing the plan. This is a good idea.

While it is undoubtedly true that some countries lack the capacity to draft PRSPs, it is not a fair complaint. When the capacity is lacking or not forthcoming, experience suggests that Bank and Fund teams will step in and assist. It is hard to see how this outcome is worse than the alternative in which Bank and Fund teams initially draft all the plans for all the countries. The other alternative, conditional on not being able to magically create local capacity in an instant, is to make the PRSP approach less demanding. I would reject this alternative. It is true that a careful analysis of the distributional impact of myriad policies with an emphasis on quantitative analysis is difficult. But relaxing these requirements is a bad idea. If hard quantitative goals and metrics for success are absent, it is too easy for the PRSP approach to be waylaid by political concerns with proclamations of success or failure motivated by dogma rather than evidence.

The focus on poverty as opposed to, say, broadly defined economic growth, is so pervasive in the PRSP approach that it could almost go unmentioned. This focus is real, not just marketing, and it permeates almost every aspect of the process. It is an obviously good idea. An implication of the focus on poverty is that it requires very detailed household-level (if not individual-level) data. Detailed data is required to identify the poor, and even more data is required to identify transitions from or into poverty. These data are needed for several aspects of a successful PRSP implementation. In particular:

1. Data on household income or expenditure are needed to determine just who the poor are. This is not as readily available as one might think. There are many examples of household surveys in which expenditure data is scarce and in which income data is either not reported, reported only in broad bands (which makes identifying the very poor hard) or reported only incompletely. (For example, income from self-production is sometimes poorly reported, as are transfers from non-resident household members.) These data are usefully supplemented with data on self-reported measures of well-being and other capabilities-based measures.
2. Data on household expenditure is needed to determine how poor house-holds might be affected by various policy options that are part of PRSPs. For example, the PRSP Sourcebook notes that what a household con-sumes will influence how it is affected by trade policy. Similarly, consump-tion patterns will be important to the analysis of the distributional impact of price changes that might arise from shifts in food-pricing policy or other tax-related policies. Expenditure data are generally more scarce than income data but they are essential.
3. Data on the household use of public services is needed to determine the distributional impact of government-provided programs and services. That is to say, to know whether health clinics or clean running water investments will help the very poor, one requires data on the use of these services by the poor.
4. Data on the income sources of the very poor are needed to ascertain how the employment effects of various macroeconomic policy options are likely to affect the very poor. This means knowing more than just a household's income, instead knowing the source(s) of that income, also often by sector of employment.

All of the above data are needed to establish baseline estimates of poverty and its correlates. To evaluate effectively the impact of PRSP policies, one needs either repeated cross-sectional data on the above items or, ideally, panel data. In most developing countries, the former are more available than the latter. Nationally representative panel surveys are pretty rare. Cross-sectional surveys (often annual) are more available, but are by no means common. If panel data is absent, it is impossible to investigate transitions into or out of poverty. Questions about whether the poor are a stable population, or are comprised of different households moving into and out of poverty, remain unanswerable.

The PRSP documentation is admirably upfront about the need for good household data to be able to identify the poor and monitor changes in their (individual or collective) welfare. There are myriad references to the necessity of using and, in many cases, collecting household-level data. This is exactly the right way to focus the evaluation of the PRSP plans. By focusing on poverty, which occurs at the level of the household or individual and not at the level of the nation, the PRSP approach redirects attention to micro-data and away from macroeconomic data. This is a good thing. Micro-data are required for most poverty-related policy analysis and with the Bank and Fund arguing for its collection, it is more likely that such data will be collected.

With very little micro-data available, one might wonder whether the PRSP approach can be evaluated. It happens that there is a surprising amount of data out there. On a helpful web page titled 'Household Surveys for Poverty Monitoring', the Bank notes that fully 97 per cent of the population of low and middle-income countries are covered by at least one survey with data on consumption and/or income as of the year 2000. Furthermore, the comparable figure is 86 per cent for those covered by comparable data for at least two points in time. In Africa, where some of the poorest countries are, 93 per cent of the population is covered by at least one survey measuring income and/or consumption, while 51 per cent is covered by comparable data for at least two points in time. These are hopeful figures. They suggest that it is, in practice as well as in principle, possible to evaluate the efficacy of the PRSP approach over time.

In order to conduct the evaluation of the approach, it will be necessary to continue to collect household survey data and not just rely on the existing stock of data. This is acknowledged in the PRSP documentation and, assuming it happens, is a nice side-benefit of the approach.

In the Bank and Fund's common review of the PRSP framework, it is too early to say whether the approach is working. That is why they focus instead on best practices. The quantitative evaluation that is presented is minimal and does not really address the issue of how changes in government spending are affecting poverty-related outcomes. The NGO reviews do not contain even bad quantitative analysis. At the end of the day, there seem to be *no* evaluations of a particular PRSP program that really examine the effectiveness of the program at the level of detail that the program recommends.

Finally, just as it is useful to highlight best practices so that other countries can learn from the experiences of the first completed PRSPs, it would be helpful if the Bank and Fund, or an NGO, could provide one (just *one*) careful, detailed and rigorous analysis of a PRSP program. Such an analysis would identify the poor and note the usefulness (or not) of expansive definitions of poverty relative to more narrow ones. The analysis would look carefully at how the poor spend their incomes and from where the incomes derive. It would examine the distributional consequences of government spending and would try to distinguish between marginal changes in policy and expenditures or programs and results that would have happened anyway. Ideally, this analysis would be based on multiple waves of a household survey. The results would of course be preliminary. Still, providing an example of how it is done would be a helpful addition to an ambitious and, on the whole, admirable program. The Bank and Fund have the expertise and resources to conduct such an analysis, have access to the necessary data, and presumably know what constitutes a convincing analysis of a PRSP-supported reform program.

Notes

1 This paper was prepared as part of the research program of the Intergovernmental Group of Twenty-Four on International Monetary Affairs and Development (G24), with financial support from the International Development Research Centre of Canada (IDRC). It was first published by UNCTAD as no. 21 of the G24 Discussion Paper Series. The views expressed and the designations and terminology employed are those of the author and do not necessarily reflect the views of the G24, IDRC and UNCTAD.

2 The review of the PRSP is available at www.worldbank.org/poverty/strategies/overview.htm.

3 Much of this section is drawn from material on the World Bank's PRSP website. This website, devoted to the PRSP, is a tremendous resource. There, one can find links to all the original PRSP reports, the interim reports, the evaluation of these reports, the many contributed papers evaluating the PRSP, and hundreds of related links. The URL is: http://www.worldbank.org/poverty/strategies/index.htm.

4 Countries can still obtain concessional lending before their PRSP is complete and one way to do this is to prepare what is called an Interim PRSP (I-PRSP). This is basically like a PRSP but much shorter, less detailed, and easier to prepare. It is a kind of draft mini-PRSP.

5 In some documents, there are five key principles, in others there are six or seven. In the interest of brevity, I am selecting the shortest list, but in substance all the lists are quite similar. To the Bank and Fund's credit, there is a clear set of expectations associated with what the PRSPs are supposed to accomplish. I have taken the list of principles from the PRSP Sourcebook draft of April 2001. This seems to be the most recent draft available to the public. It is a very, very long document and is available online at http://www.worldbank.org/poverty/strategies/sourctoc.htm

6 See p. 6 of the Overview chapter of the PRSP Sourcebook, April 2001 draft for public comments.

7 Taken verbatim from the PRSP Sourcebook, p. 17 in the Overview section.

8 The PRSP Sourcebook makes explicit reference to the well-publicized findings of Dollar and Kray and their contention that open trade regimes promote growth, which alleviates poverty. No mention is made of the careful and fairly devastating critique of that work.

9 The review has its own homepage http://www.worldbank.org/poverty/strategies/
   review/. The 103-page review is downloadable at: http://www.worldbank.org/
   poverty/strategies/review/earlyexp.pdf

10 Another review of the PRSP approach is scheduled for 2005 and in the 2002 review it
   is noted that the next review will need to 'examine changes in poverty outcomes'.

11 See paragraph 42 of the internal Bank and Fund review, cited above.

12 The same would apply to expenditure-based measures. While economists tend to differentiate between the two and prefer expenditure-based measures since they are more
   resilient to transient shocks, the complaints about income-based measures seem to
   apply to expenditure-based measures too.

13 'Review of the Poverty Reduction Strategy Paper Initiative', December 2001, Catholic
   Relief Services, p. 12. Available on-line at: http://www.worldbank.org/poverty/
   strategies/review/crs1.pdf

14 This review is available on line at: http://www.worldbank.org/poverty/strategies/
   review/scuk1.pdf.

15 The EURODAD report is available on line at: http://www.worldbank.org/poverty/
   strategies/review/eurodad1a.pdf. and http://www.worldbank.org/poverty/strategies
   /review/eurodad1b.pdf.

16 Several NGOs also make this point. A more subtle question is whether, conditional on
   the requirement that a PRSP be completed to obtain concessional lending, is it perhaps
   good public policy to rush the completion of the document in order to get the needed
   funds to then move forward with the real business of poverty alleviation and economic
   growth.

17 The IDB review is available on line at: http://www.worldbank.org/poverty/
   strategies/review/imfieo1.pdf.

18 Although it is too trivial to really qualify as a 'quibble', it sure would be nice if the
   PRSP process could avoid the use of more acronyms than a Tom Clancy novel. To the
   uninitiated, the approach has its own language.

19 See, for example, the brief discussion of sequencing in the Overview chapter of the
   PRSP Sourcebook, page 18.

20 This is available online, like all the chapters. The overview of the trade chapter is on
   line at: http://www.worldbank.org/poverty/strategies/chapters/trade/trade.htm

21 The entire chapter is available at: http://www.worldbank.org/poverty/strategies/
   chapters/trade/trad0613.pdf.

22 This project has its own web page. The address is: http://www.worldbank.org/
   poverty/voices/index.htm.

23 See http://www.worldbank.org/poverty/data/index.htm and http://www.world-
   bank.org/poverty/data/census/part2.htm#Findings as well as the links contained
   there. These are very useful resource pages for those looking for household-level data.

Bibliography

[All references in this paper are available online and may be accessed via the world-wide-
web. Addresses are included below.]

Catholic Relief Services, 'Review of the Poverty Reduction Strategy Paper Initiative',
   December 2001, www.worldbank.org/poverty/strategies.review/crs1.pdf.

EURODAD, 'Many Dollars, Any Change?' October 2001, www.worldbank.org/poverty/strategies.review/eurodad1a.pdf and www.worldbank.org/poverty/strategies.review/eurodad1b.pdf.

International Monetary Fund, IMF Independent Evaluations Office, 'Synopsis of Contributions to the PRSP Review', 2001, www.worldbank.org/poverty/strategies.review/imfieo1.pdf.

Jubilee South, Focus on the Global South, AWEPON, and the Centor do Estudios Internacionales, and The World Council of Churches, 'The World Bank and the PRSP: Flawed Thinking and Failing Experiences', 2001, www.worldbank.org/poverty/strategies/review/jsouth1.pdf.

Save the Children UK, 'Save the Children UK submission to the IMF/WB review of PRSPs', December 2001, www.worldbank.org/poverty/strategies.review/scuk1.pdf

The World Bank, 'Overview of Poverty Reduction Strategies', www.worldbank.org/poverty/strategies/overview.htm (Last accessed 21 November, 2002.)

The World Bank, 'Poverty Reduction Strategies and PRSPs', www.worldbank.org/poverty/strategies/index.htm (Last accessed 21 November, 2002.)

The World Bank, 'Comprehensive Development Framework', www.worldbank.org/cdf/cdfprsplink.pdf (Last accessed 21 November, 2002.)

The World Bank, 'Overview and Background of the Comprehensive Development Framework', www.worldbank.org/cdf/overview.htm (Last accessed 21 November, 2002.)

The World Bank, 'PRSP Sourcebook', (April 2001 draft.) www.worldbank.org/poverty/strategies/courctoc.htm.

The World Bank, 'IMF/World Bank PRSP Comprehensive Review Homepage', www.worldbank.org/poverty/strategies/review/ (Last accessed 21 November, 2002.)

The World Bank, 'Review of the Poverty Reduction Strategy Paper (PRSP) Approach: Early Experience with Interim PRSPs and Full PRSPs', 26 March, 2002, www.worldbank.org/poverty/strategies/review/earlyexp.pdf. (Last accessed 21 November, 2002.)

World Bank, 'Poverty Reduction Strategy Sourcebook, Overview of Trade Policy', www.worldbank.org/poverty/strategies/chapters/trade/trade.htm. (Last accessed on 21 November, 2002.)

World Bank, 'Voices of the Poor', www.worldbank.org/poverty/voices/index.htm. (Last accessed 21 November, 2002.)

World Bank, 'Household Surveys for Poverty Monitoring', www.worldbank.org/poverty/index.htm. (Last accessed on 20 August, 2002.)

6

CAPITAL MANAGEMENT TECHNIQUES IN DEVELOPING COUNTRIES*

Gerald Epstein, Ilene Grabel and KS Jomo

Abstract

We examine the experiences of five developing countries that employed various capital management techniques during the 1990s. By 'capital management techniques' we refer to policies of prudential financial regulation and controls that affect international capital flows to achieve national economic goals. One key finding is that by employing a diverse set of capital management techniques, policymakers in Chile, Colombia, Taiwan Province of China, Singapore and Malaysia were able to achieve critical macroeconomic objectives. These included the prevention of maturity and locational mismatch; attraction of favored forms of foreign investment; reduction in overall financial fragility, currency risk, and speculative pressures in the economy; insulation from the contagion effects of financial crises and enhancement of the autonomy of economic and social policy. We also examine the structural factors that contributed to these achievements and consider the costs associated with the capital management techniques employed. We conclude by considering the policy lessons of these experiences and the political prospects for other developing countries that wish to apply them.

1. Introduction

Developing countries can use capital management techniques to strengthen financial stability, support good macroeconomic and microeconomic policies

---

* This paper is also published by UNCTAD as G24 Discussion Paper no. 25, United Nations, New York and Geneva (forthcoming).

and boost investment. Countries have, in fact, employed these techniques during the 1990s; and so we consider the experiences of five such countries.

We use the term capital management techniques (CMTs) to refer to two complementary (and often overlapping) types of financial policies: policies that govern international private capital flows, called capital controls, and those that enforce prudential management of domestic financial institutions. A strict bifurcation between capital controls and prudential regulations often cannot be maintained in practice.[2] Policymakers frequently implement multi-faceted regimes of capital management, as no single measure can achieve the diverse objectives.

Moreover, the effectiveness of any single management technique magnifies the effectiveness of other techniques and enhances the efficacy of the entire regime of capital management. For example, certain prudential financial regulations magnify the effectiveness of capital controls (and vice versa). In this case, the stabilizing aspect of prudential regulation reduces the need for the most stringent form of capital control. Thus, a program of complementary CMTs reduces the necessary severity of any one technique and magnifies the effectiveness of the regime of financial control.

A number of characteristics of capital management techniques are worth noting. CMTs can be static or dynamic. Static management techniques are those that authorities do not modify in response to changes in circumstances. Examples of static management techniques include restrictions on the convertibility of the currency or maintenance of minimum-stay requirements on foreign investment. By contrast, dynamic CMTs can be activated or adjusted as circumstances warrant. Several types of circumstances trigger implementation of management techniques or lead the authorities to strengthen or adjust existing regulations. CMTs are typically activated in response to changes in the economic environment, or to prevent identified vulnerabilities from culminating in a financial crisis, or to reduce the severity of such a crisis;[3] they are strengthened or modified as authorities attempt to close loopholes in existing measures.

Policymakers use CMTs to achieve some or all of the following four objectives:

- promote financial stability
- encourage desirable investment and financing arrangements
- enhance policy autonomy
- enhance democracy.[4]

CMTs can promote financial stability through their ability to reduce currency, flight, fragility and/or contagion risks, thereby reducing the potential for financial crisis and attendant economic and social devastation. They can also influence the composition of the economy's aggregate investment portfolio and can influence the financing arrangements that underpin these investments. Moreover, CMTs can promote desirable types of investment and financing strategies by rewarding investors and borrowers for engaging in them. Desirable types of investment are those that create employment, improve living standards, promote greater income equality, technology transfer, learning by doing and/or long-term growth. Desirable types of financing are those that are long-term, stable and sustainable. Capital management can discourage less socially useful types of investment and financing strategies by increasing their cost or precluding them altogether.

CMTs can enhance policy autonomy in a number of ways: they can reduce the severity of currency risk and can thereby allow authorities to protect a currency peg, and they can create space for the government and/or the central bank to pursue growth-promoting and/or reflationary macroeconomic policies by neutralizing the threat of capital flight. By reducing the risk of financial crisis in the first place, CMTs can reduce the likelihood that governments are compelled to use contractionary macroeconomic, microeconomic and social policy to attract foreign investment back to the country or as a precondition for IMF assistance. Finally, CMTs can reduce the specter of foreign control or ownership of domestic resources.

It follows from the above that capital management can enhance democracy by reducing the potential for speculators and external actors to exercise undue influence over domestic decision-making directly or indirectly (via the threat of capital flight). CMTs can reduce the veto power of the financial community and the IMF and create scope for other groups (such as advocates for the poor) to play a role in the design of policy. They can thus be said to enhance democracy because they create the opportunity for pluralism in policy design.

2. Case studies

We now present five case studies that analyse the CMTs employed during the 1990s in Chile, Colombia, Malaysia, Singapore and Taiwan Province of China (POC).[5] The presentation of these case studies is guided by five principal goals. First, to provide a detailed institutional guide to the CMTs pursued in diverse areas of the world from the 1990s to the present. Second, to examine the extent to which these management techniques achieved the objectives of their architects. Third, to elaborate the underlying structural factors that explain the success or failure of the techniques employed. Fourth, to examine the costs associated with these measures. And fifth, to draw general conclusions about the desirability and feasibility of replicating or adapting particular techniques to developing countries outside of our sample.

We have limited our examination to the 1990s because this period is distinguished by the *combination* of high levels of financial integration, a global norm of financial and economic liberalization, an increase in the power and autonomy of the global financial community and significant advances in telecommunications technology. It is widely accepted that any one of these factors (let alone their combined presence) frustrates the possibility of successful capital management. We have selected these five cases because policymakers employed diverse CMTs (in line with levels of state capacity and sovereignty) with different objectives and disparate degrees of success. (Table 1, p. 166, presents a summary of the major CMTs and their objectives for each of our cases.)

2.1 CMTs in Chile and Colombia[6]

In the aftermath of the Asian crisis, heterodox and even prominent mainstream economists, for example Eichengreen, focused a great deal of attention on the 'Chilean model', a term that was used to refer to a policy regime that the Chilean and Colombian authorities began to implement in June 1991 and September 1993 respectively.[7] During the 1990s, policymakers in Chile and Colombia sought to improve investor confidence and to promote stable, sustainable economic and export growth. The CMTs of the 1990s were an integral component of the overall economic plan in both countries. CMTs in Chile and Colombia can perhaps be best understood in the context of the economic challenges that confronted the region's economies during the 1970s and 1980s. These problems included high inflation, severe currency and banking instability, financial crises, high levels of external debt and capital flight and low levels of investor confidence.

2.1.1 Chilean context

Chile experienced a 'boom–bust cycle' in the two decades that preceded the CMTs of the 1990s. During the neoliberal experiment of the 1970s, surges in foreign capital inflows led to a consumption boom and created significant pressure for currency appreciation. Experience with the 'Dutch disease'[8] in the 1970s reinforced policymakers' commitment to preventing the fallout from surges in private capital inflows in the 1990s. The financial implosion, reduction in international capital flows and deep recession of the early to mid-1980s also played a powerful role in the design of CMTs in the 1990s. Thus, the experiences of the 1970s and 1980s created a consensus around the idea that it was necessary to insulate the economy from volatile international capital flows.

Preventing the Dutch disease was of paramount importance in the 1990s because of the government's commitment to an export-led economic model. Chilean economic policy in the 1990s is difficult to characterize. In some senses, it was rather strongly neoliberal. For instance, the country's status as a pioneer in the area of pension-fund privatization earned it much respect in the international investment community. The government also pursued a vigorous program of trade liberalization and privatization of state-owned enterprises. But at the same time, the government also provided education and income support to the poor and unemployed and maintained a stringent regime of CMTs. Also, the health of the country's banking system improved significantly during the 1990s, thanks to a number of prudential banking and regulatory reforms.

2.1.2 Colombian context

As in Chile, the architects of Colombia's CMTs in the 1990s were influenced by the economic problems of the previous two decades. The promotion of investor confidence was a far more daunting task in Colombia than in Chile because of the country's political and civil uncertainties. Inflation was also a severe problem in Colombia in the 1970s and 1980s (and indeed remained a problem during the 1990s). The 1990s were a time of far-reaching economic reform in Colombia. The authorities sought to attract international capital flows, and promote trade and price stability through a number of structural reforms. These reforms included trade liberalization, increased exchange-rate flexibility, tax reductions, labor market liberalization, partial privatization of social security and state-owned enterprises and central bank independence. Most of the economic reforms in the 1990s were in the direction of neo-liberalism; however, the CMTs and the increases in public expenditure were important exceptions in this regard.

2.1.3 Objectives of CMTs in Chile and Colombia

Though there were national differences in policy design, Chilean and Colombian policies shared the same objectives. The policy regime sought to balance the challenges and opportunities of financial integration, lengthen the maturity structure and stabilize capital inflows, mitigate the effect of large volumes of inflows on the currency and exports, and protect the economy from the instability associated with speculative excess and the sudden withdrawal of external finance.

2.1.3.1 Chile, 1991–9

Financial integration in Chile was regulated through a number of complementary, dynamic measures (the most important of which are described
here). During the lifetime of the Chilean model, the authorities widened and
revalued the crawling exchange-rate band that was initially adopted in the
early 1980s. The monetary effects of the rapid accumulation of international
reserves were also largely sterilized.

Central to the success of the Chilean model was a multifaceted program of
inflows management. Foreign loans faced a tax of 1.2 per cent a year. Foreign
direct investment (FDI) and private investment faced a one-year residence
requirement. And from May 1992 to October 1998, the Chilean authorities
imposed a non-interest bearing reserve requirement of 30 per cent on all types
of external credits and all foreign financial investments in the country. Note
that the level and scope of the reserve requirement ratio was, in fact, changed
several times during the lifespan of this policy regime in response to changes
in the economic environment and to identified channels of evasion. The
required reserves were held at the central bank for one year, regardless of the
maturity of the obligation.

The central bank eliminated the management of inflows (and other
controls over international capital flows) in several steps beginning in
September 1998. The authorities made this decision because the country
confronted a radical reduction in inflows in the post-Asian/Russian/Brazilian
crisis environment (rendering flight risk not immediately relevant). The
Chilean authorities determined that the attraction of international private
capital flows was a regrettable necessity in light of declining copper prices and
a rising current-account deficit. Critics of the Chilean model heralded its
demise as proof of its failure.

Others, however, viewed the dismantling of the model as evidence of its
success insofar as the economy had outgrown the need for protections. For
example, Eichengreen notes that by the summer of 1998 it was no longer necessary to provide disincentives to foreign funding because the Chilean banking system was on such a strong footing following a number of improvements
in bank regulation.[9] In our view, the decision to terminate inflow and other
controls over international capital flows was imprudent given the substantial
risks of a future surge in capital inflows to the country and the risk that the
country could experience contagion from financial instability in Argentina,
Brazil, Paraguay and Uruguay. It would have been far more desirable to
maintain the controls at a low level while addressing the current-account
deficit and the need to attract inflows through other means. Indeed, flexible
deployment of the inflows policy was a hallmark of the Chilean model (consis-

tent with the dynamic approach to capital management), and it is regrettable that the authorities moved away from this strategy.

2.1.3.2 Colombia, 1993–9

Colombia's inflows management policies relating to foreign borrowing were similar to (though blunter than) those in Chile. This difference may be attributable to limitations on state capacity in Colombia. Beginning in September 1993, Colombia's central bank required that non-interest-bearing reserves of 47 per cent be held for one year against foreign loans with maturities of 18 months or less (this was extended to loans with a maturity of up to five years in August 1994). Foreign borrowing related to real estate was prohibited. Moreover, foreigners were simply precluded from purchasing debt instruments and corporate equity (there were no comparable restrictions on FDI). Colombian policy also sought to discourage the accretion of external obligations in the form of import payments by increasing the cost of import financing. The authorities experimented with a variety of measures to protect exports from currency appreciation induced by inflows. These measures ranged from a limited sterilization of inflows, to maintenance of a managed float, to a crawling peg. As in Chile, regulations on international capital flows were gradually eliminated following the reduction in flows after the Asian crisis.

2.1.4 Assessment of CMTs in Chile and Colombia

The array of CMTs that constitute the Chilean model represent a highly effective means for achieving the economic objectives identified by the architects of these policies. The CMTs achieved these objectives via their effect on currency, flight, fragility and contagion risks.

The Chilean authorities managed currency risk via adjustments to its crawling peg, sterilization and inflows management. Taken together, these measures greatly reduced the likelihood that the currency would appreciate to such a degree as to jeopardize the current account, and the policies made it difficult for investor flight to induce a currency collapse. Indeed, the appreciation of the Chilean currency and the current-account deficit (as a share of GDP) were smaller than in other Latin American countries that were also recipients of large capital inflows.[10] Moreover, the currency never came under attack following the Mexican and Asian crises.

Colombian efforts to manage currency risk were less successful than those in Chile for three reasons. There was a lack of consistency in the exchange-rate regime in Colombia as a consequence of the frequent changes in the exchange rate strategy employed (for example, managed float, crawling peg);

inflow sterilization was rather limited in scope relative to sterilization in Chile and inflation continued to be a problem in Colombia during the 1990s. Nonetheless, currency and inflows management offered some protection to exports in Colombia when the country was receiving relatively large capital inflows. The currency also held up fairly well following the Mexican crisis.

Chilean and Colombian policies reduced the likelihood of a sudden exit of foreign investors by discouraging those inflows that introduce the highest degree of flight risk. The reserve requirement tax in Chile was designed to discourage such flows by raising the cost of these investments. The Chilean minimum-stay policy governing FDI reinforced the strategy of encouraging longer-term investments while also preventing short-term flows disguised as FDI. Colombian policy precluded the possibility of an exit of foreign investors from liquid investment by prohibiting their participation in debt and equity markets (while maintaining their access to FDI). The reduction in flight risk in both countries complemented efforts to reduce currency risk – particularly in Chile where policy effectively targeted currency risk.

Chilean and Colombian inflows management also mitigated fragility risk. The regime reduced the opportunity for maturity mismatch by demonstrating an effective bias against short-term, unstable, capital inflows. In Chile, taxes on foreign borrowing were designed precisely to discourage the financing strategies that introduced so much fragility risk to Asian economies and Mexico. In Colombia, the rather large reserve requirement tax on foreign borrowing and the prohibition on foreign borrowing for real estate played this role too.

Numerous empirical studies find that inflows management in Chile and Colombia played a constructive role in changing the composition and maturity structure (though not the volume) of net capital inflows, particularly after the controls were strengthened in 1994–5.[11] These studies also find that leakages from these regulations had no macroeconomic significance. Following implementation of these policies in both countries, the maturity structure of foreign debt lengthened and external financing in general moved from debt to FDI. Moreover, Chile received a larger supply of external finance (relative to GDP) than other countries in the region, and FDI became a much larger proportion of inflows than in many other developing economies. Colombia's prohibition on foreign equity and bond-market participation dramatically reduced the relative importance of short-term, liquid forms of finance. More strikingly, foreign direct investment became a major source of finance in the country despite political turbulence and blunt financial controls.

The move toward FDI and away from short-term, highly liquid debt and private investment flows is a clear achievement of the Chilean model. It bears noting, however, that FDI is not without its problems. It can, and has, introduced sovereignty risk in some important cases (such as Chile's earlier experience with ITT) and can introduce other problems for developing countries.[12]

The Chilean model also reduced the vulnerability to contagion by fostering macroeconomic stability. It is noteworthy that the transmission effects of the Asian crisis in Chile and Colombia were quite mild compared with those in other Latin countries (such as Brazil), let alone elsewhere. The decline in capital flows in Chile and Colombia following the Mexican and Asian crises was rather orderly and did not trigger currency, asset and investment collapse. Contrary to the experience in East Asia, the decision to float the currency in Chile and Colombia (in the post-Asian crisis environment) did not induce instability.

Some analysts challenge the generally sanguine assessment of the Chilean model. Edwards, for example, argues that the effectiveness of the model has been exaggerated.[13] However, a year later, De Gregorio, Edwards and Valdés concluded that the Chilean controls affected the composition and maturity of inflows, but not their volume.[14] The De Gregorio et al. result is confirmed for Chile in other studies that claim to demonstrate the failure of the model, even though their reported results show just the opposite.[15] As Eichengreen aptly remarks, that the controls affected only the composition and maturity and not the volume of inflows is 'hardly a devastating critique', since this was precisely their purpose.[16]

2.1.5 Supporting factors

The architects of CMTs in both Chile and Colombia were able to achieve their economic objectives for several reasons. The policies were well designed, consistent and reasonably transparent throughout their life span. Policymakers in both countries were 'nimble', in the sense that they dynamically modified CMTs as the economic environment changed[17] and as loopholes in the policies were revealed.[18] Both countries offered investors attractive opportunities and growing markets, such that investors were willing to commit funds despite the constraints imposed by the capital management regime.

Chile certainly had advantages over Colombia. The greater degree of state capacity in Chile may well explain why its policies (particularly with regard to exchange rate management) were more successful. Moreover, Chile's status as a large developing economy certainly rendered it more attractive to foreign investors, and may have granted the country a greater degree of policy autonomy than was available to Colombia. The general soundness of its banking system and macroeconomic policy, the maintenance of price stability and the high level of official reserves were important sources of investor confidence in Chile. Finally, international support for the neoliberal aspects of Chile's economic reforms provided the government with the political space to experiment with CMTs.

2.1.6 Costs

Compelling evidence on the costs of CMTs in Chile and Colombia is still not available. Indeed, the two most comprehensive studies of this issue deal only with Chile (and not very well).

Forbes is the most extensive study available on the microeconomic costs of the Chilean CMTs.[19] Using a variety of empirical tests (and sensitivity analysis thereof), Forbes shows that CMTs in Chile resulted in an increase in capital costs to small-sized enterprises.[20] Forbes is careful to note that the results themselves must be treated cautiously because of limitations on data availability.

In a broad study of the macroeconomic effects of the Chilean CMTs, Edwards notes in passing that CMTs increased capital costs for the SMEs that had difficulty evading controls on capital inflows.[21] He reports that the cost of funds to smaller enterprises in Chile was more than 21 per cent and 19 per cent a year, in dollar terms, in 1996 and 1997 respectively. Edwards does not, however, place these data into the necessary comparative context, rendering them entirely unpersuasive as an indictment of the Chilean CMTs.

Both Forbes and Edwards conclude their studies with the argument that the cost to smaller firms of the Chilean CMTs is a far from trivial matter because these enterprises play an important role in investment, growth and employment creation in developing countries. Neither study provides empirical support for the argument that these firms do, in fact, play a significant role in macroeconomic performance. And neither study provides unambiguous evidence that the macroeconomic benefits of the Chilean CMTs failed to outweigh even this modest evidence of their microeconomic costs (much the same could be said of Colombian experience).

On the issue of costs versus benefits, Forbes remains agnostic on the relative importance of microeconomic costs versus macroeconomic benefits. Edwards, by contrast, is entirely clear on this matter.[22] He argues that proponents of Chilean CMTs vastly overstate their macroeconomic benefits and fail to acknowledge their microeconomic costs. On this basis, Edwards argues that the Chilean CMTs should not serve as a model for other developing countries. We find the empirical basis for this conclusion entirely unconvincing.

2.1.7 Other achievements

As discussed above, the CMTs associated with the Chilean model achieved the most important goals of its architects (though to a greater extent in Chile than in Colombia). Additionally, the CMTs in both countries can be credited with enhancing the sovereignty of macroeconomic, microeconomic and social policy. The importance of this achievement warrants discussion.

The CMTs of the Chilean model afforded policymakers insulation from potential challenges to macro, microeconomic and social policy sovereignty through the reduction in various types of risks (particularly, through reduction in flight and fragility risks). Both countries were able to maintain relatively autonomous, somewhat restrictive, monetary policies because of the protections afforded by the CMTs.[23] Moreover, the protection from flight risk afforded by the CMTs made it possible for policymakers to implement some growth-oriented fiscal policies.[24] Finally, as LeFort and Budenvich argue, the protections and advantages conferred on both countries by their CMTs were essential to the success of the entire regime of macro and microeconomic policy.[25] For example, the attraction of certain types of international capital flows promoted economic growth in both countries, and the protection from currency appreciation (to a large extent in Chile, and to a modest extent in Colombia) contributed to success in current-account performance.

The insulation afforded to both countries by the CMTs also meant that the monetary authorities were able to navigate the transition to a floating exchange rate far more smoothly. In many other countries (such as in East Asia), the transition to a floating rate involved significant currency depreciation and financial instability.

The CMTs employed in both countries also reduced the risk of financial crisis and thereby buttressed the sovereignty of economic and social policies in both countries. CMTs reduced the potential for IMF involvement in both countries. Policymakers were therefore never pressed to change the direction of (macro or micro) economic or social policy to satisfy the demands of the IMF or to calm investors.

2.2 Taiwan Province of China (POC)

2.2.1 Context

The CMTs employed in Taiwan POC can only be understood in the context of a 'developmentalist state' and an extended notion of national security that includes economic and financial stability.[26] That is, CMTs are an integral component of the macroeconomic and security objectives of Taiwan POC.

These economic and security objectives were, and are largely still, the guiding forces behind extensive regulation of domestic financial institutions and credit flows, monetary and exchange-rate policy and controls over international capital flows. Taiwan POC built its industrial base on the basis of restrictive policies toward FDI in 'strategic sectors' (for details, see Chang and Grabel, forthcoming). CMTs played a critical role in promoting industrialization and export performance.

2.2.2 Objectives

Prior to the mid-1980s, Taiwan POC's policymakers employed a multi-faceted set of CMTs in the service of three aims: promoting industrialization and export supremacy, economic growth and economic stability. Since the goal of industrialization was achieved by the mid-1980s, CMTs are now directed toward growth and stability objectives. CMTs that restrict investment in unproductive assets are critical in this regard.

Extensive CMTs are still in use, though policymakers began to liberalize aspects of the financial sector and loosen some controls over international capital flows in 1995 as part of the Asia Pacific Regional Operations Center Plan (APROC) and with the goal of joining the World Trade Organization (WTO). The APROC aimed at making Taiwan POC a regional center for high value-added manufacturing, transportation, finance, telecommunications and several other areas. However, as Chin and Nordhaug make clear, financial liberalization in Taiwan POC in the 1990s in no way weakened prudential financial regulation in the country.[27]

2.2.3 CMTs in Taiwan POC

As noted above, Taiwan POC maintains an extensive set of CMTs that are tied to economic and security objectives.[28] Policymakers maintain rather tight reins on the domestic currency, the New Taiwan dollar (NT dollar), and on currency risk more generally. Most important among the CMTs that relate to currency risk is the lack of convertibility of the NT dollar. The Central Bank of China (the CBC) manages the NT dollar in a number of other ways. Prior to September 1994, foreign nationals (without residency visas) were prohibited from opening NT dollar accounts. However, as of September 1994, the CBC permitted non-resident foreign nationals and corporations to hold savings accounts denominated in NT dollars, although the use of these is limited to domestic spending or to the purchase of imports, and these accounts may not be used to purchase foreign exchange or for securities trading. The CBC also adjusts the reserve ratios that must be held against foreign currency deposits to prevent inflows of foreign investment from leading to an appreciation of the NT dollar.

The domestic banking system is highly regulated by the state. Indeed, domestic banks in Taiwan POC were owned primarily by the state until the early 1990s. In 1995, 71.9 per cent of Taiwan POC's total banking assets were housed in banks that were controlled fully or partly by the government; in the same year, 62.2 per cent of overall credit was provided by government-controlled credit and financial institutions.[29] The authorities maintain restrictions on bank participation in speculative activities. Bank involvement in securities holdings is limited. In 1989, the central bank imposed a 20 per cent ceiling on bank lending to the real estate sector for six years, following problems associated with a real estate bubble in the 1980s.

The authorities also regulate foreign borrowing. Foreign-owned companies must apply to the CBC and the Investment Commission of the Ministry of Economic Affairs to secure government approval for borrowing from abroad. Control over foreign borrowing aims to concentrate most private foreign borrowing from international banks in Taiwan POC's banks rather than in the hands of individuals. In fact, at the end of June 1997, 62 per cent of all private foreign borrowing in the country went to its banks.[30]

Foreign investment in Taiwan POC remains tightly regulated. During the 1990s certain strategic sectors were off limits to foreign investors. These restrictions were loosened considerably in March 1996, but the authorities retain the ability to manage foreign investment. At present 'qualified foreign institutional investors' are subject to a ceiling on maximum investment; foreign individual investors are also subject to a ceiling on maximum investment and must receive approval from the CBC.

The stock market and private investment are closely regulated as well. Chin and Nordhaug point out that Taiwan POC's stock bubble in the 1980s exposed some regulatory weaknesses, leading the authorities to improve the quality of capital market regulation and to increase control over private investment inflows. They also note that a number of events in the 1990s reinforced the CBC's regulatory caution toward the stock market and private investment inflows. These events also encouraged the CBC to develop new strategies for discouraging speculation and channeling capital toward developmentally productive uses. The CBC's power to regulate the stock market and private investment inflows increased following the country's stock market crash in 1990; it also increased following the CBC's interventions to support the currency and the stock market in the aftermath of the cross-strait tensions and the ensuing missile crisis from August 1995 to March 1996. The CBC also monitored evasion of its regulations and had the political will to enforce penalties when malfeasance was uncovered. For example, in 1995 the

CBC closed Taiwan POC's foreign exchange market for one year when it was discovered that a major share of the foreign inflows that it had approved for equity investment had been used to speculate against the currency. During the Asian financial crisis, the Taiwan POC authorities also took steps to prevent illegal trading of funds by financier George Soros (because these funds were blamed for causing the stock market to fall).

Taiwan POC's stock market was not very 'internationalized' during the 1990s as a direct result of its policies toward private investment. In 1997, according to Chin and Nordhaug, foreign investors held only 4 per cent of stocks on the domestic exchange. Moreover, the authorities maintained firm entry and exit barriers and high withholding taxes on dividends (in 1996 the tax rate on dividends was 35 per cent). Today, buying stocks on margin and short-selling are still prohibited.

2.2.4 Assessment

Taiwan POC's CMTs have clearly achieved the objectives of their architects. The regime of capital management plays an essential role in Taiwan POC's industrialization, export performance, economic growth and economic and financial stability. The strategic stance toward FDI was critical to industrialization.

CMTs are central to Taiwan POC's financial stability. The restrictions on currency convertibility mean that it is difficult for Taiwan POC to experience a currency collapse (and related currency-induced fragility risk). Investors have little reason to fear a collapse of currency values, and they behave accordingly (as was evident during the regional crisis of 1997–8). Thus, even a decline in asset values – for example, stocks – is unlikely to translate into a currency crash.

Taiwan POC's exposure to currency, fragility and flight risks is reduced by the restrictions on foreign investors' ability to use the currency for speculation. The regulation of the stock market (for example, prohibitions on buying on margin and short-selling) and the cautious stance toward private investment curtail the fragility and flight risks to which Taiwan POC is exposed. It is notable that regulatory authorities have responded to the evasion of financial controls and the appearance of regulatory gaps by dynamically refashioning their CMTs.

The regulations that govern banks and foreign lending support the objective of promoting financial and economic stability. Banks in Taiwan POC do not have a high exposure to securities and real estate transactions. As a consequence, banks do not hold a large portfolio of non-performing or under-collateralized loans. Curbs on foreign lending also reduce fragility in the economy and render the risk of lender flight not terribly important.

Taiwan POC's resilience during the Asian financial crisis is in no small part due to the economic and financial stability fostered by its CMTs. The economy was simply not vulnerable to the currency, flight or fragility risks that proved so devastating to many countries in the region.

2.2.5 Supporting Factors

The achievements of Taiwan POC's CMTs were facilitated by a number of structural and geopolitical factors.[31] Critical among these are the high degree of regulatory capacity and the independence of the CBC from political bodies. This independence allowed the CBC to exercise its authority to curb speculation, close loopholes in policy and resist international and external pressures to liberalize the financial system imprudently. The policy independence of the CBC stemmed from its backing by the President and the government's historic commitment to financial stability. National security concerns and geopolitical uncertainties reinforced the commitment to financial stability, as stability is seen as essential for withstanding diplomatic, military and/or economic shocks. The reaction of the CBC to several events in the 1990s 'served as an unplanned rehearsal for the subsequent 1997–8 regional financial crisis'.[32]

As part of its national development vision, Taiwan POC channeled rents to promote exports and upgrade industry, and these efforts were accompanied by strict performance criteria and disciplinary measures. In this context, stringent and dynamic CMTs were essential to the promotion of productive investment and industrial dynamism.

2.2.6 Costs

Scant evidence is available on the costs of Taiwan POC's CMTs. A report by the Institute for International Economics (1998), for example, reports that CMTs in Taiwan POC have created a concentration of credit in large firms and an illiquid financial system, have provided incentives for a rather large informal financial sector to flourish and have reinforced conservatism on the part of its banks. Chin and Nordhaug report that this conservatism leads banks to favor short-term lending backed by tangible collateral, such as real estate.[33] This study also reports that banks are limited in their ability to engage in project, company and credit assessments, and do not have reliable accounting and auditing systems.

Clearly, the evidence on costs reviewed here is limited and anecdotal. Even if one were to fully accept this evidence, these costs in no way outweigh the macroeconomic benefits afforded to Taiwan POC by its CMTs.

2.2.7 Other Achievements

CMTs afforded Taiwan POC insulation from the Asian financial crisis. This insulation, coupled with China's vast resources, meant that Taiwan POC did not confront challenges to the sovereignty of macroeconomic, microeconomic and social policy associated with IMF involvement or with the need to regain investor confidence.

2.3 Singapore[34]

Singapore is widely believed to have a completely free and open capital account, a 'fact' that is often cited as an essential component of Singapore's outward-oriented economic policy and its rapid postwar economic growth.[35] It is true that Singapore eliminated its exchange controls in 1978, and since that time, both residents and non-residents have been free to engage in a broad range of international financial market activities. However, it is less well known that the 'Monetary Authority of Singapore (MAS) has a long-standing policy of not encouraging the internationalization of the Singapore dollar (S$)'.[36] The S$ 'non-internationalization policy' limits the borrowing of S$ by residents and non-residents for 'currency speculation'.[37] This policy is clearly a type of CMT, and has evidently been successful in contributing to Singapore's macroeconomic and industrial policy and economic stability.

2.3.1 Context

By virtually any measure, Singapore's economy has been a major success story of postwar economic development. To cite just one statistic, per capita income in Singapore has more than quadrupled in less than twenty years, from $5,200 in 1981 to $23,000 in 1999. Moreover, Singapore's economy has been relatively stable for the last twenty years, notably escaping the worst ravages of the Asian financial crisis of the late 1990s.[38] The government of Singapore has used a creative mix of macroeconomic tools and other government policies to achieve these outcomes. Macroeconomic policy has been rather conservative in a number of ways. The government has sought to maintain fiscal surpluses and low rates of inflation and to attract large amounts of foreign direct investment. Few would deny the success of these policies. To take just one example, between 1981 and 1999, Singapore attracted FDI in an amount equivalent to more than 9 per cent of its GDP, far higher than any of its neighbors.

At the same time, the government of Singapore has projected an image of greater adherence to economic orthodoxy than is actually the case. For example, Singapore has pursued a very successful industrial policy, huge infrastructure investments and large investment in public housing for its population, all of which have contributed to a rapid growth of living standards. Most importantly for our purposes, the government has pursued a managed exchange-rate policy designed to stabilize the exchange rate and maintain the competitiveness of Singapore's industry. It turns out that Singapore's CMTs have played an important, but little understood, role in many of these successful policies.[39]

2.3.2 Objectives

According to the MAS, the aim of the policy of non-internationalization of the Singapore dollar 'is to prevent the exchange rate from being de-stabilized and to ensure the effective conduct of our monetary policy'.[40] The policy is also designed to help Singapore maintain the 'soft peg' that has been crucial for its export-led strategy of development. Singapore's successful maintenance of its soft peg defies the conventional wisdom that soft pegs are not viable.[41]

2.3.3 CMTs in Singapore

Singapore progressively dismantled exchange controls in the 1970s until virtually all restrictions were removed in 1978. In 1981, the MAS moved to an exchange rate-centered monetary policy. As the MAS put it: 'the absence of exchange or capital controls, coupled with the small size and openness of our economy, made the conduct of monetary policy that much more difficult when Singapore shifted to an exchange-rate-centered monetary policy in 1981'.[42]

To support this policy, the MAS instituted an explicit policy of discouraging the internationalization of the Singapore dollar by discouraging 'the use of the S$ outside Singapore for activities unrelated to its real economy'. In 1983, when the policy was first codified, financial institutions located in Singapore were forbidden to lend S$ to any residents or non-residents that planned to take the S$ outside the country. Moreover, there were restrictions on equities and foreign bond listings by foreign companies in S$ to limit the development of an internationally connected domestic capital market denominated in Singapore dollars. After nine years, in 1992, the policy was loosened somewhat when it was amended to allow the extension of S$ credit facilities of any amount to non-residents, provided that the S$ funds were used for real activities in Singapore.[43] Under this amendment, non-residents can only borrow S$ to finance their activities outside Singapore providing the S$ proceeds are swapped into foreign currency.[44] In addition, some restrictions were placed on inter-bank S$ derivatives, such as foreign exchange, currency and interest-rate swaps and options, which could facilitate the leveraging or hedging of S$ positions. As the MAS puts it, 'These restrictions made it harder for potential speculators to short the S$ and signaled unambiguously our disapproval of such speculation'.[45]

In response to pressures from the domestic and foreign financial sectors for more liberalization, the MAS has reviewed the non-internationalization policy four times since 1998, and has liberalized it to some extent during these years. In August 1998, the MAS issued a new directive, 'MAS 757', reaffirming the basic thrust of the non-internationalization policy, but establishing clearer and more explicit provisions than previously. These more explicit regulations reduced the need for banks to consult the MAS, and then, to some extent, reduced the ability of the MAS to implement 'moral suasion' and 'supervision'. Moreover, some activities, specifically in relation to the arrangement of S$ equities listings and bond issues of foreign companies, were relaxed to foster the development of the capital market in Singapore.[46]

In late 1999, Singapore dollar interest-rate derivatives were liberalized further. Foreign companies were allowed to list S$ equity, provided the proceeds are converted into foreign currency before being used outside Singapore. Furthermore, in late 2000, key changes were made to MAS 757 to allow banks to lend S$ to non-residents for investment purposes in Singapore. These changes to MAS 757 were intended to allow non-residents to obtain S$ funding for investment in S$ equities, bonds and real estate and to broaden the investor base for S$ assets. They also extended S$ credit facilities to non-residents to fund offshore activities, as long as the S$ proceeds were first swapped into foreign currency before being used outside Singapore. Finally, in March of 2002, the policy was liberalized again, exempting individuals and non-financial entities from the S$ lending restrictions, 'recognizing ... that such entities were not usually the prime drivers of destabilizing currency speculation'.[47] The amendments significantly loosened restrictions on non-resident financial entities to transact freely in asset swaps, cross-currency swaps and cross-currency *repos*. They also ended any amount of S$-denominated securities in exchange for both S$ or foreign currency-denominated collateral. Previously, lending of S$ securities exceeding $5 million had to be fully collateralized by S$ collateral; transact freely in S$ foreign-exchange options with non-resident entities. Previously, such transactions had been allowed only if they were supported by underlying economic and financial activities in Singapore.

Thus, following the revisions of March 2002, only two core requirements of the policy remain. First, financial institutions may not extend S$ credit facilities in excess of S$5 million to non-resident financial entities, where 'they have reason to believe that the proceeds may be used for speculation against the S$'. This continues to be necessary to prevent offshore speculators from accessing the liquidity in Singapore's onshore foreign-exchange swaps and money markets. Second, for a S$ loan to a non-resident financial entity exceeding S$5 million, or for a S$ equity or bond issue by a non-resident entity, which is used to fund overseas activities, the S$ proceeds must be swapped or converted into foreign currency before use outside Singapore.

2.3.4 Assessment

Observers attribute at least part of the success of Singapore's macroeconomic policy to the significant CMTs that have hindered speculation against the S$ and allowed authorities to pursue a managed exchange rate. The MAS itself finds its CMTs extremely useful. A recent report states that: 'The S$ has served Singapore well. The strength and stability of the S$ have instilled confidence and kept inflation low. These have in turn provided the foundation for sustained economic growth as well as continued strengthening of the S$'.[48]

According to the MAS, interest rates in S$ instruments have generally been lower than corresponding US dollar rates. This has helped keep the cost of capital low in Singapore. Moreover, as a result, domestic banks and corporations did not suffer from the currency and maturity mismatches that existed in other emerging-market economies.[49] Part of the reason that the MAS was able to keep lower interest rates was the expectation of exchange rate appreciation. Singapore avoided the familiar problems associated with expectations of appreciation, namely, massive capital inflows, overvaluation and then crash.[50] It seems likely that Singapore's CMTs, which discouraged speculation against the currency, helped the country avoid that all too familiar malady. It also helped support Singapore's export-led model by keeping the exchange rate from becoming excessively overvalued.

2.3.5 Supporting factors

The success of this policy is due partly to the ability of the MAS to use 'moral suasion' to discourage banks and other financial institutions from using the Singapore currency for speculating against (or in favor of) the local currency. Close, ongoing interaction between the MAS and international and domestic financial institutions has allowed the MAS to shape and monitor implementation of what appear to be deliberately vague formal regulations. Moral suasion allows the MAS to make sure that loans are 'tied to economic activities in Singapore'. Singapore's 'strong fundamentals' are often cited as the key to its policy success. These include low inflation, fiscal surpluses, stable unit labor costs and current-account surpluses-factors that are undoubtedly important.[51] But what is often ignored is the role of CMTs in enhancing these fundamentals. In short, Singapore's experience demonstrates that there is two-way causation between CMTs and fundamentals.

2.3.6 Costs

No systematic analysis of the costs of Singapore's CMTs has been taken; only qualitative guesses exist. Some have argued that the restrictions have hindered the development of Singapore's capital markets, especially the bond markets, and may have also reduced the inflow of foreign investment, though there is little hard evidence to support these assertions.[52] Another possible cost is that the government of Singapore forgoes the opportunity to earn seignorage from the international use of the S$, but there have been no quantitative estimates of these costs to date.

2.3.7 Other Achievements

Singapore has been able to maintain a high level of foreign direct investment and political stability. The country's CMTs have contributed to this success by allowing the MAS to maintain a stable exchange rate and avoid the financial crises that have generated so much instability elsewhere in the region.

2.4 Malaysia[53]

2.4.1 Context

In the first two thirds of the 1990s, Malaysia experienced rapid economic growth attributable to growth in spending on infrastructure, FDI and exports. During this period, the Malaysian capital account was so liberalized that there was an offshore market in ringgit, perhaps the only case of an offshore market in an emerging-market currency.[54] Rapid economic growth in Malaysia came to a halt with the Asian financial crisis of 1997. The Malaysian government bucked trends in the region and, rather than implement an IMF stabilization program, implemented capital controls and adopted an expansionary monetary policy 14 months after September 1998. Malaysia's introduction of capital controls was widely seen as a major departure from its long-sustained reputation for maintaining a liberal capital account.

2.4.2 Objectives

The goals of the 1998 controls were to facilitate expansionary macroeconomic policy while defending the exchange rate, reduce capital flight, preserve foreign exchange reserves and avoid an IMF stabilization program.[55]

2.4.3 CMTs in Malaysia in September 1998

The policy package is generally recognized as having been comprehensive and well designed to limit foreign exchange outflows and ringgit speculation by non-residents as well as residents, while not adversely affecting foreign direct investors. The offshore ringgit market had facilitated exchange rate turbulence in 1997–8. Thus, the measures were designed to eliminate this source of disturbance.

The measures introduced on 1 September 1998 were designed to achieve the following objectives:[56]

1. Eliminate the offshore ringgit market by prohibiting the transfer of funds into the country from externally held ringgit accounts except for investment in Malaysia (excluding credit to residents), or for purchase of goods in Malaysia.
2. Eliminate access by non-residents to domestic ringgit sources by prohibiting ringgit credit facilities to them. All trade transactions had to be settled in foreign currencies, and only authorized depository institutions were allowed to handle transactions in ringgit financial assets.
3. Shut down the offshore market in Malaysian shares conducted through the Central Limit Order Book (CLOB) in Singapore.
4. Obstruct speculative outward capital flows by requiring prior approval for Malaysian residents to invest abroad in any form, and limiting exports of foreign currency by residents for other than valid current account purposes.
5. Protect the ringgit's value and raise foreign exchange reserves by requiring repatriation of export proceeds within six months from the time of export.
6. Further insulate monetary policy from the foreign exchange market by imposing a 12-month ban on the outflow of external portfolio capital (only on the principal; interest and dividend payments could be freely repatriated).

The September 1998 measures imposed a 12-month waiting period for repatriation of investment proceeds from the liquidation of external portfolio investments. To preempt a large-scale outflow at the end of the 12-month period in September 1999, and to try to attract new portfolio investments from abroad, a system of graduated exit levies was introduced beginning 15 February 1999, with different rules for capital already in the country and for capital brought in after that date. For capital already in the country, there was an exit tax inversely proportional to the duration of stay within the earlier stipulated period of 12 months. Capital that had entered the country before 15 February 1998 was free to leave without paying any exit tax. For new capital yet to come in, the levy would only be imposed on profits, defined to exclude dividends and interest, also graduated by length of stay. In effect, profits were being defined by the new rules as realized capital gains.

Credit facilities for share as well as property purchases were actually increased as part of the package. The government has even encouraged its employees to take second mortgages for additional property purchases at its heavily discounted interest rate. The exchange controls, still in place, limit access to ringgit for non-residents, preventing the re-emergence of an offshore ringgit market. Free movement from ringgit to dollars for residents is possible, but dollars must be held in foreign exchange accounts in Malaysia (for example, at the officially approved foreign currency offshore banking center on Labuan).

2.4.4 Assessment

Did Malaysia's September 1998 selective capital control measures succeed? They clearly succeeded in meeting some of the government's objectives. The offshore ringgit market was eliminated by the September 1998 measures. By late 1999, international rating agencies had begun restoring Malaysia's credit rating – for example, the Malaysian market was reinserted on the Morgan Stanley Capital International Indices in May 2000.

But did these controls succeed in the sense of allowing more rapid recovery of the Malaysian economy? The merits and demerits of the Malaysian government's regime of capital controls to deal with the regional currency and financial crises will continue to be debated for a long time to come. Proponents claim that the economic and stock-market decline came to a stop soon after the controls were implemented.[57] On the other hand, opponents argue that such reversals have been more pronounced in the rest of the region. Kaplan and Rodrik present strong evidence that the controls did have a significant positive effect on the ability of Malaysia to weather the 1997 crisis and reflate its economy. While this debate is likely to go on for some time, our reading of the evidence suggests that Kaplan and Rodrik are correct: controls segmented financial markets and provided breathing room for domestic monetary and financial policies. They also allowed for a speedier recovery than would have been possible via the orthodox IMF route.

2.4.5 Supporting Factors

In the other cases we discuss above, prior experience with CMTs has been important to the success of capital management in the 1990s. However, the case of Malaysia seems quite different: the country had a highly liberalized capital account prior to the 1990s. Nonetheless, the government was able to implement numerous CMTs, all under rather difficult circumstances. This suggests that a history of capital management is not a necessary prerequisite for policy success.

2.4.6 Costs

It is difficult to identify any significant costs associated with the short-lived 1994 controls. The most important cost of the 1998 controls was the political favoritism associated with their implementation. It is difficult, however, to estimate the economic costs of political favoritism.[58] Moreover, these costs (if quantified) must be weighed against the significant evidence of the macro-economic benefits of the 1998 controls.

2.4.7 Other achievements

The Malaysian experience enriches debate on the policy options available to developing countries. It demonstrates that it is possible for outflow controls to achieve their objectives.

3. Lessons and opportunities for capital management in developing countries

What policy lessons can be derived from these case studies? Before turning to *positive* lessons, we consider four commonly held mistaken claims about CMTs.

1. Capital management can only work in the 'short run' but not the 'long run'. With the exception of Malaysia, however, all of our cases show that management can achieve important objectives over a significant number of years. Singapore, for example, employed CMTs for more than a decade in the service of important policy objectives.
2. For capital management to work for a long period of time, measures have to be consistently strengthened. In fact, the reality is much more complex than this. As the cases of Malaysia and Chile show, in times of stress, it may be necessary to strengthen controls to address leakages that are exploited by the private sector. As these same cases demonstrate, however, controls

can be loosened when a crisis subsides or when the international environment changes, and then reinstated or strengthened as necessary. More generally, looking at a broad cross-section of country experiences, one finds that dynamic capital management evolves endogenously according to the economic environment and the evolution of government goals. In Chile, for example, CMTs were adjusted several times (and ultimately abandoned) during the 1990s in response to changes in the economic environment. During its 2003 bilateral trade negotiations with the USA, Chilean policymakers sought and won the right to reinstate these controls during financial crises. In Malaysia, capital management was strengthened to address evasion during the Asian financial crisis, and was then eventually loosened. In Singapore, the government strengthens enforcement and moral suasion during times of stress, and then steps away from this strategy when the situation changes.

3. Controls on capital inflows work while those on outflows do not. However, our cases reveal that this not always true. For example, Chile and Colombia maintained controls on inflows while Malaysia maintained controls on outflows. In addition, Singapore and Taiwan POC maintain controls on the ability of residents and non-residents to use domestic currency offshore for purposes of speculating against the home currency. This constitutes a control on outflows that has successfully insulated these countries from crises and has helped governments manage their exchange rates.

4. CMTs impose significant costs by leading to higher costs of capital, especially for small firms. As we have seen, in some cases these arguments may have some merit. But much more evidence needs to be presented before this is established as a widespread problem.[59]

The positive lessons are as follows.

1. First and most generally, we find that CMTs can contribute to currency and financial stability, macro and microeconomic policy autonomy, stable long-term investment, and sound current-account performance. CMTs also entail some costs. Specifically, there is evidence that in some countries the cost of capital to small firms is increased, and capital management can create scope for corruption.

2. Successful implementation of controls over a significant period of time depends on the presence of a sound policy environment and strong fundamentals. These include a relatively low debt ratio, moderate rates of inflation, sustainable current account and fiscal balances, consistent exchange-rate policies, a public sector that functions well enough to be

able to implement coherent policies (that is, *administrative capacity*) and governments that are sufficiently independent of narrow political interests that they can maintain some degree of control over the financial sector (that is, *state capacity*).

3. Our cases show that causation works both ways: from good fundamentals to successful CMTs, and from successful CMTs to good fundamentals. Good fundamentals are important to the long-run success of CMTs because they reduce the stress on these controls, and thereby enhance their chance of success. On the other hand, these techniques also improve fundamentals. Thus, there is a synergy between CMTs and fundamentals.

4. The dynamic aspects of CMTs are perhaps their most important features. Policymakers need to retain the ability to implement a variety of management techniques and alter them as circumstances warrant. Nimble and flexible capital management is very desirable. Chile and Taiwan POC's experience with these techniques is a good example of this type of flexibility. Countries with successful experiences with controls must maintain the option to continue using them as circumstances warrant.

5. CMTs work best when they are coherent and consistent with the overall aims of the economic policy regime, or better yet, when they are an integral part of a national economic vision. To be clear, this vision does not have to be one of widespread state control over economic activity. Singapore is a good example of an economy that is highly liberalized in some ways, but also where CMTs are an integral part of an overall vision of economic policy and development.[60]

6. Prudential regulations are often an important complement to capital controls traditionally defined, and vice versa. In Singapore, for example, government moral suasion aimed at discouraging banks from lending to firms or individuals intending to speculate against the currency is an example of an effective prudential regulation. In Chile, taxes on short-term inflows that prevent maturity mismatches is an example of a capital control that also serves as a prudential regulation. Our case studies present many such examples.

7. There is not one type of CMT that works best for all countries: in other words, there is no one 'best practice' when it comes to CMTs. We have found a variety of strategies that work in countries with very different levels of state and administrative capacities, with financial systems that differ according to their depth and degree of liberalization, with different mixes of dynamic and static controls and with different combinations of prudential financial regulations and capital controls.

Many countries that have had extensive controls in the past are now liberalizing them. Do our case studies offer any insight as to whether countries that employ extensive CMTs should begin to abandon them? Our research suggests, that in many cases, it is not in the interests of developing countries to seek full capital-account liberalization. The lesson of dynamic capital management is that countries need to have the flexibility to both *tighten* and *loosen* controls.

If countries completely liberalize their capital accounts, however, they might find it very difficult to re-establish any degree of control when the situation warrants or even demands it. This is because market actors might see the attempt to re-establish capital management as *abandonment* of a liberalized capital account, and then might react rather radically to this perceived change. By contrast, if investors understand that a country is maintaining a system of dynamic capital management they will expect management to tighten and loosen over time. It is therefore less likely that investors will over-react if management techniques are tightened.

In sum, we have shown that the CMTs employed in five developing countries during the 1990s have achieved many important objectives. The achievements of these CMTs therefore warrant close examination by policy-makers in developing countries.

Table 1. **Types and objectives of CMTs employed during the 1990s***

Country	Types of CMTs	Objectives of CMTs
Chile	**Inflows** • FDI and private investment: One-year Residence Requirement • 30% URR • Tax on foreign loans: 1.2% a year **Outflows:** No significant restrictions **Domestic financial Regulations:** Strong regulatory measures	• Lengthen maturity structures and stabilize inflows • Help manage exchange rates to maintain export competitiveness • Protect economy from financial instability

Colombia	Similar to Chile	Similar to Chile
Taiwan POC	**Inflows** *Non-residents* • Bank accounts can only be used for domestic spending, not financial speculation • Foreign participation in stock market regulated • FDI tightly regulated *Residents* • Regulation of foreign borrowing **Outflows** • Exchange controls **Domestic Financial Regulations** • Restrictions on lending for real estate and other speculative purposes	• Promote industrialization • Help manage exchange for export competitiveness • Maintain financial stability and insulate from foreign financial crises
Singapore	**'Non-Internationalization' of Singapore $ inflows** **Outflows** *Non-residents* • Financial institutions can't extend S$ credit to non-residents if they are likely to use for speculation • Non-residents: if they borrow for use abroad, must swap first into foreign currency	• Prevent speculation against Singapore $ • Support 'soft peg' of S$ • Help maintain export competitiveness • Help insulate Singapore from foreign financial crises

Country	Types of CMTs	Objectives of CMTs
	Domestic Financial Regulations • Restrictions on creation of swaps, and other derivatives that could be used for speculation against S$	
Malaysia (1998)	**Inflows** • Restrictions on foreign borrowing **Outflows** *Non-residents* • 12-month repatriation waiting period • Graduated exit levies inversely proportional to length of stay *Residents* • Exchange controls **Domestic financial regulations** *Non-residents* • Restrict access to ringgit *Residents* • encourage to borrow domestically and invest	• Maintain political and economic sovereignity • Kill the offshore ringgit market • Shut down offshore share market • Help reflate the economy • Help create financial stability and insulate the economy from contagion

Table 2. **Assessment of the CMTs employed during the 1990s***

Country	Achievements	Supporting Factors	Costs
Chile	• altered composition and maturity of inflows • currency stability • reduced vulnerability to contagion	• well-designed policies and sound fundamentals • neoliberal economic policy in many domains • offered foreign investors good returns • state and administrative capacity • dynamic capital management	• limited evidence of higher capital costs for small and medium-sized enterprises (SMEs)
Colombia	• similar to Chile, but less successful in several respects	• less state and administrative capacity than in Chile meant that blunter policies were employed • economic reforms in the direction of neoliberalism	• no evidence available
Taiwan POC	• debt burdens and financial fragility are insignificant • competitive exchange rate and stable currency • insulated from financial crises • enhanced economic sovereignty	• high levels of state and administrative capacity • policy independence of the CBC • dynamic capital management	• limited evidence of concentration of lending to large firms, conservatism of banks, inadequate auditing and risk and project assessment capabilities • large informal financial sector

			• limited evidence of inadequate liquidity in financial system
Singapore	• insulated from disruptive speculation • protection of soft peg • financial stability	• strong state capacity and ability to use moral suasion • strong economic fundamentals	• possibly undermined financial sector development • loss of seignorage
Malaysia (1998)	• facilitated macroeconomic reflation • helped to maintain domestic economic sovereignty	• public support for policies • strong state and administrative capacity • dynamic capital management	• possibly contributed to cronyism and corruption

Notes

1 This paper was prepared as part of the research program of the Intergovernmental Group of Twenty-Four on International Monetary Affairs and Development (G24), with financial support from the International Development Research Centre of Canada (IDRC). It was first published by UNCTAD as no. 25 of the G24 Discussion Paper Series. The views expressed and the designations and terminology employed are those of the author and do not necessarily reflect the views of the G24, IDRC and UNCTAD. Epstein acknowledges the financial support of the Ford and Rockefeller Foundations. In addition, we thank Arjun Jadayev and Peter Zawadzki for excellent research assistance and Jayadev for his contribution to the India case study. We are grateful to Professor Dani Rodrik for his help at the early stages of this project. We are also grateful to the participants at the TGM for helpful comments (especially, Ariel Buira, Aziz Ali Mohammed, Esteban Perez and Benu Schneider.

2 Ocampo 2002 and Schneider 2001.

3 Grabel 1999, 2003a, proposes 'trip wires and speed bumps' as a framework for dynamic capital management.

4 Discussion of objectives and costs draws on Chang and Grabel, forthcoming: ch. 10, and Grabel 2003b; discussion of the means by which CMTs attain their objectives draws on Grabel, 2003a.

5 Epstein, Grabel and Jomo 2003, also include case studies of China and India, omitted here because of space constraints.

6 This case study draws heavily on Grabel 2003a. Details and assessment of Chilean and Colombian CMTs are drawn from: Agonsin 1998; Eichengreen 1999; Ffrench-Davis and Reisen 1998; LeFort and Budenvich 1997; Ocampo 2002; and Palma 2000.

7 Eichengreen 1999.

8 Generally refers to a situation where a country's apparent good economic fortune has detrimental effects.

9 Nevertheless, Eichengreen 1999 makes clear that authorities erred in terminating inflows management.

10 Agonsin 1998.

11 Ffrench-Davis and Reisen 1998; LeFort and Budenvich 1997; Ocampo and Tovar 1998; Palma 2000.

12 See Chang and Grabel, forthcoming: ch. 10; Singh 2002.

13 Edwards 1999.

14 De Gregorio, Edwards and Valdés 2000.

15 Ariyoshi et al. 2000; Valdés-Prieto and Soto 1998.

16 Eichengreen 1999.

17 For example, Chile's reserve requirement was adjusted several times because of changes in the volume of capital flows. See Massad 1998 for discussion of the Chilean case.

18 Ocampo 2002 points out that the frequency with which authorities changed the rules pertaining to exchange rates in Chile and reserve requirements in Colombia were not without cost, however.

19 Forbes 2002.

20 To date (Forbes 2002), findings have not been challenged in the literature. This, however, is not surprising given that the draft paper only became available in November 2002.

21 Edwards 1999.

22 Forbes 2002; Edwards 1999.

23 Even Edwards 1999, a prominent critic of CMTs in Chile, shows that they increased the autonomy of monetary policy in the country. However, he argues the extent of increased autonomy was trivial insofar as the small benefit accruing from increased monetary policy autonomy was outweighed by the increase in capital costs that were associated with the CMTs.

24 LeFort and Budenvich 1997.

25 Note, however, that CMTs and macroeconomic policy did not succeed in promoting price stability in Colombia, LeFort and Budenvich 1997.

26 See Chin and Nordhaug 2002 on the extended notion of security in Taiwan POC and, more generally, for a rich discussion of the broader context of its economic and financial policies.

27 Chin and Nordhaug 2002, p. 82.

28 The description of CMTs draws heavily on Chin and Nordhaug 2002. Details are also drawn from the EIU 2002 and the US Commercial Service 2002.

29 Chin and Noedhaug 2002.

30 op. cit.

31 This discussion draws heavily on Chin and Nordhaug 2002, which provides an in-depth historical examination of relevant structural considerations.

32 Chin and Nordhaug 2002.

33 op. cit.

34 This section draws heavily on MAS 2001; 2002, Errico and Musalem 1999, IMF 1999; 2001, McCauley, 2001 and Ishi et. al. 2001.

35 See IMF 1999; 2001 for useful surveys of the Singapore economy during this period.

36 MAS 2002.

37 op. cit.
38 See MAS 2001.
39 Since 1981, monetary policy in Singapore has been centered on exchange-rate management. First, the exchange rate is managed against a basket of currencies of Singapore's major trading partners. The composition of the basket is revised periodically to take account of Singapore's trade patterns. Second, the MAS operates a managed float. The trade-weighted exchange rate is allowed to fluctuate within an undisclosed policy band. If the exchange rate moves outside the band, the MAS will step in, buying or selling foreign exchange to steer the exchange rate back within the band. In conducting this policy, the MAS has generally given up control over domestic interest rates in order to maintain its exchange rate within its target band. McCauley 2001 argues that the main target of this policy is inflation.
40 ibid.
41 Eichengreen 1999.
42 MAS 2002.
43 op. cit.
44 MAS 2001.
45 MAS 2002.
46 ibid.
47 ibid.
48 ibid.
49 MAS 2001.
50 See, for example, Taylor 2002.
51 IMF 2001 emphasizes the role of fundamentals and discounts the importance of capital management.
52 MAS 2001.
53 This section draws mainly on Jomo 2001; BNM, various years; Kaplan and Rodrik 2002; Rajamaran 2001; Mahathir 2001.
54 Rajaraman 2001.
55 Kaplan and Rodrik 2002.
56 Rajaraman 2001; Bank Negara Malaysia; Mahathir 2001; Jomo 2001.
57 Kaplan and Rodrik 2002; Jomo 2001; Palma 2000; Dornbusch 2002.
58 Jomo 2001; Kaplan and Rodrik 2002; Johnson and Mitton 2002.
59 In any case, this observation says nothing about the balance of costs and benefits. As economists are fond of pointing out, there are always trade-offs. Our cases demonstrate that CMTs can have important macroeconomic or prudential benefits. Of course, these benefits must be weighed against the micro costs. But as James Tobin was fond of remarking, 'It takes a lot of Harberger Triangles to fill an Okun Gap'.
60 See Nembhard 1992 for an excellent discussion of these issues.

Bibliography

Angosin, Manuel and Ffrench-Davis, Ricardo, 1996, 'Managing Capital Inflows in Latin America', in Mahbub ul Haq, et al., *The Tobin Tax*, New York, Oxford University Press.

Angosin, Manuel R, 1998, 'Capital Inflows and Investment Performance: in the 1990s' in Ffrench Davis et al., *Capital Flows and Investment Performance: Lessons From Latin America in the 1990s*, Santiago, ECLAC.

Ariyoshi, Akira, Habermeier, Karl, Laurens, Bernard, Otker-Robe, Inci, Ivan Canales-Kriljenko, Jorge, and Kirilenko, Andrei, 2000, *Capital Controls: Country Experiences with their Use and Liberalization*, IMF Occasional Paper, no. 190.

Bank Negara Malaysia, various years, *Annual Reports*, Kuala Lampur, Bank Negara Malaysia.

Carlson, Mark and Hernandez, Leonardo, 2002, 'Determinants and Repercussions of the Composition of Capital Inflows', IMF Working Paper, WP/02/86.

Chang, Ha-Joon and Grabel, Ilene, forthcoming 2004, *Reclaiming Development: an Economic Policy Handbook for Activists and Policymakers*, London, Zed Press.

Chin, Kok Fay and Nordhaug, Kristen, 2002, 'Why Are There Differences in the Resilience of Malaysia and Taiwan to Financial Crisis?' *European Journal of Development Research*, vol. 14, no.1, pp. 77–100.

De Gregorio, Jose, Edwards, Sebastian, and Valdes, Rodrigo, 2000, 'Controls On Capital Inflows: Do they Work?', NBER Working Paper, no. 7645.

De Gregorio, Jose and Valdes, Rodrigo O, 2001, 'Crisis Transmission: Evidence from the Debt, Tequila and Asian Flu Crises', *World Bank Economic Review*, vol. 15, no. 2, pp. 289–314.

Dornbusch, R, 2002, 'Malaysia's Crisis: Was it Different?' in Sebastian Edwards and Jeffrey A Frankel, eds, *Preventing Currency Crises in Emerging Markets*, Chicago, The University of Chicago Press, pp. 441–60.

Economist Intelligence Unit (EIU), 2002, Country report, Taiwan, http://biz.yahoo. com/ifc/tw/forex.html

Edwards, S, 1999, 'How effective are capital controls?', *Journal of Economic Perspectives*, vol. 13, no. 4.

Edwards, S, 2001, 'Capital Mobility and Economic Performance: Are Emerging Economies Different?', NBER Working Paper, no. 8076.

Epstein, Gerald, Grabel, Ilene and Jomo, KS, 2003, 'Capital Management Techniques for Developing Countries: An Assessment of Experiences from the 1990s and Lessons for the Future' (http: //www.g24.org/tgpapers.htm).

Errico, Luca and Musalem, Alberto, 1999, 'Offshore Banking: An Analysis of Micro – and Macro – Prudential Issues', IMF Working Paper, WP/99/5.

Ffrench-Davis, R and Reisen, H, eds, 1998, *Capital Flows and Investment Performance*, Paris, UN/ECLAC Development Centre of the OECD.

Forbes, Kristin, 2002, 'One Cost of the Chilean Capital Controls: Increased Financial Constraints for Small Firms', MIT-Sloan School of Management and NBER, unpublished paper, November.

Grabel, Ilene, 1999, 'Rejecting Exceptionalism: Reinterpreting the Asian Financial Crises', in J Michie and JG Smith, 1999, eds, *Global Instability: The Political Economy of World Economic Governance*, London, Routledge, pp. 37–67.

—, 2003a, 'Averting Crisis: Assessing Measures to Manage Financial Integration in Emerging Economies', *Cambridge Journal of Economics*, vol. 27, no. 3, pp. 317–36.

—, 2003b, 'International Private Capital Flows and Developing Countries' in Ha-Joon Chang, ed., *Rethinking Development Economics*, London, Anthem Press.

Gregorio, Edwards and Valdes, 2000, 'Controls on Capital Inflows: Do They Work?', NBER Working Paper, no. 7645.

Institute for International Economics (IIE), 1998, 'Financial Services Liberalization in the WTO', Taiwan, Washington, DC, www.iie.com/CATALOG/CaseStudies/DOB SON/dobtaiwa.htm.

International Monetary Fund, 1999, 'Singapore: Selected Issues', IMF Country Report no. 99/35.

International Monetary Fund, 2000, *Annual Report on Exchange Arrangements and Exchange Restrictions*, Washington, DC.

International Monetary Fund, 2001, 'Singapore: Selected Issues', IMF Country Report no. 01/177.

Ishi, Shogo, Otker-Robe, Inci and Cui, Li, 2001, 'Measures to Limit the Offshore Use of Currencies: Pros and Cons', IMF Working Paper, WP/01/43.

Johnson, Simon and Mitton, Todd, 2003, 'Cronyism and Capital Controls: Evidence from Malaysia', *Journal of Financial Economics*, no. 67, pp. 351–82.

Johnston, R Barry, with Swinburne, Mark, Kyei, Alexander, Laurens, Bernard, Mitchem, David, Otker, Inci, Sosa, Susana and Tamirisa, Natalia, 1999, *Exchange Rate Arrangements and Currency Convertibility: Developments and Issues,* Washington, DC, International Monetary Fund.

Jomo, KS, ed., 2001, *Malaysian Eclipse,* Zed Press.

Kaplan, E and Rodrik, D, 2002, 'Did the Malaysian Capital Controls Work?' in Sebastian Edwards and Jeffrey A Frankel, eds, *Preventing Currency Crises in Emerging Markets,* Chicago, The University of Chicago Press, pp. 393–441.

Krugman, P, 1998, 'Open letter to Mr. Mahathir', *Fortune,* September 28.

Le Fort, VG and Budenich, C, 1997, 'Capital Account Regulations and Macroeconomic Policy: Two Latin American Experiences', *International Monetary and Financial Issues for the 1990s,* Research Papers from the Group of 24, vol. viii.

Massad, Carlos, 1998, 'The Liberalization of the Capital Account: Chile in the 1990s' in 'Should the IMF Pursue Capital-Account Convertibility?', *Princeton Essays in International Finance,* no. 207, pp. 34–46.

McCauley, Robert N, 2001, 'Setting Monetary Policy in East Asia: Goals, Developments and Polices', Basel, Bank for International Settlements.

Mohamad, Mahathir, 2001, *The Malaysian Currency Crisis: How and Why it Happened,* Pelanduk, Petaling Jaya.

Monetary Authority of Singapore (MAS), 2001, 'Singapore's Exchange Rate Policy', February.

Monetary Authority of Singapore (MAS), 2002, 'Singapore: Policy of Non-Internationalization of the S$ and the Asian Dollar Market', paper presented to the BIS/SAFE Seminar on Capital Account Liberalization, 12–13 September, Beijing, China.

Nembhard, Jessica Gordon, 1996, *Capital Control, Financial Policy and Industrial Policy in South Korea and Brazil,* New York: Praeger Press.

Ocampo, JA, 2002, 'Capital-Account and Counter-Cyclical Prudential Regulations in Developing Countries', UNU/WIDER Discussion Paper, August.

Palma, Gabriel, 2000, 'The Three Routes to Financial Crises: The Need for Capital Controls', CEPA Working Paper Series III, no. 18.

Schneider, Benu, 2000, 'Conference Report: Conference on Capital Account Liberalization – A Developing Country Perspective', Overseas Development Institute.

Schneider, Benu, 2001, *Issues in Capital Account Convertibility in Developing Countries,* vol. 19, no. 1, pp. 31–84.

Singh, Ajit, 2002, 'Capital Account Liberalization, Free Long-Term Capital Flows, Financial Crises and Economic Development', paper presented to IDEAS Conference, Chennai, India.

US Commercial Service, 2002, Taiwan Country Commercial Guide FY2002, Washington, DC, www.usatrade.gov/Website/CCG.nsf/CCGurl/CCG-TAIWAN 2002-CH-7:-00443.

Valdes-Prieto, S and Soto, M, 1998, 'The Effectiveness of Capital Controls: Theory and Evidence from Chile', *Empirica,* vol. 25, no. 2.

7

INTERNATIONAL RESERVES TO SHORT-TERM EXTERNAL DEBT AS AN INDICATOR OF EXTERNAL VULNERABILITY: THE EXPERIENCE OF MEXICO AND OTHER EMERGING ECONOMIES

Javier Guzmán Calafell
Rodolfo Padilla del Bosque[*]

Abstract

How robust has the ratio of international reserves to short-term external debt been as an early warning indicator of external vulnerability and currency crisis? We examine this issue and, in particular, analyse the significance of the reserve ratio's predictive power and its sensitivity to the database used by estimating regression coefficients for a number of explanatory variables using *Probit* and *Logit* methods. The data cover 15 episodes of crisis during 1985 to 2001 in nine emerging-market countries from Latin America and Asia. Our econometric results firmly support the notion that the reserve ratio is a strong indicator of currency crisis and external vulnerability, but its relative significance varies with the source of the data on short-term debt. We also estimate the vulnerability threshold value of the reserve ratio and draw a highly unconventional conclusion: The minimum threshold value of approximately 1 is a reasonable guide to an emerging-market country's reserves policy; higher levels of reserve ratio, while costly to maintain, do not make a country less vulnerable to external crises. Finally, we examine the predictive power of the reserve ratio by using alternative measures of international reserves and short-term debt in the case of 1994 Mexican crisis. Two key findings emerge. First, some of the methodological adjustments recommended by the IMF for calculating the reserve ratio are indeed highly significant. Second, the market amortization component of short-term debt (amortizations of external debt held by private foreign investors scheduled over the next 12 months) is a much more powerful indicator of potential liquidity problem that total short-term external debt (total amortizations over the next 12 months).

1. Introduction

Recent crises in emerging markets have highlighted the importance of maintaining adequate levels of international reserves, and of identifying reliable indicators to assess both the current levels of reserves and any possible future pressures on them. Until relatively recently, the indicators most often used for this purpose were measurements such as the ratio of international reserves to merchandise imports or to a particular monetary aggregate. However, as capital movements have gained importance in emerging economies, the usefulness of indicators based on balance of trade flows has decreased markedly. In addition, in view of the instability of the demand for money and the use of increasingly sophisticated financial instruments, the value added of ratios focused on the relationship between international reserves and a monetary aggregate has been cast into doubt. The consequent interest in finding alternative indicators comes as no surprise. Against this background, special attention has been placed on the relation between international reserves and short-term external debt (IR–STED).

This chapter has four objectives:

- To provide evidence on the usefulness of the IR–STED indicator in predicting economic crises
- To deepen the analysis of the limitations faced when using this ratio, taking into account both the ideal characteristics its components should display and the data available to calculate these components
- To contribute to the discussion on the values of this ratio that can provide reasonable coverage in the event of economic shocks
- To analyse the adjustments that could be introduced to increase the usefulness of the ratio as a tool for crisis prevention, using more timely and detailed data for Mexico.

Section II of the chapter briefly describes how interest in this variable has increased in recent years and outlines the merits and limitations attributed to it in general. Section III describes the methodology proposed by the International Monetary Fund (IMF) to calculate the indicator. Section IV features an analysis of the ratio's predictive power and its sensitivity to the database employed on the basis of a *Probit* model for a group of emerging countries in Latin America (Argentina, Brazil, Colombia, Chile and Mexico) and Asia (South Korea, Indonesia, Malaysia and Thailand). Econometric estimations are supplemented by graphic analysis for each country and the existence of vulnerability thresholds is assessed empirically. Section V estimates the IR–STED ratio for Mexico, contrasts projections based on data from international and official national databases and introduces a variant that allows a more timely detection of periods of economic vulnerability. Concluding remarks are presented in Section VI.

2. Background

The difficulties involved in using traditional models to effectively explain the economic crises observed in South East Asia in 1997 led to the conclusion that alternative variables had to be found to provide a clearer understanding of this phenomenon. As a result, various authors began to emphasize that the excessive accumulation of short-term external debt vis-à-vis levels of international reserves was a common characteristic of these crises.

In this context, economists such as Furman and Stiglitz and Radelet and Sachs focus on analysing the importance of this variable in greater depth.[1] They conclude that the IR–STED ratio was one of the determining factors of the Asian crises in the second half of the 1990s.

Interest in using the IR–STED ratio as a vulnerability indicator became even more pronounced as a result of the importance attached to it by several distinguished economists.[2] Thus, additional empirical support emerged for the ratio's role in the Asian crisis and in crisis episodes in other emerging markets.[3] These studies support the superiority of the IR–STED ratio over other coefficients (such as monetary aggregate–reserves ratios and ratios based on import coverage) as an indicator of an economy's liquidity position under current circumstances. In addition, the IMF has incorporated this variable into the series of indicators used in its early warning systems and the Bank of International Settlements has also begun to pay more attention to this ratio.[4]

In light of the evidence supporting the use of the IR–STED ratio as a vulnerability indicator, the reasons underlying its importance have become increasingly obvious:

1. A country with a low IR–STED ratio is more vulnerable to speculative attacks or external shocks owing to the more limited availability of foreign exchange.

2. A low IR–STED ratio may indicate that imprudent macroeconomic policies are being pursued.
3. An economic crisis will tend to be more severe if this ratio is low, as the current-account and exchange-rate adjustments required to balance the macroeconomic accounts are magnified.
4. An appropriate level for this ratio may provide the international community with substantial benefits. This would limit the size of international support packages to countries in crisis, since the amount of these packages is very much linked to the level of a country's short-term liabilities vis-à-vis its international reserves.

If these potential benefits are to become reality, however, at least three obstacles must be overcome when calculating the indicator. First, it must be borne in mind that defining the IR–STED components is not an easy task. Second, the availability of the statistics needed to estimate this indicator appropriately is limited, as recording private external debt is not mandatory in many countries and data on external debt amortizations are published with a lag of several months. In addition, differences in the methodologies and coverage of external debt statistics in individual countries render comparative analysis difficult. Furthermore, most international sources on external debt provide only annual data (with a lag of up to two years in some cases) and there are substantial differences in debt-instrument coverage. Third, although it has been generally noted that the ratio of international reserves to short-term external debt must be at least equal to 1 to enable an economy to withstand shocks, it is necessary to evaluate whether this assertion is adequately supported by empirical evidence.[5]

3. IMF methodology for calculating the appropriate vulnerability indicator

As a result of the growing importance of the IR–STED ratio in recent years, the IMF has provided a detailed definition of the ideal characteristics both components of the ratio should display if it is to serve as a vulnerability indicator.[6]

IMF recommendations for international reserves may be summarized as follows:

1. International reserves should be equivalent to all external assets controlled by the monetary authorities.
2. Undrawn, unconditional external credit lines should be included as international reserves.

3. The definition of official reserve assets should only cover the total amount of immediately-available liquid external assets. In other words, pre-determined and contingent future 'drains' on reserves should be taken into account in the definition.

The methodology proposed by the IMF recommends that short-term external debt should:

- be classified by residual maturity
- cover both public sector or public-sector-guaranteed external debt and private-sector external debt
- include all debt instruments held by nonresidents (irrespective of the currency in which the debt is denominated), rather than simply all debt instruments issued abroad
- include all credits linked to foreign trade
- consider monetary authority liabilities, including those stemming from derivative transactions.

The IMF recommends that emerging countries wishing to minimize their external vulnerability seek, as a starting point, a ratio of IR–STED measured by residual maturity equal to 1. Naturally, a number of factors may enhance or mitigate the need for reserves in a particular country compared to such a benchmark.[7]

4. Estimating the vulnerability indicator for a sample of countries

We now explore the availability of data to apply the criteria established by the IMF, analyse the usefulness of the IR–STED ratio as a vulnerability indicator and the extent to which data limitations detract from the benefits of its use, and conduct an empirical analysis of vulnerability thresholds.

4.1 Available data sources

The availability of appropriate statistics is a problem that affects both components of the IR–STED ratio, although the nature of the problems involved is different for each component. In the case of international reserves, the limiting factors are more the result of problems associated with transparency, while data availability per se is the main restriction with regard to short-term external liabilities. Given that the latter is the only variable for which alternative data sources are available, this chapter focuses on the implications for the ratio of using different databases for short-term external debt.

The main external data sources used in estimating the IR–STED ratio denominator are:

- Statistics prepared jointly by the Bank of International Settlements, IMF, Organization for Economic Cooperation and Development and World Bank (BIS-IMF-OECD-WB).[8]
- World Bank statistics[9]
- OECD statistics[10]
- Institute of International Finance (IIF) statistics.[11]

The following comments concerning these databases are relevant:

1. The BIS-IMF-OECD-WB database is the only source that estimates total short-term external debt balances on the basis of residual maturities. This database also has the advantage of supplying half-yearly data (quarterly data became available as from 2000). Consequently, it is the most used of all databases, although it does contain some gaps in instrument coverage (bilateral and multilateral debt, liabilities with banks located in countries that do not report to the BIS, non-officially guaranteed suppliers' credit not channeled through banks, private placements of debt securities abroad and domestically issued public debt held by nonresidents are not included).

2. Although IIF data partly offset BIS-IMF-OECD-WB gaps in instrument coverage by including the full range of bank and non-bank export credits (with and without official guarantees), domestically issued public securities held by nonresidents and payments related to interest in arrears, as well as providing two-year forecasts, the main shortcomings of this database are that it classifies debt on the basis of original maturities and only provides annual data.

3. The World Bank and OECD databases estimate debt balances on the basis of original maturities, and instrument coverage is greatly restricted. As a result, foreign currency liquidity requirements are largely understated. In addition, these databases only provide annual data and operate with a lag of approximately two years.

In view of the fact that World Bank and OECD short-term external debt statistics are characterized by serious limitations, data from these sources is not used in the empirical analysis undertaken in the next section.

4.2 Analysis of the IR–STED ratio as a vulnerability indicator

We conducted econometric analysis of the factors explaining economic crises with a view to analysing the extent to which the IR–STED ratio is useful as a vulnerability indicator, and to assess the degree to which the use of this indicator is affected by the limitations faced in estimating each of its components adequately. We used alternative databases in this process. The latter was supplemented by graphic analysis aimed at considering in greater depth the impact of the IR–STED ratio on a country-by-country basis.

The crisis episodes we examined were identified on the basis of the definition proposed by Kaminsky, Lizondo and Reinhart, and also used by Kamin, Schindler and Samuel, Edison and in IMF crisis early warning models.[12] According to the definition, a crisis occurs when the weighted average of the monthly depreciation of the nominal exchange rate and the monthly loss in the level of international reserves exceed the mean by more than three standard deviations. On this basis, 15 crises were identified for the period 1985–2001, as follows: Argentina in 1989; Brazil in 1990, 1991 and 1999; Colombia in 1985, 1997, 1998 and 1999; Chile in 1985; Mexico in 1994; South Korea in 1997; Indonesia in 1986 and 1997; Malaysia in 1997 and Thailand in 1997.

4.2.1 Econometric analysis

Once the specific crisis episodes were identified, a vector of explanatory variables was selected. These variables were chosen on the basis of their theoretical support and the results obtained in other empirical studies. A *Probit* method was used for the estimations. In this context, the dependent variable is dichotomic and equal to 1 when a country suffers a currency crisis, or 0 if this is not the case. The method applied in this econometric analysis is similar to that used in the empirical literature on currency and financial crises.[13] However, as explained below, in contrast to other studies, this paper analyses the sensitivity of the estimations to alternative databases and conducts an empirical assessment of possible vulnerability thresholds.

The results obtained using BIS and IIF statistical databases for short-term external liabilities are presented in Tables 1 and 2. The equation that provides the best results (reference equation) is presented in column 1 in these tables. It should be noted that all reference equation coefficients have the expected signs and are statistically significant at the 5 per cent level. They are also jointly significant at 0.00001 per cent, as indicated in the P-value line. The coefficients are stable in general, and their level of statistical significance remains high even if new variables are introduced. Pseudo-R^2 values (generally low in this type of econometric model) are similar to values obtained in equivalent exercises conducted by other authors.[14] In addition, we offer the following comments:

1. The IR–STED variable is highly significant and features the expected sign

in all regressions estimated. This conclusion holds true regardless of the variables included in the equation (Tables 1 and 2).

Table 1. **Determinants of Currency Crises (1985–2001) Based on BIS Source Data Regression Coefficients[1], z value***

Variable2	(1)	(2)	(3)	(4)
IR/STED	-0.010791 *	-0.009797 *	-0.0113546 *	-0.0115039 *
	-2.538	*-2.622*	*-2.537*	*-2.574*
RERM	0.0257201 *	0.0241268 *	0.0279571 *	0.0270948 *
	2.826	*2.853*	*2.832*	*2.876*
MB/GDP	0.1416732 *	0.1046809 *	0.1479893 *	0.1632191 *
	2.494	*2.033*	*2.409*	*2.368*
TT	-0.0717893 *	-0.0616194 *	-0.0788794 *	-0.0769214 *
	-2.609	*-2.416*	*-2.735*	*-2.628*
CA/GDP	-0.2972633 *		-0.2910725 *	-0.285 *
	-3.122		*-2.744*	*-2.948*
CAAP/GDP		0.1406936 *		
		2.739		
PSBC/GDP			0.0034019	
			0.609	
PSBR/GDP				0.0101147
				0.556
No. of Obs.	153	153	140	153
P-value				
(Ho: Coefs=0)	0.0000	0.0000	0.0000	0.0000
Pseudo-R^2	0.3838	0.3344	0.4058	0.3871

*/ Statistically significant at a level of less than or equal to 5 percent.
[1] Constants are included in all regressions.
[2] Variables are identified by the following signs:
IR/STED = International reserves as a percentage of short-term external debt.
RERM = Real exchange rate misalignment.
MB/GDP = Annual absolute variation in the nominal monetary base as a proportion of GDP.
PSBC/GDP = Private sector bank credit as a proportion of GDP.
TT = Terms of trade percentage variation.
CA/GDP = Current account balance as a proportion of GDP, with a one-year lag.
CAAP/GDP = Capital account balance as a proportion of GDP, with a one-year lag.
PSBR/GDP = Public sector borrowing requirement as a proportion of GDP.

2. The IR–STED variable coefficients are database-sensitive, with regressions using BIS statistics resulting in higher ratios than those obtained using IIF data.
3. The regressions produce a small IR–STED coefficient compared with the coefficients obtained for the other variables. However, the relative size of

Table 2. **Determinants of Currency Crises (1985–2001) Based on IIF Source Data Regression Coefficients[1], z value***

Variable[2]	1)	(2)	(3)	(4)
IR/STED	**-0.0070715** *	**-0.0065206** *	**-0.0065748** *	**-0.0074012** *
	-2.241	*-2.24*	*-2.095*	*-2.251*
RERM	**0.0249508** *	**0.0245309** *	**0.0262512** *	**0.025785** *
	2.765	*2.896*	*2.69*	*2.771*
MB/GDP	**0.1078307** *	**0.086036** *	**0.1121668** *	**0.1200389** *
	2.127	*1.967*	*2.08*	*1.969*
TT	**-0.0702069** *	**-0.0602641** *	**-0.0742858** *	**-0.0734181** *
	-2.593	*-2.405*	*-2.652*	*-2.56*
CA/GDP	**-0.2571751** *		* **-0.2544489** *	**-0.2489171** *
	-3.045		*-2.64*	*-2.87*
CAAP/ GDP		**0.1184578** *		
		2.627		
PSBC/GDP			**0.0012841**	
			0.241	
PSBR/GDP				**0.0062154**
				0.362
No. of Obs.	153	153	140	153
P-value (Ho: Coefs=0)	0.0000	0.0000	0.0000	0.0000
Pseudo-R^2	0.3540	0.3038	0.3618	0.3554

*/ Statistically significant at a level of less than or equal to 5 percent.
[1]/ Constants are included in all regressions.
[2]/ Variables are identified by the following signs:
IR/STED=International reserves as a percentage of short-term external debt.
RERM=Real exchange rate misalignment.
MB/GDP=Annual absolute variation in the nominal monetary base as a proportion of GDP.
PSBC/GDP=Private sector bank credit as a proportion of GDP.
TT=Terms of trade percentage variation.
CA/GDP=Current account balance as a proportion of GDP, with a one-year lag.
CAAP/GDP=Capital account balance as a proportion of GDP, with a one-year lag.
PSBR/GDP=Public sector borrowing requirement as a proportion of GDP.

this coefficient must be interpreted with caution, as the data available does not allow a precise calculation of this parameter, and as this indicator has become increasingly relevant in recent years.[15]

4. The current account balance as a proportion of GDP is the main variable for explaining economic crises in the exercises performed. Moreover, although the current- and the-capital account balances yield similar results, those obtained with the former were generally better.

5. The ratio of the monetary base to GDP is high and significant. However, this result is greatly influenced by figures from Argentina and Brazil, and the fact that both these countries recorded high levels of inflation and monetization for several years. If estimations for Argentina and Brazil are eliminated from the regressions, the ratio plummets and its statistical significance is reduced drastically.

6. Public-sector borrowing requirements and private-sector bank credit are often mentioned as determinants of currency crises. However, these variables did not prove significant and affected neither the coefficients nor the level of statistical significance of the other variables considered.

We conducted additional estimations aimed at testing the results of the model using the *Logit* method and data from the BIS and the IIF. The results of these exercises are presented in Table 3. In general, the *Probit* and *Logit* methods produce the same results (there is practically no variation in coefficient[16] values, signs and statistical significance levels). Moreover, the results remain sensitive to the database selected regardless of the method used. This confirms that the estimations do not depend on the methodology followed.

In sum, the econometric analysis provides firm support for the assertion that the IR–STED ratio is important in explaining currency crises and, conse-quently, represents a vulnerability indicator that must be carefully monitored. Furthermore, this conclusion holds firm irrespective of the database used in the estimations.

The regressions show that the ratio's relevance, however, is linked to the statistics used in its calculation. The problems stemming from the availability of statistics may, of course, be far more serious if the analysis is conducted for individual countries. To illustrate this point, Charts 1–9 present the behavior of the IR–STED indicator for the group of countries and the period described in the previous section.

Despite the different methodology and degree of coverage of the databases employed, the charts show that the trend of this vulnerability indicator was generally similar for both data sources in six of the nine countries analysed (Colombia, Mexico, South Korea, Indonesia, Malaysia and Thailand). This is not the case for the three remaining countries (Argentina, Brazil and Chile), where the differences in indicator behavior depending on the source used are more obvious for certain periods. In some economies (for example Argentina during 1995–2000), an increasing divergence between the ratios can be observed, while in others (Chile during 1991–2001) ratio trends are so different that they cast doubts about the usefulness of the data utilized. Possibly the most worrisome case can however be observed in economies in which the tracking of ratios estimated on the basis of alternative statistical sources may have led to contradictory conclusions on the very eve of a crisis (Brazil in 1990 and 1999, and Colombia in 1997).

Table 3. **Estimation Methods and Sources of Data**

| Variable[2] | Regression Coefficients[1], z value* | | | |
| | *Probit* | | *Logit*[3] | |
	BIS	IIF	BIS	IIF
IR/STED	**-0.011**	**-0.007**	**-0.011**	**-0.007**
	-2.538	*-2.241*	*-2.481*	*-2.223*
RERM	**0.026**	**0.025**	**0.025**	**0.025**
	2.826	*2.765*	*2.904*	*2.800*
MB/GDP	**0.142**	**0.108**	**0.139**	**0.108**
	2.494	*2.127*	*2.576*	*2.227*
TT	**-0.072**	**-0.070**	**-0.073**	**-0.072**
	-2.609	*-2.593*	*-2.658*	*-2.659*
CA/GDP	**-0.297**	**-0.257**	**-0.290**	**-0.250**
	-3.122	*-3.045*	*-3.167*	*-3.090*
Observations	153	153	153	153
P- value	0.0	0.0	0.0	0.0
Pseudo-R[2]	0.384	0.354	0.378	0.347

* All coefficients are statistically significant at a level of less than or equal to 5 percent.

1/ Constants are included in all regressions.

2/ Variables are identified by the following signs:

　　IR/STED = International reserves as a percentage of short-term external debt.

　　RERM = Real exchange rate misalignment.

　　MB/GDP = Annual absolute variation in the nominal monetary base as a proportion of GDP.

　　TT = Terms of trade percentage variation.

　　CA/GDP = Current account balance as a proportion of GDP, with a one-year lag.

3/ Coefficients are divided by 1.8138 for comparison with coefficients obtained using the *Probit* model.

IR-STLO RATIO

Chart 1

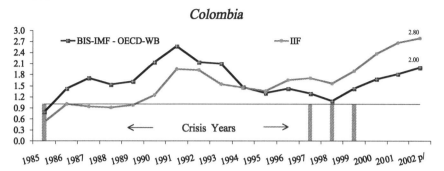

Chart 2

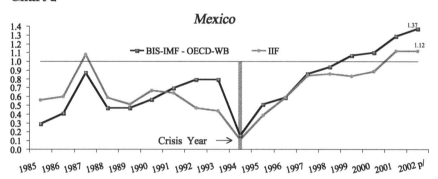

Chart 3

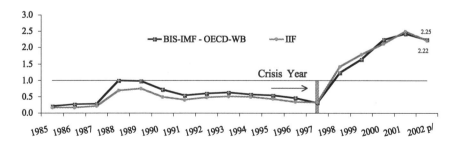

p/ BIS data are as of June 2002 while IIF data cover estimations as of end 2002.

IR-STED RATIO

Chart 4

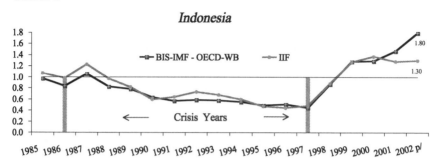

Chart 5

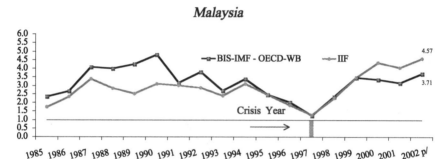

Chart 6

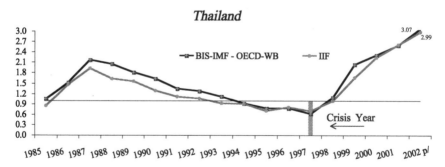

p/ BIS data are as of June 2002 while IIF data cover estimations as of end 2002.

IR-STED RATIO

Chart 7

Chart 8

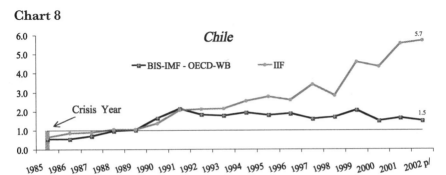

Chart 9

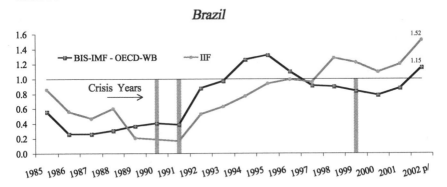

p/ BIS data are as of June 2002 while IIF data cover estimations as of end 2002.

The charts clearly illustrate the severe limitations that may arise for some countries in certain periods if the IR–STED ratio is estimated with the international statistics available. As is shown below, the restrictions faced by these data sources can be rendered even more obvious when results are compared with those obtained from national sources.

4.2.2 Vulnerability threshold

Interest in the IR–STED ratio as an indicator of external vulnerability has been accompanied by proposals as to what the value of this indicator should be to ensure adequate safety margins (that is, where to establish the vulnerability threshold). As mentioned above, it has often been suggested that the latter should have a minimum value of 1.

We undertook several exercises in an attempt to contribute to drawing general conclusions in this regard. We preferred BIS data over data from other sources owing to their higher opportunity and half-yearly periodicity. The method described below was applied.

In a *Probit* model the dependent variable 'y' can only have two values ($y=1$ or $y=0$), and the model used for the probability of observing a value of 1 is formulated as follows:

$$Pr(y=1) = \alpha\,(\beta'\times)$$

where α denotes the standard normal distribution function and β reflects the impact on the probability of a crisis of any change in the explanatory variable 'x' matrix. The model was modified for the analysis of vulnerability thresholds as follows:

$$Pr\,(y=1) = \alpha\,(\beta'\times\phi) \qquad\qquad \text{where } \phi \text{ is a constant.}$$

In the specific analysis of the relevance of the IR–STED variable, the threshold was defined as U and the following values were assigned to the constant ϕ:

$\phi=1$ *if IR/STED≤U,*   and

$\phi=0$ *if IR/STED>U*

Regression results are presented in Table 4. Estimations obtained using the reference equation are also included for comparison purposes. The value range for thresholds for which regressions were run is 0.5 to 4.4. It can be seen from the table that, when the model is estimated with low IR–STED values, the relative significance of this variable as a determining factor of crises increases considerably compared with the values obtained using the reference equation.[17] This should not be surprising, since the lower the ratio the higher the probability that a country will suffer an economic crisis.

In addition, the regressions display a characteristic pattern for a threshold of 1.3. In particular, the IR–STED ratio plummets to levels even below those observed using the reference equation and loses its significance altogether. How should these results be interpreted? The most viable explanation is that, for the estimations performed, the IR–STED variable ceases to be relevant in explaining economic crises from a level of 1.3 onward. For this reason, the coefficient value at this threshold is not larger than that obtained in the reference equation. When this is combined with the relatively low number of observations featuring a value other than zero for this threshold, the variable loses significance. Of course, if the number of observations containing values other than zero increases, regression quality improves and the variable becomes significant. Table 4 shows that this is the case for thresholds of 2.2 onward, as the results obtained for this level are practically identical to those obtained using the reference equation.

The above has a further important implication. Given that the impact of the IR–STED variable on the likelihood of a crisis does not diminish for thresholds above a certain value, there is not much point in setting as policy goal to achieve ratios above this level. In other words, the vulnerability threshold not only has a lower limit (floor) as suggested by the IMF, it also has an upper limit (ceiling).

Let us now consider the inferences to be drawn from the exercises to determine the possible lower threshold limit. The econometric calculations do not provide any conclusive data in this respect. Although the ratio value generally diminishes as the threshold increases, it is not possible to establish a criterion that automatically results in the selection of a specific threshold on the basis of the exercises performed. The most conservative approach would be to select the IR–STED value that lies as close as possible to the 'ceiling' as the lower threshold limit. Bearing in mind that the coefficient estimated for the IR–STED ratio remains practically constant for all thresholds in the 0.9 to 1.2 range, and the practical advantages of using a reference value of 1, it would seem useful to regard the value of 1 as the minimum.

Table 4. Vulnerability Thresholds (1985–2001, based on BIS source data)

THRESHOLD	VARIABLE										P-value	Pseudo R²
Criterion <:	IR/STED		RERM		MB/GDP		TT		CA/GDP			
Basic equation	-0.011	*	0.026	*	0.142	*	-0.072	*	-0.297	*	0.0000	0.384
	-2.538		2.826		2.494		-2.609		-3.122			
0.5	-0.072		0.075		0.365		0.000		-0.857		0.0002	0.243
	-0.982		1.538		1.412		-0.005		-1.373			
0.6	-0.041		0.072	*	0.251	*	-0.004		-0.379	**	0.0001	0.273
	-1.445		2.173		2.102		-0.057		-1.693			
0.7	-0.049	**	0.066	*	0.262	*	-0.022		-0.476	*	0.0000	0.308
	-1.625		2.305		2.347		-0.343		-2.032			
0.8	-0.026	*	0.032	*	0.185	*	-0.020		-0.318	*	0.0002	0.246
	-2.071		2.685		2.856		-0.482		-2.477			
0.9	-0.019	**	0.026	*	0.149	*	-0.081	*	-0.323	*	0.0001	0.277
	-1.829		2.525		2.582		-2.563		-2.822			
1.0	-0.020	*	0.026	*	0.151	*	-0.083	*	-0.330	*	0.0000	0.284
	-2.089		2.559		2.635		-2.683		-2.929			
1.1	-0.018	*	0.027	*	0.142	*	-0.088	*	-0.338	*	0.0000	0.322
	-2.051		2.750		2.576		-2.946		-3.124			
1.2	-0.019	*	0.027	*	0.143	*	-0.089	*	-0.340	*	0.0000	0.322
	-2.114		2.779		2.588		-2.976		-3.127			
1.3	-0.007		0.026	*	0.164	*	-0.078	*	-0.311	*	0.0000	0.377
	-1.204		2.968		2.979		-2.874		-3.357			
1.4	-0.009		0.027	*	0.167	*	-0.078	*	-0.307	*	0.0000	0.368
	-1.419		2.994		3.027		-2.878		-3.329			
1.5	-0.004		0.028	*	0.193	*	-0.082	*	-0.340	*	0.0000	0.415
	-0.638		3.005		3.156		-2.911		-3.465			
1.6	-0.004		0.028	*	0.190	*	-0.083	*	-0.343	*	0.0000	0.411
	-0.825		3.007		3.123		-2.952		-3.479			
1.7	-0.006		0.028	*	0.186	*	-0.083	*	-0.353	*	0.0000	0.402
	-1.259		3.066		3.152		-2.959		-3.583			
1.8	-0.007		0.028	*	0.185	*	-0.082	*	-0.356	*	0.0000	0.401
	-1.413		3.059		3.131		-2.938		-3.632			
1.9	-0.008	**	0.028	*	0.183	*	-0.080	*	-0.361	*	0.0000	0.397
	-1.677		3.048		3.090		-2.884		-3.699			
2.0	-0.008	**	0.028	*	0.183	*	-0.081	*	-0.361	*	0.0000	0.396
	-1.719		3.050		3.080		-2.925		-3.698			
2.2	-0.010	*	0.027	*	0.157	*	-0.078	*	-0.323	*	0.0000	0.377
	-2.136		3.022		2.843		-2.868		-3.540			
2.4	-0.010	*	0.027	*	0.155	*	-0.077	*	-0.320	*	0.0000	0.378
	-2.181		2.996		2.802		-2.835		-3.491			
2.6	-0.010	*	0.027	*	0.153	*	-0.076	*	-0.316	*	0.0000	0.379
	-2.242		2.970		2.747		-2.800		-3.428			
2.8	-0.009	*	0.027	*	0.152	*	-0.077	*	-0.314	*	0.0000	0.383
	-2.069		2.991		2.735		-2.809		-3.445			
3.0	-0.010	*	0.027	*	0.152	*	-0.076	*	-0.314	*	0.0000	0.380
	-2.290		2.953		2.721		-2.774		-3.403			
3.2	-0.010	*	0.027	*	0.151	*	-0.075	*	-0.313	*	0.0000	0.380
	-2.295		2.943		2.704		-2.761		-3.382			
3.4	-0.010	*	0.026	*	0.149	*	-0.074	*	-0.309	*	0.0000	0.381
	-2.314		2.910		2.646		-2.720		-3.313			
3.6	-0.010	*	0.026	*	0.148	*	-0.074	*	-0.307	*	0.0000	0.382
	-2.319		2.897		2.625		-2.705		-3.287			
3.8	-0.010	*	0.026	*	0.148	*	-0.074	*	-0.307	*	0.0000	0.382
	-2.319		2.897		2.625		-2.705		-3.287			
4.0	-0.011	*	0.026	*	0.145	*	-0.073	*	-0.303	*	0.0000	0.382
	-2.537		2.874		2.573		-2.670		-3.220			
4.2	-0.011	*	0.026	*	0.144	*	-0.073	*	-0.302	*	0.0000	0.383
	-2.537		2.859		2.549		-2.651		-3.189			
4.4	-0.011	*	0.026	*	0.143	*	-0.072	*	-0.299	*	0.0000	0.383
	-2.538		2.843		2.522		-2.631		-3.156			

* Statistically significant at a level less than or equal to 5 per cent.
** Statistically significant at a level less than or equal to 10 per cent.

Two points emerging from these exercises bear highlighting:

1. When defining the vulnerability threshold, it should be borne in mind that the latter must not simply be regarded as a minimum value. Above a certain level, the threshold ceases to provide additional protection for an economy. This is no trivial matter, as accumulating international reserves can involve considerable costs.

2. It has already been emphasized that any empirical analysis of vulnerability thresholds must be conducted with extreme caution owing to the statistical limitations and the different characteristics of each economy. Nonetheless, for the group of countries analysed in this chapter, the econometric estimations suggest that, as an overall criterion and depending on the specific conditions governing each economy, establishing a minimum level of 1 for the IR–STED ratio as a means of reducing external vulnerability is by no means an irrational goal.

5. Estimating the vulnerability indicator for Mexico

We now conduct three types of exercises for Mexico. First, we combine BIS and IIF statistics with official national data to incorporate some of the methodological adjustments recommended by the IMF. Second, we estimate the IR–STED ratio exclusively on the basis of official national data. Third, we use the breakdown of official national data on short-term amortizations to construct an 'adjusted' version of the IR–STED ratio, which allows a more timely detection of emerging liquidity problems.

5.1 Exercises conducted using international databases

In the previous section, the IR–STED ratio for Mexico and other countries was estimated using BIS-IMF-OECD-WB and IIF data. In this section, we supplement estimations for Mexico based on these sources by calculating an IR–STED* ratio for each database, to bring these databases as closely into line as possible with the methodology proposed by the IMF. The IR–STED* ratio features the following differences with respect to the IR–STED ratio:

1. The stock of international reserves includes the undisbursed component of the credit line agreed with the United States and Canada in April 1994 (NAFA credit line), and the contingency liquidity credit line negotiated with 33 international financial institutions from 10 countries in November 1997.[18]

2. Short-term public external debt includes the balance in circulation of fixed-income government securities issued domestically and held by non-residents.[19]

Chart 10

Mexico

Vulnerability indicator based on data from BIS-IMF-OECD-WB database

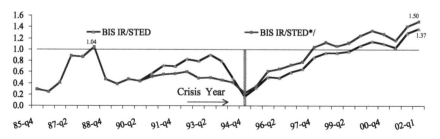

* Includes nonresident holdings of peso-denominated domestically-issued government securities, the NAFA credit line, and the liquidity credit line available from commercial banks.

The behavior of these indicators is presented in Charts 10 and 11. Chart 10 shows that, if BIS-IMF-OECD-WB data are used, a marked difference is observed between IR–STED and IR–STED* indicator levels for the period 1990–4 (during which non-resident holdings of domestically-issued government securities were considerable). Although it can be concluded that both ratios foresaw the possibility of a crisis prior to the close of 1994, in that they recorded a downward trend for several consecutive semesters and stood at very low levels, the IR–STED* indicator is more useful, as its downtrend began before that for IR–STED, and the IR–STED* value was lower for most of this period and thus suggested a higher element of risk.[20]

When IIF data are used to estimate the IR–STED ratio (Chart 11), it can be observed that a marked downtrend sets in as early as 1991 and reaches levels that culminate in the 1994 crisis. In this case, there is practically no difference between the predictive power of the IR–STED and IR–STED* indicators.[21] In addition, once BIS figures are adjusted to include domestic currency-denominated securities held by nonresidents, the results are very similar to those obtained using IIF data.

Chart 11

Mexico

Vulnerability indicator based on data from IIF database

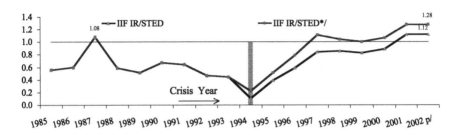

* Includes the NAFA credit line and the liquidity credit line available from commercial banks .

p/ IIF data are for estimations as at end-2002.

5.2 Exercises conducted using official national databases

We obtained two estimations of the short-term external debt stock measured by residual maturity on the basis of data published by the Ministry of Finance and Public Credit (SHCP):[22]

1. *Total Amortizations.* Short-term external debt at the end of each year is equivalent to total amortizations scheduled for the next 12 months[23] (as opposed to BIS and IIF figures that provide only partial coverage). In addition, we assume that Mexican commercial banks must amortize their total liabilities in less than one year.
2. *Market Amortizations.* Short-term external debt only includes components with a higher degree of sensitivity to changes in the perception of the economic climate in Mexico, that is, amortizations scheduled for the next 12 months for:

  • public-sector debt liabilities in capital markets (bond placements and private issues) and liabilities stemming from debt restructuring
  • non-bank private-sector debt liabilities with the commercial banking sector and international capital markets (bond issues and commercial paper).

In accordance with this methodology, the definition of debt excludes:

- public-sector debt amortizations with multilateral creditors and the IMF, as well as foreign trade debt amortizations
- non-bank private-sector foreign trade debt amortizations
- all private banking sector external liabilities.

The IR–STED ratios obtained on the basis of these data are supplemented by IR–STED* ratios that incorporate contingency liquidity credit lines with other governments and the banking sector as international reserves. They include amortizations of domestically-issued fixed-income government securities held by nonresidents among short-term liabilities.

The most relevant results of these exercises are as follows:

1. The IR–STED and IR–STED* ratios both clearly reflect the 1994 Mexican crisis ex-post in all calculations performed. However, estimations that incorporate data on the balance in circulation of domestically-issued government securities held by non-residents and on contingency liquidity credit lines prove to be more useful in predicting this crisis, as they record a downtrend and feature very low values in the several years leading up to the crisis (Charts 12 and 13). In fact, the IR–STED ratio is of no use in detecting the 1994 crisis, as it records an upward trend in the preceding years in both versions (total amortizations and market amortizations).

2. The second aspect worth emphasizing is the usefulness of IR–STED* data based on market amortizations ('adjusted' IR–STED*). As can be observed in Chart 13, this indicator drops sharply from 4.8 to approximately 1 in the period 1987–93. Not only is this decline much more pronounced than that based on total amortizations; it is also observed much earlier. In conjunction with a persistently low IR–STED* ratio estimated on the basis of total amortizations, a drop of this magnitude should have triggered a 'yellow flag' regarding the liquidity problems confronting the Mexican economy from the early 1990s onward.

3. The great advantage of the market amortization-based indicator lies in its higher degree of sensitivity to changes in liquidity availability, which allows it to detect the risk of problems with external payments in a more timely manner. However, as this indicator only provides a low level of coverage, is it advisable to use data obtained by this means in conjunction with broader indicators, such as the total amortizations indicator.

Chart 12

Vulnerability indicator based on data from official national databases

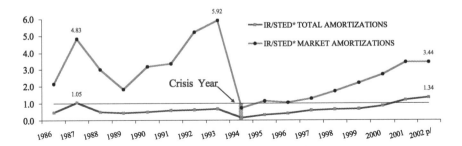

p/ Forecast prepared using the stock of international reserves as of June 2002 and the
    Data Book external debt amortization schedule for the second half of 2002, and 50 per
    cent of total external debt amortizations scheduled for 2003, based on the external
    debt balance as of June 2002.

Chart 13

Vulnerability indicator based on data from official national databases

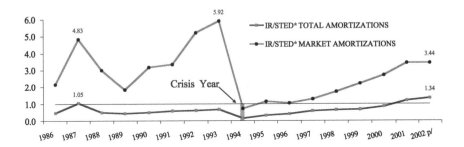

*   Includes nonresident holdings of peso-denominated domestically-issued government
    securities, the NAFA credit line, and the liquidity credit line available from commer-
    cial banks .
p/ Forecast prepared using the stock of international reserves as at June 2002 and the
    Data Book external debt amortization schedule for the second half of 2002, and 50 per
    cent of total external debt amortizations scheduled for 2003, based on the external
    debt balance as at June 2002.

Chart 14

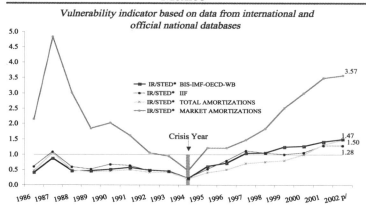

Mexico

Vulnerability indicator based on data from international and
official national databases

* Includes nonresident holdings of peso-denominated domestically–issued government securities, the NAFA credit line, and the liquidity credit line available from commercial banks.

p BIS data are as at June 2002, while IIF data cover estimations as at end of 2002. Total external debt amortization and market amortization forecasts were prepared using the stock of international reserves as of June 2002, the Data Book external debt amortization schedule for the second half of 2002, and 50 per cent of total amortizations scheduled for 2003, based on the external debt balance as of June 2002.

Chart 14 presents the evolution of the IR–STED* ratio based on data from international and official national sources. It can be seen from the chart that three of the four indicators (BIS, IIF, and Total Amortizations) behave almost identically and record very similar levels for the period 1986–94. However, although they all display low values and a downward trend from 1991, none of the three predict the emergence of liquidity problems in the Mexican economy with the clarity and timeliness of the 'adjusted' ratio (IR–STED* estimated on the basis of market amortizations). Finally, all IR–STED* ratios show a marked upward trend from 1995, irrespective of the data source employed.

6. Concluding remarks

The conclusions drawn from this study may be summarized as follows:

1. Estimations based on a *Probit* model for nine emerging economies confirm that the IR–STED ratio is a highly relevant variable in explaining economic crises.

2. This conclusion holds firm regardless of the database used. However, the relative significance of the variable as an indicator of external vulnerability changes when alternative databases are employed.

3. Graphic analysis of individual cases show that, for some countries, the assessment of the IR–STED ratio as a factor in explaining crises depends fundamentally on the database used.

4. The deficiencies in the databases available and the different characteristics of each economy make it very difficult to conduct a reliable empirical analysis of vulnerability thresholds. Nevertheless, the estimation of the *Probit* model with restrictions for IR–STED values suggests, on the one hand, that this threshold must be regarded as an interval and not simply as a minimum value, as there comes a point beyond which not much is gained from increasing the value of this variable. This aspect must be borne in mind, as accumulating international reserves also implies costs. On the other hand, within the limitations mentioned earlier in this study, the econometric estimations performed support the assertion that achieving a minimum vulnerability threshold value of approximately 1 is in general a reasonable goal.

5. We analysed the Mexican case in more detail using data from international and official national sources. Two fundamental aspects emerged. First, some of the methodological adjustments recommended by the IMF for calculating the IR–STED ratio may be crucial for ensuring that this ratio proves useful as a tool for crisis prevention. For instance, calculating this indicator without considering domestically-issued fixed-income government securities held by nonresidents serves no purpose in predicting the 1994 Mexican crisis. Second, although it is worth incorporating total amortizations in determining the indicator's STED component, the sensitivity of this variable to changes in external conditions may be limited. Early detection of a downward trend in the IR–STED ratio is, of course, indispensable if this ratio is to be of any use. The Mexican case study proves that if only the market amortizations component of the STED variable is considered (that is, external funds that have to be refinanced in international capital markets), the risk of potential liquidity problems can be detected in a much more timely manner. It would therefore seem important to analyse the relevance of indicators of this nature for other countries.

The above conclusions make clear that, although the IR–STED ratio may be very useful in crisis prevention, in order to perform this function it must display a number of characteristics that are not always easily obtained. Consequently, in analysing the external vulnerability of an economy, this indicator must be handled with caution and supported by official national and international databases, incorporating the methodological adjustments needed to redefine both ratio components, and including ratio variants that take into account its sensitivity to changes in external conditions. Of course, the limitations faced by indicators of this type and the need to include a broad set of economic variables in any analysis of external vulnerability must not be ignored in this process.

Notes

* The views expressed in this paper are those of the authors and do not necessarily reflect those of the Banco de Mexico.

1 Furman and Stiglitz 1998; Radelet and Sachs 1998.
2 Greenspan 1999.
3 Rodrik and Velasco 1999; Bussière and Mulder 1999; and De Beaufort Wijnholds and Kapteyn 2001.
4 Berg, et al. 1999 and IMF 2002; Hawkins and Klau 2000.
5 Several IMF studies provide some empirical support for this conclusion (IMF 2000 and Bussière and Mulder 1999), but the determination of the vulnerability threshold clearly requires further work.
6 IMF 2000.
7 The IMF includes among the latter the exchange-rate regime, the currency denomination of external debt, other macroeconomic fundamentals, the microeconomic conditions that affect the soundness of the private-sector debt position and the possibility of capital flight by residents, IMF 2000.
8 'Joint BIS-IMF-OECD-World Bank Statistics on External Debt', BIS.
9 'Global Development Finance', World Bank.
10 'External Debt Statistics, Historical Data', OECD.
11 'Economic Reports', The Institute of International Finance.
12 Kaminsky, Lizondo and Reinhart 1998; Kamin, Schindler and Samuel 2001; Edison 2000; IMF 2000.
13 See, for example: Frankel and Rose 1996; Radelet and Sachs 1998; Rodrik and Velasco 1999; Esquivel and Larraín 1998, among others.
14 See the first three studies listed in the previous footnote.
15 When analysing regression coefficients using a *Probit* method, it must be taken into account that the normalization applied in *Probit* model estimations generally leads to coefficients on an arbitrary scale. In this context, the relative magnitude of the coefficients involved, rather than their absolute value, is the relevant factor. Pindyck and Rubinfeld 1986.
16 In accordance with the usual procedure, coefficients obtained using the *Logit* model are divided by 1.8138 ($\pi/3$?) for comparison with coefficients obtained using the *Probit* method.
17 Although coefficients estimated using *Probit* models do not provide data on the marginal effect on the dependent variable, they do make it possible to identify the relative significance of each variable in calculating the probability of a crisis.
18 This liquidity line was disbursed in full in September 1998 and was not renewed.
19 This modification only applies to BIS-IMF-OECD-WB data, as IIF data already include this type of debt. It is assumed that all debt instruments included in the stock of fixed-income government securities issued domestically and held by nonresidents are short-term.

20 The IR–STED* indicator is higher than the IR–STED beginning in the second half of 1994. This is because the balance of non-resident holdings of domestically-issued government securities falls drastically and the credit line opened with the USA and Canada becomes relevant.

21 As the IIF data include domestically-issued fixed-income government securities held by nonresidents, the only adjustment made to the IR–STED* ratio is related to credit lines available from foreign banks and other countries.

22 SHCP, 'Mexico: Economic and Financial Statistics, Data Book'.

23 The IR–STED ratio is thus calculated on the basis of gross international reserves at the end of each year and total external debt amortizations scheduled for the following year.

Bibliography

Bank for International Settlements, 'Joint BIS-IMF-OECD-World Bank Statistics on External Debt', several editions.

Berg, Andrew, Borensztien, Eduardo, Milesi-Ferreti, Gian Maria and Patillo, Catherine, 1999, 'Anticipating Balance of Payments Crisis: The Role of Early Warning Systems', Occasional Paper 186, IMF.

Bussière, Matthieu and Mulder, Christian, 1999, 'External Vulnerability in Emerging Market Economies: How High Liquidity Can Offset Weak Fundamentals and the Effects of Contagion', IMF Working Papers, no. 99/88, July.

De Beaufort Wijnholds, Onno, J and Kapteyn, Arend, 2001, 'Reserve Adequacy in Emerging Market Economies', IMF Working Papers, no. 01/143, September.

Edison, Hali J, 2000, 'Do Indicators of Financial Crisis Work? An Evaluation of An Early Warning System', Board of Governors of the Federal Reserve System, International Finance Discussion Papers, no. 675, July.

Esquivel, Gerardo and Larraín, Felipe B, 1998, 'Explaining Currency Crisis', Harvard University Development Discussion Paper, no. 666, November.

Frankel, Jeffrey and Rose, Andrew K, 1996, 'Currency Crashes in Emerging Markets: An Empirical Treatment', Journal of International Economics, no. 41, November, pp. 351–66.

Furman, J and Stiglitz, J, 1998, 'Economic Crisis: Evidence and Insights from East Asia', Brooking Papers on Economic Activity, no. 98:2, pp. 1–114.

Glick, Reuven and Rose, Andrew, 1998, 'Contagion and Trade: Why Are Currency Crises Regional?', Journal of International Money and Finance, vol. 18, no. 4, pp. 603–18, August.

Greenspan, Alan, 1999, 'Currency Markets and Debt', Remarks at the World Bank Conference on Recent Trends in Reserve Management, Washington, DC, 29 April.

Guidotti, Pablo, 1999, 'Remarks at G-33 Seminar in Bonn', April.

Hawkins, John and Klau, Marc, 2000, 'Measuring Potential Vulnerabilities in Emerging Market Economies', BIS Working Papers, no. 91, October.

Hawkins, John and Turner, Philip, 2000, 'Managing Foreign Debt and Liquidity Risks in Emerging Economies: An Overview', BIS Policy Papers, no. 8, September.

Institute for International Finance, 'Economic Reports', several editions.

International Monetary Fund, 2002, Global Financial Stability Report, Market Developments and Issues, IMF World Economic and Financial Surveys, March.

International Monetary Fund, 2001, 'Issues in Reserves Adequacy and Management', Prepared by the Monetary and Exchange Affairs Department and Policy Development and Review Department in consultation with others departments, October.

International Monetary Fund, 2000, 'Debt and Reserve-Related Indicators of External

Vulnerability', Prepared by the Policy Development and Review Department in consultation with others departments, March.

International Monetary Fund, *International Financial Statistics*, several editions.

Kamin Steven B, Schindler, John W and Samuel, Shawna L, 2001, 'The Contribution of Domestic and External Factors to Emerging Market Devaluation Crisis: An Early Warning Systems Approach', Board of Governors of the Federal Reserve System, International Finance Discussion Papers, no. 711, September.

Kaminsky, Graciela, Lizondo, Saúl and Reinhart, Carmen M, 1998, 'Leading Indicators of Currency Crises', *IMF Staff Papers*, vol. 45, no. 1, pp. 1–48, March.

Kaminsky, Graciela and Reinhart, Carmen M, 1996, 'The Twin Crisis: The Causes of Banking and Balance-of Payments Problems', Board of Governors of the Federal Reserve System, International Finance Discussion Papers, no. 544, March.

Mahoney, C, 1999, 'What Have We Learned? Explaining the World Financial Crisis', Moody's Investors Service, Report Number 43599, March.

Organization for Economic Cooperation and Development, *External Debt Statistics*, several editions.

Pindyck, Robert S and Rubinfeld, Daniel L, 1986, *Econometric Models and Economic Forecast*, McGraw-Hill Book Co., Second Edition.

Radelet, Steven and Sachs, Jeffrey, 1998, 'The East Asian Financial Crisis: Diagnosis, Remedies, Prospects', Brookings Papers on Economic Activity, 1, pp. 1–74.

Rodrik, Dani and Velasco, Andrés, 1999, 'Short-Term Capital Flows', National Bureau of Economic Research, Working Papers, no. 7364, September.

Ministry of Finance and Public Credit, Mexico: *Economic and Financial Statistics*, Data Book, several editions.

Sidaoui, José, 2000, 'Macroeconomic Aspects of the Management of External Debt and Liquidity: Reflections on the Mexican Experience', BIS Policy Papers, no. 8, September.

World Bank, *Global Development Finance*, several editions.

8

MECHANISMS FOR DIALOGUE AND DEBT-CRISIS WORKOUT THAT CAN STRENGTHEN SOVEREIGN LENDING TO DEVELOPING COUNTRIES

Barry Herman[1]

Abstract

A positive future for foreign private lending to developing countries requires reducing perceived risk through mechanisms for more permanent debtor-creditor 'conversation', and an accepted and effective 'bankruptcy' approach to orderly workouts from unavoidable sovereign defaults. The IMF began a serious debate on this issue by proposing a Sovereign Debt Restructuring Mechanism (SDRM) for orderly workouts of sovereign debts in default. Somewhat surprisingly, the creditor banks, the US Treasury, and the emerging market countries have all rejected the Fund's SDRM approach to debt restructuring. The emerging market countries are concerned that the SDRM approach would significantly increase the high 'spread' or the risk premium they already have to pay for foreign loans. The chapter makes certain suggestions and revisions to the Fund's SDRM approach to make it more acceptable to all parties involved, and to preserve its bite. For example, the chapter advocates including bilateral official creditors in SDRM negotiations, making a mediation service available to negotiating countries, retaining an effective but temporary 'stay' mechanism and, most importantly, separating the mechanism as a whole from the IMF by seeking to enact an international law through a stand-alone treaty. I conclude by warning that premature closure around this controversial, but extremely important, proposal could rob the international system of measures for increasing investor and citizen confidence. I thus call for further consideration of the matter in all relevant forums.

1. Introduction

Reducible market uncertainty makes the perceived risk in foreign lending to the governments of developing countries higher than it need be. In part, the culprit is the shift in the composition of creditors in syndicated loans toward buyers of bonds. The open information and communication needs of bond investors are larger than those of multinational banks, which were the main intermediaries for international lending in earlier decades, and the mechanisms to work out from a default on sovereign bonds are not as developed as they have been for default on international bank loans. There are also controversies and thus uncertainties about how losses in a work out from a crisis should be shared among the various private and official creditors of a defaulting government, and between the country and its creditors as a whole.

In this chapter, I argue that the uncertainty can be reduced through a regular, ongoing dialogue between the borrowing government and its creditors, and that mechanisms can be conceived for carrying this out. Also, the uncertainty over how creditor claims would be treated in the event of default can be addressed through a more assured and comprehensive mechanism for organizing a debt work out.

An additional source of the high uncertainty is that the governments of the major industrial countries no longer want to handle sovereign debt crises as in the 1990s, when they provided massive loans – bilaterally and through the multilateral financial institutions – to try to stave off debtor-country defaults. Political opposition in industrial countries to additional 'bailouts' is understandable, as they provided opportunities for private creditors to be rescued from countries receiving such loans. Opponents see the bailouts as having substituted public debt for private debt, and in certain cases as only postponing eventual default. Although the official creditors have not lost any resources from debtor-country bailouts – all such loans have been repaid with interest – it is legitimate to ask whether bailouts are an appropriate use of 'taxpayer money'. The answer is that in cases of liquidity crisis, they are definitely a warranted use of official resources, under appropriate safeguards. Indeed, helping countries through liquidity crises is a major reason for the existence of the International Monetary Fund (IMF).[2] Admittedly, however, it is often difficult to distinguish liquidity from solvency crises, when large-scale official lending would not be warranted.

While building new mechanisms for dialogue between a government and its creditors is easily accepted, at least in principle, designing a mechanism for

the prompt, effective and equitable resolution of debt crises is more complicated. Currently, many financial-markets participants and debtor-country
governments argue against going too far in the direction of formal processes
for debt-crisis resolution, certainly not as far as creating an international
sovereign bankruptcy mechanism. Indeed, in April 2003, the IMF ministerial
committee found that it was not feasible to take steps toward establishing a
Sovereign Debt Restructuring Mechanism (SDRM), as proposed by the IMF
staff.[3] The private creditors who lobbied hard with their governments against
the SDRM seemed to prefer retaining their full contractual rights to pursue
uncertain legal remedies against a defaulting sovereign, rather than risk weakening them to develop more formal, if collaborative, mechanisms to contain
their losses under a default settlement. Debtor-country governments were
hardly in a position to argue with them. They could only insist that they had
absolutely no intention to ever default. It is not that either group was necessarily right, but that neither was ready for big changes. That does not,
however, lessen the need for such changes.

In what follows, I argue for mechanisms that create regular opportunities
for frank conversations between a government and its creditors, beginning
well before a crisis threatens. In addition, effective and fair negotiation
processes are needed to handle the events of sovereign default that do occur.
Given all the attention directed to the SDRM in 2002 and 2003, it has
become the obvious starting point for further discussions of such processes.
However, significant changes are recommended in the design, affecting
both how such a mechanism might work in a defaulting country and how it
might be implemented internationally. Finally, a plea is made to keep the
international and intergovernmental conversation going on these issues.
It is not enough to have a fairly broad recognition that a problem exists. We
also need to advance toward agreement on what constitutes an effective
solution.

2. The value of a continuous conversation on crisis prevention

A major part of the strategy that the international community established
for crisis prevention in developing countries since the mid-1990s has been
to increase the information in the hands of international creditors and government policymakers. The focus has been above all on quick release of
standardized information and encouraging official commitment to operate
various functions of government according to a set of international standards
and codes of good practice. While this is undoubtedly beneficial, when the
IMF opened a channel for interaction with the international financial community, the first matter chosen for joint analysis reflected a different approach

– namely, how to facilitate 'investor relations programs', which are forums for individual government discussion with its private creditors and investors.[4]

Major international banks and investment houses, ratings agencies and other industry specialist firms have their own private access to senior officials of sovereign borrowers, which they use to gather relevant information. But such information, or the most valuable part of it, is usually confidential for political reasons. This suits the private interlocutors, as the information is also a potential source of income to the firms receiving it.[5] Thus, an independent and cost-effective mechanism for carrying out such conversations with the larger investing community on a regular basis, as well as on the initiative of either debtor or creditors, would add an important instrument for reducing investor and government uncertainty and thus insecurity. Such communications can be especially important when macroeconomic and debt difficulties emerge and creditor concerns begin to build. They may provide a channel through which the government can explain the steps it is taking to stem the drain on resources for debt servicing. They may also provide a forum in which the financing needs of the country or government could be debated and assessed, and thereby facilitate reaching a decision on, say, whether an upcoming bulge in principal payments needs to be re-profiled or bridging finance arranged. In other words, there is value in creating the means by which a government and its diverse private creditors can have the kinds of conversations that enterprises have with their bankers. Whatever the formal legal protections of contracts, finance first and foremost operates on a relationship of trust built between lenders (or their agents and advisors in the case of market finance) and borrowers.

After a sovereign default happens and a concerted debt-restructuring mechanism is brought into play, it is equally important that it incorporate or facilitate an open channel of communication through which creditors can express their views to the debtor government on its policies and be made aware of the government's policy priorities and constraints. Indeed, this channel should be created well before the crisis so that it is already operating to build confidence that each side – the private creditor community and the debtor government – will act accountably. This is certainly important to have when debt restructuring becomes necessary.

A well-established dialogue between the debtor government and the official international community is already ongoing, undertaken through regular IMF policy surveillance and through negotiations that governments undertake when they seek IMF-supported adjustment programs. Although IMF surveillance reports and Letters of Intent of borrower countries seeking adjustment programs are increasingly available to the public on the IMF's website, giving creditors a perspective on policy choices made, it is not the same as the give-and-take evident in a conversation. Having a channel for continuing dialogue between the government and its private creditor community would achieve the internationally desired 'constructive engagement of the private sector by the official sector', and serve as a concrete part of the process for 'private-sector involvement' in crisis prevention and crisis resolution.[6]

The Monterrey Consensus, adopted by the Heads of State and Government and other senior officials at the International Conference on Financing for Development in March 2002, highlighted such 'consultation mechanisms'. It also encouraged 'public/private initiatives that enhance the ease of access, accuracy, timeliness and coverage of information on countries and financial markets, which strengthen capacities for risk assessment'.[7] One concrete proposal in this regard, presented at the International Business Forum of the Monterrey Conference, was to create an independent global clearinghouse of multi-sourced information on developing countries and relevant industries. The clearinghouse would have an investor-friendly 'user interface', to which could be affiliated a series of internet-based government-investor communication networks linking together creditors in different parts of the world with various government officials in specific debtor countries on an ongoing basis.[8]

Conversation is good, but the issue of a government–investor dialogue can be delicate. Foreign creditors are not 'stakeholders' in the political process of the borrowing country. They have no right even to an indirect role, or responsibility, in determining the policies followed by the government. Participation of the actual stakeholders in policy formation – including different departments of government, the legislature, civil society and the press – are not only proper but also essential for effective national ownership of economic policies and programs. Nonetheless, creditors will want, and should have, a 'voice' in the policy dialogue, one that will help retain their confidence in the government, perhaps facilitate informal processes for temporarily easing debt-servicing obligations without default, and perhaps even help broadly structure a debt reduction agreement before default becomes necessary, leapfrogging some of the steps in standard debt-restructuring negotiations. This 'voice' through dialogue might also help rebuild confidence after it is lost through default, an essential step in the eventual return of the debtor to normal external borrowing relationships. The political task of government leaders is to gain and hold such confidence without risking loss of the confidence of their domestic stakeholders.

3. Policy in the event of sovereign default

Although the incidence of sovereign default can be reduced with mechanisms such as those discussed above, it is widely accepted that debt crises will still occasionally occur. What then? In the past, official and private creditors eschewed formal mechanisms for dealing with sovereign default. The Paris Club of bilateral official creditors is an informal arrangement – at best, a cartel with a conscience – with procedures that private observers find opaque and presumptuous for according generally temporary relief from servicing official loans.[9] It also has no way to 'bind in' bilateral official creditors that are not Paris Club members other than through moral suasion. London Clubs or Bank Advisory Committees for restructuring international bank loans are also informal arrangements, although they are now less central than they were in the 1980s when bank lending dominated private-sector financing. Bondholders, a globally more dispersed population, have thus far been handled in ad hoc ways in default situations, with debtor governments employing legal devices that do not require international bankruptcy arrangements, such as the 'exit consent' strategy from US corporate bond restructuring.[10] The international discussions in 2002–03 on creating a statutory international mechanism for debt workouts were very heated, but they reflected agreement on one (perhaps only one) point: the old approaches were not enough. What, however, should be the essential aspects of a new approach?

3.1 A 'stay' during crises so creditors behave collectively

Most private creditors to a bankrupt entity, governmental or private, do not see themselves as having a long-run stake in that entity. Rather, each individual creditor tries to recover as much of its loans to the entity as fast as possible, assuming that all other creditors are thinking the same way. In reality, the average creditor will recover more of its loans by working together with other creditors, although the fleet-footed creditor that is willing to risk expensive legal costs can come out better (or worse) than the average. In the USA, bankruptcy court proceedings – particularly for processes under Chapters 11 and 9 of the Federal Bankruptcy Code (Title 11 of the United States Code) – are aimed precisely at forcing the creditors together for 'collective action' by limiting their ability to act individually. A major instrument for this is the 'stay on litigation' against the bankrupt firm (Chapter 11) or municipality (Chapter 9) while it is under the court's protection. On this analogy, a stay on litigation has been proposed as a tool to promote collective action in the case of sovereign bankruptcies.[11]

In its work on a framework for orderly workouts from debt crises, the IMF has developed guidelines under which it accepts that sometimes a government needs to suspend its debt servicing to private creditors. The IMF would signal its acquiescence in such situations by continuing to make its own loan disbursements to the government after the government had suspended foreign private-debt servicing. The IMF refers to this as 'lending into arrears'.[12] However, 'lending into arrears' does not protect the debtor government from the courts of the creditors.

One may ask, as this gap in legal protection of the sovereign has existed for over 50 years of the IMF existence, why was it never filled? The answer seems to be that, until recently, creditors rarely sued defaulting sovereigns. For countries whose creditors have been primarily official institutions, except for financing of trade, a formal stay is unnecessary, as short-term trade credits are largely self-financing and long-term ones are often insured by official export credit agencies that cover the losses of the private lenders in the event of default. Neither the official export credit agencies that end up holding the insured claims nor other official creditors will attempt to force immediate payment, by the sovereign in crisis, through the courts.

In addition, after the 1970s, and as the boom in private lending ended in the 1980s, creditors did not, as a rule, attempt to immediately collect on their defaulted loans through the courts; thus, there was no pressure for a formal international stay arrangement. The defaulted private lenders had been primarily banks (indeed, most of the bond issues outstanding continued to be serviced even when countries defaulted on their bank loans), and banks were not under pressure to immediately resolve the situation. For one thing, banks do not have to immediately take an accounting reserve against bad debt or write down the value of the loans carried on their books, as they do not publish balance sheets daily. For another, many of the foreign bank creditors had business interests in the defaulting country (for example, retail, investment or private banking businesses) and thus had reasons not to antagonize local government officials with legal action. For a third thing, 'sharing' clauses in multi-bank syndicated loans – the most common instrument for large loans – required that if a bank was successful in its suit it had to share the proceeds with the other lending banks. In other words, banks holding defaulted external debt enjoyed the time and incentives to try to resolve the debt crisis through privately organized collective action. They did not need to bring to bear any formal bankruptcy mechanism.

Moreover, organizing themselves into Advisory Committees and London Clubs to address defaulted government debt was made easier by the relative concentration of the international banking industry and because the bulk of the lending was in the form of syndicated loans, as noted above (sometimes, a few lead managers would represent 500 or more banks in a single syndicate).

The difference today is that a large percentage of the private financing of emerging economies is in the form of bonds. Bond financing is much more a market phenomenon than bank lending, as the number of bondholders is usually far larger than the banks in a syndicated loan and bonds are more easily traded than bank loans.[13] Also, mechanisms for organizing bondholders to restructure a loan are far less developed than for banks. Individual bondholders might thus feel less confident that their interests will be protected than might a small bank whose syndicate was participating in a London Club restructuring negotiation.[14] Individual bondholders might thus look more quickly than bank managements at trying to protect their interests through the courts.

In contrast to bank loans, bonds have to be 'marked to market' every day. This means that the owners of the securities have to immediately reflect the weakness of defaulted debt in their portfolio of securities. Moreover, most securities investors in emerging markets have little ongoing business interest in the country. This makes more credible the threat that some number of them would seek individual redress in the courts of the country where the securities were issued, or a small group might file a class-action suit, as has happened in Argentina.[15] It is not obvious that a court would give satisfaction to such creditors, but several ongoing court proceedings in various jurisdictions might well complicate negotiations on behalf of all bondholders to arrive at an agreed restructuring with the debtor. A legal 'stay' means not having to deal with this complication during the period of the stay.

At the same time, the stay should be temporary when it is invoked. While the threat of the stay encourages creditors to take a collective approach to resolving the debt crisis, a long stay would give the debtor the opportunity to delay negotiations. One approach might thus be to empower the debtor government to declare an initial stay, valid, say, for only 60 days (perhaps subject to IMF Executive Board endorsement after enactment), after which it would expire. In that period, the creditors would need to form themselves into creditor committees and should begin negotiations with the debtor. The creditors represented by the committees should be empowered to extend the stay as needed, say, in 60-day intervals. This would give the creditors, collectively represented by the committees, the power to prevent defections, and it would be in their interest to do so as long as the negotiations and the economic adjustment program were judged to be making adequate progress. There might be an upper limit to the number of extensions, however, as there is also a need to create strong incentives to bring the full negotiation to a close.[16]

Organizations representing private creditors have opposed including the stay in any new sovereign debt-restructuring mechanism. They believe it unduly compromises 'creditor rights'.[17] Indeed, its purpose is precisely to restrict individual creditor actions in order to increase the recovery by an entire class of creditors. Another reason for opposition to a stay is a fear that, before default, the government might more readily threaten suspension of debt servicing or actually default when it was not yet inescapable, knowing the stay would protect it.

In sum, although there is a point to the case against a stay, there is also much to argue for it. Perhaps given the creditor concerns, a more refined legal instrument that does not broadly challenge creditors' rights to go to court could substitute for a stay, but it should have an equivalent effect to a stay in preventing creditor litigation during the debt negotiations.[18] What is essential is that individual creditors should be unable to disrupt or delay the resolution of the sovereign's debt crisis. What is most desirable is if all creditors see that their individual interest is best served through their collective interaction with the indebted sovereign.

3.2 Rules for organizing a sovereign's debt renegotiation

The general strategy in complex debt-restructuring cases has been for the debtor government to negotiate with separate and self-organized classes of creditors – such as commercial banks, bondholders (if at all), domestic creditors (if required), and the Paris Club – usually in the context of an IMF-supported macroeconomic adjustment program. Although IMF approval of the adjustment program usually comes before the debt negotiations are completed (and is a precondition for the Paris Club to act), the IMF-supported program is itself a compromise between proposed adjustment policies, the financial resources required to support their implementation and the amount of funds and debt relief judged likely to be supplied by official and private sources.

The aim is a coherent and adequate package of policy measures, financing and debt relief that brings the country to a sustainable situation at the end point of the adjustment process. The adjustment path should be 'growth oriented' and contribute to the struggle to eradicate poverty. Design of the package thus entails a judgment about what a sustainable overall level of debt would be for the country and how quickly the country might move to the sustainable situation. It depends on the outlook for the international and domestic economy, the amount of new financing that official or private inflows might provide (for example, through foreign direct investment), the socially and politically tolerable rate of structural adjustment and the need to maintain basic social services, indeed, in many cases to increase spending on them.

No magic formula yields the 'correct' package of actions, and experience over the past 25 years suggests that often several economically and socially costly attempts have been needed – sometimes spanning many years – before sufficient steps are taken to enable a country to 'graduate' from debt-crisis status, if then.[19] There is good reason to seek an improved way to arrive at the warranted package of actions, one that also shortens the time needed for the country to renegotiate its debt burden.

3.2.1 Collective action clauses

The major debt-reform proposals that have circulated in recent years have focused on improving the way to arrive at the debt restructuring part of the full policy package. The least ambitious proposal, albeit with the strongest political momentum, is to insert or strengthen 'collective action clauses' (CACs) in sovereign bond contracts. The clauses would address how to mobilize the holders of any specific bond issue and bind-in its potentially recalcitrant members, principally by specifying the precise majority required to change the financial terms of the bond.[20] They would also commit the issuing government to appropriate standards of behavior in its relations with bondholders, by endorsing a particular 'code of conduct'.

One may pose a question, however, about the CACs proposal. Given that the international community has endorsed CACs in one form or another since 1996, and although no international action is required for bond buyers or market professionals to demand them and for sovereign issuers to introduce them, why has their use not increased?[21] The 'revealed preference' of the buyers and issuers in the international bond market suggests a possible concern that CACs would weaken creditor interests in a default situation relative to current standard bond contracts. It might even be that advocates of CACs in the business community, which opposed them until recently, began to see them mainly as a weapon with which to defeat the stronger SDRM proposal.

Meanwhile, bond-issuing emerging economy governments feared that adopting CACs in their bond documents would send a signal to international investors that default was more likely, raising risk judgments and thus interest costs. The logic is not clear, as few insurance companies believe that purchasers of dual airbags for automobiles intend to smash their cars into trees or other cars. But the concern is about market psychology and not logic. Indeed, the fears appear to have been exaggerated, especially since the government of Mexico floated a bond issue under New York law with a CAC in late February 2003 that had no perceptible premium for additional risk priced into the bond.

One important shortcoming – and frequently made criticism – is that

CACs beg the question of how to organize the multiple classes of creditors of a single country for negotiations with the debtor, let alone how to bring together into a single class the holders of bonds issued in different currencies and under the laws of different financial markets. Proponents of CACs have recently responded to this criticism by advocating the formation of 'an informal, country-specific advisory group comprised of leading market participants from a broad spectrum of financial institutions'. Such an advisory group would enter into discussions with the authorities in a country in difficulty and if 'broad debt restructuring' were required, could 'give way to constructive dialogue between the debtor country and a broad spectrum of creditors reflected in a creditor group'.[22] Such an informal advisory group could emerge smoothly from the 'continuous conversation' mechanism discussed above; one might wonder, however, about how representative its members might be in the actual negotiations if they were self-appointed, as seems to be indicated.

3.2.2 Building on the SDRM proposal

While intergovernmental consideration of the Sovereign Debt Restructuring Mechanism proposed by the IMF was effectively put on hold in April 2003, it is an obvious starting point for considering what a comprehensive debt-restructuring mechanism might look like. Indeed, the private-sector proposal noted above to encourage formation of an advisory/negotiating creditor group in complex cases was essentially a form of the 'creditor committee' feature of the SDRM proposal.

Under the SDRM, all creditors that would participate in the restructuring of the sovereign's debt would be formed into separate classes. A new international legal mechanism, the Sovereign Debt Dispute Resolution Forum (SDDRF) would oversee the formation of the classes, validate the claims of individual creditors and resolve disputes on the allocation of individual creditors to the classes. It would also oversee creditor voting within each class on such matters as who should represent them in their negotiations. The chosen class negotiators would be charged with developing, with the sovereign, a precise restructuring proposal for their class. In addition, a steering committee of the various classes of creditors might be formed to coordinate their various negotiations and check on the coherence of the overall financial package that emerges. The sovereign would then formally propose the component draft agreements to each class, which would formally vote on them, all of this, again, overseen by the SDDRF. The overall debt agreement would be considered adopted when approved by 75 per cent of the outstanding principal of registered claims in each class.[23]

While this seems to be a powerful overall approach, it has a number of shortcomings, which, if addressed, would significantly strengthen it. For example, as currently proposed, an important group of creditors for many developing countries would not be included, namely official bilateral creditors. The IMF staff instead envisaged a parallel process of negotiations in the Paris Club, apparently following its existing practices and precedents.[24] One reason for keeping the Paris Club separate is that the results of its negotiations would be hard to reconcile with those of the SDRM. Above all, unlike private creditors, the Paris Club has been very reluctant to grant 'stock of debt' reductions, except for the poorest countries. Rather, it reschedules debt-servicing obligations in arrears and falling due during limited future periods. In addition, each Paris Club arrangement is only an informal 'Agreed Minute', which then has to be negotiated into individual debt-relief agreements with the authorities of each Paris Club member. The indebted country must, therefore, undertake repeated sets of Paris Club negotiations over time. Moreover, the debtor is expected to seek comparable treatment from its other bilateral official creditors that are not Paris Club members, which are often other developing countries. This is a high-cost mechanism, especially for the debtor, and would not allow for closure on the question of whether the country will have eliminated its debt overhang when it completes its SDRM arrangement.

In fact, the Paris Club could make new rules so that its agreements were more like those arrived at under an SDRM mechanism. It seems that once such a mechanism is created, however, the Paris Club will have outlived its usefulness. The Paris Club treats mainly two types of official loans: export credits and direct loans by its member governments, including official development assistance (ODA). Each type could be treated as a separate creditor class within the SDRM process. While ODA loans involve a policy matter that might warrant special guidelines or a special class within the SDRM, the other loans are essentially commercial activities of states. The latter mainly promote the exports of countries through advantaged terms of export financing, typically for large-scale purchases such as airplanes, nuclear power stations and capital equipment. As essentially commercial activities, albeit governmental, these should be treated like other commercial credits. That is, the export credit agencies (both Paris Club members and non-members) could be grouped together under the SDRM as a mandatory separate class. Not only would this better facilitate an appropriate overall package for the debtor, it would also bind in non-Paris Club members and reduce the expenses of the export credit agencies themselves in negotiating each Paris Club bilateral round. Instead, they would settle their claims on the debtor in one relatively quick negotiation. This would take account of the inter-creditor equity issues among bilateral agencies that underlie the formation of the Paris Club in the first place.

It should also be possible for the steering committee to raise questions about the overall adequacy of the country's proposed adjustment program and its financing envelope.[25] The steering committee could conceivably even conclude that the overall financial and policy package would not lead the country to a sustainable debt situation, in which case their post-agreement credits would be of uncertain value. The committee might thus urge the debtor government to reopen its discussions with IMF.

As the overall package would have usually been supported and endorsed by the IMF, it might be seen that the closeness of the IMF to the SDRM is a problem. What happens if the creditors conclude that sustainability requires relief from servicing debt owed to the multilateral financial institutions? Those institutions could reject this argument, but it should be addressed on its merits. It is not clear, however, where that debate would take place. It does not appear that such concerns could be addressed to the SDDRF. Perhaps the only avenue open to the creditors would be to reject the debt restructuring package reached under the SDRM by voting it down, which is not an attractive option.

At this point, one may return to the more general question: how would one know that the overall package, of which the debt-relief agreement is a part, would be adequate or appropriate? It would have resulted from a complex negotiation and reflect the relative bargaining strengths and strategies of the negotiators. Indeed, a group of civil-society organizations has argued that an SDRM-type of process would not produce an adequate outcome and has instead proposed a different approach, called an International Fair and Transparent Arbitration Process (FTAP). It would replace the negotiations between debtor and creditors with an arbitration process.[26] In this model, a panel of five arbitrators, chosen in a particular way that aims to ensure their independence and balance, would hear testimony of all relevant stakeholders in the sovereign's debt crisis, including representatives of the poor, and then determine a fair solution. The argument here is that instead of negotiations among unequally backed parties, arbitrators (assisted by internationally supplied staff) would reach a better solution.

Usually, when arbitral proceedings are used to settle financial disputes, provision for them is made in the original contract or in the governing law or administrative regulations. Operating at the international level, the FTAP would have to be created by treaty, as it would apply in principle across the board to all financial obligations of the sovereign, regardless of the terms of individual loan agreements. Creditors who worry about the abridgement of their rights during a temporary stay of litigation under an SDRM would presumably be apoplectic over this proposal. What it serves to do, however, is focus on the matter of the adequacy of the overall agreement in terms of its economic and social implications – and this is an essential point. Also, by recommending use of an arbitral panel, the FTAP proposal suggests that there is value in bringing to bear the viewpoints of reputable individuals who are outside the process of the direct negotiations.

This points to another possible amendment of the SDRM proposal. Instead of FTAP arbitrators, mediators might serve as external advisors to the SDRM process. Mediation works when all sides to a dispute believe that the mediator's suggestions are competent, unbiased and aimed at an effective solution. The mediator's main function is not to get a 'better deal' for one party or another to a dispute, but to facilitate effective settlement. Mediators can save all disputants time and resources (a major advantage of mediation) as they develop a sense of how far the different negotiators would be willing to go on the various aspects of the contest, and thus where the true middle ground might lie. Not being participants in the negotiations themselves, they can more easily see and assess the overall adequacy of the evolving package, or at least respond to concerns about adequacy raised by one group of actors or another.

Mediation would be available as a service that participants in the negotiations to restructure a sovereign's debt might (or might not) draw upon to advance more expeditiously to a comprehensive and effective solution. In fact, no formal bankruptcy regime is needed for negotiators to avail themselves of mediation if they jointly so decide and they can identify a mutually acceptable mediator.

Finally, the advocates of FTAP are absolutely right about the need to be concerned about poverty and development in debt-crisis countries. The nations of the world committed themselves in the Millennium Declaration to achieving a set of social and economic goals, and the international institutions are committed to realizing those goals.[27] The agreed international follow up includes in-country reviews, as well as global monitoring. When any country is seen as not being on track to achieve the goals, it behoves policy analysts in the country and in the international community to explore why. If the reason is even partly attributable to a debt crisis, that concern should inform the process for restructuring the country's debt position.[28]

3.3 International legal and oversight issues

The IMF presented the SDRM as a 'statutory' approach to sovereign debt restructuring, meaning that it would become part of international law and would have a number of mandatory features. Central among them are the processes described above for reaching the debt-restructuring agreement once the debtor government invokes the SDRM, as well as the decisions of the Sovereign Debt Dispute Resolution Forum (SDDRF). Wary of the radical change that would be embodied in a strong, new, international process that oversaw sovereign bankruptcies, the IMF proposed strict limits on the juridical powers of the SDDRF, while also trying to assure its independence. Another legal issue is how the SDRM as a whole would be made into an international agreement having the force of law. The IMF proposed that the SDRM be adopted as an amendment to the IMF's Articles of Agreement, a treaty to which all IMF member countries are bound. Each of these issues has been highly controversial.

One advantage claimed for adopting the SDRM through an amendment to the IMF Articles is that it would not require the endorsement of all countries to which it would apply. Once the required number of countries accepted the amendment, it would be binding on all members. Given the distribution of voting power in the IMF, a large number of developing countries could oppose the draft amendment and it could still be adopted. That might improve the chances of adoption, but such an approach would violate all sense of the international pledge in the Monterrey Consensus to increase the 'effective participation' of developing countries and countries in transition in the important international efforts underway to reform the international financial architecture.[29] In other words, the standard for adoption of the SDRM or some successor mechanism should not be such that it could be adopted over the objection of a significant number of developing countries.

One additional concern of critics of the SDRM is that, as a major creditor, the IMF might not be a neutral party in the negotiations that the debtor country enters with its other creditors. The IMF would not participate directly in those negotiations, but it would be central to the development of the country's adjustment program and how it was financed with new funds and debt relief. That is, the IMF is responsible for assuring consistency between the debt relief accorded, the other financial flows, and the balance-of-payments and fiscal position of the country. This would include, naturally, assuring resources sufficient to meet the debt-servicing obligations to the IMF itself.

This potential conflict of interest was not directly addressed in the design of the SDRM, except in so far as it pertained to creating a space between the IMF and the SDDRF, and even that space was not large. The IMF proposed a complicated mechanism by which relevant international organizations and professional associations would advise the Managing Director of the IMF on prospective candidates for a 'selection panel' that would in turn recommend names to him for selection as candidates for the pool of SDDRF judges. The IMF Managing Director would thus form his list and submit it for approval or rejection as a whole by the Board of Governors.[30]

One might ask why the IMF put itself at the center of the selection of the SDDRF judges. The answer is because the SDRM would be created by an amendment of the IMF Articles. That is, it was not feasible for the IMF to engage or commit another international institution or body through an article of its own constitutional agreement. Were the SDRM adopted by a stand-alone treaty, this problem would not arise and the process for selection of the SDDRF judges could be designed in a more straightforward way. Other credible, international processes could choose them, for example, using the United Nations or a separate governance body established under a freestanding SDRM treaty. Indeed, there is nothing in the operation of the SDRM negotiations themselves that need directly involve the IMF, especially if an independent mediator were empowered to raise concerns expressed by one side or the other about the overall package. Except in the very rare cases when its own loans have to be restructured, the IMF could stay fully at arm's length from an SDRM mechanism created under a stand-alone treaty.[31]

While establishing the SDRM through such a treaty could address the criticism of the direct involvement of the IMF in the process, a treaty would still be subject to the charge that a statutory approach is not warranted for sovereign debt restructuring and would take too long to bring into force. The main suggested alternative, as noted in the discussion of CACs above, is the contractual one. That is, instead of a new international agreement that would supersede the terms of loan contracts, advocates of the contractual approach argue for changing the terms of the contracts themselves. Thus, instead of government negotiators and legislatures determining what the debt-restructuring process would be, lawyers for the creditors and the debtor would do so. In so doing, they would be guided by model clauses as have been developed by private creditor associations and which could be endorsed by an intergovernmental body. However, it seems that, barring a wholesale swap of outstanding debt, quite a number of years would be required before the stock of sovereign bonds of any country would be converted to bonds with the new clauses. In short, the CACs' approach, like the statutory one, would likely take considerable time to implement.

Moreover, as noted earlier, the contractual approach is a partial one, facilitating collective action by the investors in a particular bond issue or at most by all bondholders that would have otherwise fallen into the same class had there been an SDRM.[32] CAC advocates usually beg the question of enforcing collective action across lending instruments, other than to say that the debtor government should keep the bondholders or their representatives informed of proposed restructuring terms for other creditors (in the case of the SDRM, this would be assured by the steering committee).

Responding to this criticism, the former Chairman of the Council of Economic Advisors to the US President has recommended that comparable CACs be included in all private loan contracts (for example, bonds, bank loans and trade credits).[33] Such clauses would also specify how to aggregate votes across the different creditor classes on a package of debt-restructuring proposals covering each creditor class, paralleling the process specified in the SDRM proposal. In addition, the former CEA Chairman, acknowledging that an institution is needed to organize the negotiations and resolve disputes, proposed that an independent forum take on the function of the SDDRF, with reference to that forum also included in each loan contract. That forum, unlike the SDDRF, would be established as a voluntary body, although how it would be formed was not explained.

In fact, Richard Gitlin, a prominent American attorney, proposed creation of just such a forum at one of the 'side events' at the Monterrey Conference on Financing for Development.[34] His proposal, the Sovereign Debt Forum, would be governed by a board drawn from private creditors, sovereign issuers and international organizations, and would serve two functions. The first would be to enhance sovereign debt as an asset class through discussion among buy-side and sell-side practitioners in the bond market of the design of different lending instruments and their appropriate financial and legal terms, identifying and promoting best practices. The second would be to facilitate sovereign debt restructuring when needed. When approached by troubled debtors, the forum would help with early communication with creditors, assist in organizing the relevant parties and groups, make available facilitators or mediators from a standing panel, and provide informal adjudication processes as needed. It would also develop lessons for use in future debt restructurings based on the accumulation of experiences. Indeed, the forum could formulate principles for sovereign debt restructuring, or as other authors have described it, a code of conduct for crisis resolution. The proposal could be put into effect rather quickly on an ad hoc basis and, if backed by a significant part of the financial and official community, could quickly gain the credibility needed to be useful in resolving a pending debt crisis.

Even if a voluntary mechanism such as the one above succeeds, it may still be useful to adopt a formal SDRM to serve as a backup with legal strength. As in the domestic context, the formal bankruptcy mechanism could prompt the relevant parties to come to mutual agreement 'in the shadow' of the statutory mechanism. This does not necessarily mean, however, that the framework needs to be embodied in a treaty or amendment to the IMF Articles of Agreement.

Professor Christoph Paulus, for one, has offered an alternative approach. He emphasizes that the central issue in any bankruptcy is the collective action problem, or as he says, creating an 'enforced community' of creditors. He notes that national bankruptcy legislation establishes the process for creating that 'community' for private entities or municipalities and that it binds in not only domestic creditors but foreign ones too, and also the domestic tax authorities and even foreign states, as when the bankrupt unit owes taxes abroad.[35] The power of a national legislature to thus bind in a foreign state in a domestic bankruptcy proceeding is generally accepted. Professor Paulus then argues that the national legislature could also adopt a law specifying how the bankruptcy of the government itself should be handled. He admits that, left to itself, the legislature would probably draft the law in a way that the creditors would find unfair. His answer is that a global institution, such as the United Nations, could adopt a model law on sovereign bankruptcy, based on a text drafted in a respected technical body such as the United Nations Commission on International Trade Law (UNCITRAL). The model law would have to embody procedures that were considered fair and effective by creditors, which means, to start, involving neutral third parties in overseeing the process of restructuring the sovereign's debt, much like the role the SDDRF would play. The pool of 'third parties' would have to be maintained in a credible, independent forum, such as the International Court of Justice at The Hague, and there should be a mechanism for review and revision of the model law based on lessons learned from experience. While the practicalities of this approach would need to be investigated, it underlines that new ideas on how to effectively restructure sovereign debt are not exhausted by the CACs and SDRM proposals.

4. Conclusion: more work needed on debt restructuring

One might summarize the preceding discussion by saying that an international strategy for strengthening sovereign-risk lending to developing countries should include a focus on reducing the uncertainty faced by prospective lenders. As advocated here, that would involve first fostering an ongoing relationship between a government and its private creditors, which would facilitate access to financing in normal times, smooth the way to collaborative debt restructuring in a crisis and help speed the return to a normal relationship with foreign creditors afterward. Processes for sovereign debt restructuring should have two goals:

- to help a country that has fallen into a sovereign debt crisis to emerge from it expeditiously and with minimal social disruption

- in so doing, to help restore economic growth while preserving and strengthening the instrument of sovereign-risk lending as an important source of private finance for development.

As part of this approach, an institutional innovation seems necessary to facilitate the debt renegotiations in those few occasions, we hope, when they are required. The SDRM as proposed by the IMF would have been an important innovation in this regard, although it did not win sufficient private-creditor or debtor-government endorsement. As it also had some important shortcomings, certain features of the proposal might well be changed in a successor proposal. In particular, such changes might be the inclusion of bilateral official creditors in the negotiations, making a mediation service available to negotiating countries, retaining an effective but temporary 'stay' mechanism, and more completely separating the mechanism as a whole from the IMF by seeking to enact it through a stand-alone treaty.

In any event, establishing something like a successor SDRM is a long-term project, especially in the light of the considerable opposition to the IMF proposal and the likelihood that the changes suggested here would also be contentious. It is nevertheless important to continue investigating how to improve the SDRM proposal, as well as to consider easier-to-implement non-treaty approaches to more effective sovereign debt restructuring. Indeed, a voluntary mechanism that could be set up by interested parties relatively quickly might help resolve individual debt crises and build confidence to the extent that a statutory approach is not even needed, while an approach based on developing a model sovereign bankruptcy law is also an avenue worth exploring.

In other words, considerable work remains to be done and we should urgently take up the challenge. This requires continuing discussions in relevant international forums, including intergovernmental ones, so as to develop a workable proposal and build the requisite political momentum for its adoption.

Notes

1 An earlier version of this paper was presented at the XVIth Technical Group Meeting of the Group of 24 in Port of Spain, Trinidad and Tobago, 13–14 February 2003. That paper, like this one, has benefited from discussions over the last few years with a number of individuals from the private and official sectors. The staff of IMF involved in developing the Fund's sovereign debt restructuring proposal have also been very open in discussions with me. I appreciate as well learning from Jürgen Kaiser and Kunibert Raffer. I thank Lee Buchheit, Ariel Buira, Sergei Gorbunov, Cristián Ossa, Kunibert Raffer, Barbara Samuels and Jernej Sekolec for reading and commenting on an earlier

draft. Views expressed are those of the author and not necessarily of the United Nations.

2 The IMF recently agreed upon the criteria it will now follow in determining the conditions and degree of access to IMF resources in external financial crises, aiming to explicitly establish its policy and thereby to reduce market uncertainty about the policy (see 'IMF concludes discussion on access policy in the context of capital account crises; and review of access policies in the credit tranches and Extended Fund Facility', IMF Public Information Note 03/37, 21 March 2003).

3 See IMF, Communiqué of the International Monetary and Financial Committee (IMFC), Washington, DC, 12 April, 2003, para. 15, IMF website.

4 See IMF, 'Investor Relations Programs: Report of the Capital Markets Consultative Group (CMCG) Working Group on Creditor–Debtor Relations', 15 June 2001.

5 That is, 'sell-side' firms use the information to help market the debtor's bonds, and investment analysts use it to develop their 'buy' and 'sell' recommendations to clients; whether or not they also engage in 'insider trading' is another matter. Except for commercial banks that lend directly, the 'buy side' is often less directly informed.

6 The terms in quotation marks were prominent in the 24 September 2000 communiqué of the International Monetary and Financial Committee at the Prague Annual Meetings of the IMF and the World Bank, endorsing a framework for private sector involvement in crisis prevention and management (see *IMF Survey*, October 9, 2000, pp. 314–17).

7 United Nations, *Report of the International Conference on Financing for Development, Monterrey, Mexico, March 18–22, 2002* (A/CONF.198/11), Chapter I, Resolution 1, Annex, paras 24 and 25.

8 A prototype of the Global Clearing House was developed with Ghana and Mauritius as pilot cases, with the support of the Government of Norway and the Ford Foundation. A prototype government–investor network was also under development in 2003 (for access to the working model, contact Samuels_Barbara@bah.com). For background, see Barbara Samuels, II, 'Strengthening Information and Analysis in the Global Financial System: a Concrete Set of Proposals', United Nations Department of Economic and Social Affairs, Discussion Paper no. 23 (June 2002).

9 See Brian Caplen, 'Paris Club Comes Under Attack', *Euromoney*, September 2000, pp. 56–61 (the editorial for that issue of *Euromoney* was 'Paris Club: reform or die' [p. 7]) and 'Burden-Sharing in 2001: Now is the Time to Reform the Paris Club', Policy Paper of EMTA (Trade Association for the Emerging Markets), 13 February 2001 (at www.emta.org). Although there have been certain improvements since these commentaries appeared, the private sector seems to remain concerned about a central complaint in the EMTA paper regarding lack of 'comparable treatment' of official and private creditors by the Paris Club.

10 The typical bonds issued under New York law require full consensus to change the financial terms of the bond, but non-financial terms can be changed on a majority vote of bondholders. One device that has been used to get around this restriction is for the sovereign issuer to offer its bondholders a package deal to swap a new bond with different financial terms for the old bond and to change the non-financial terms of the old bond so bondholders not accepting the exchange offer end up with an inferior security. When this was used in Ecuador's case in 2000, it was said to have infuriated many bondholders (see Felix Salmon, 'The Buy Side Starts to Bite Back', *Euromoney*, April 2001, pp. 46–61).

11 For terminological clarity, a 'stay' is here quite different from a 'standstill' on debt servicing. A stay temporarily prevents creditors from having a court enforce a contractual obligation. A standstill is the actual suspension of debt-servicing payments (partial or full), which may be protected by a stay on creditor litigation.

12 For additional details on the current policy, see 'IMF Board Discusses the Good-Faith Criterion under the Fund Policy of Lending into Arrears to Private Creditors', IMF Public Information Note 02/107 (24 September 2002), IMF website.

13 The distinctions are not absolute, as banks, including domestic banks, may hold a large portion of a country's external bond debt, while some bond issues may be 'privately placed' and not trade over an organized exchange.

14 Even so, the secondary market in bank debt that arose in the 1980s was available as a way for banks that did not want to wait out the negotiations to sell their participation in a syndicated loan, albeit at a substantial discount from face value. In addition, banks with local operations in the debtor country, and banks that had mainly sought a financial opportunity in lending to the sovereign, followed different debt-recovery strategies. This led to the introduction of various 'exit' offers to the latter creditors in successive restructuring rounds, while the longer-term players stayed in the pool.

15 See Deepak Gopinath, 'The Debt-Crisis Crisis', *Institutional Investor*, August 2002, pp. 36–40.

16 Legal experts in bankruptcy observe that an initial, debtor-initiated stay of 60–90 days might not be needed, as it would be difficult for a creditor to mount an effective legal case, obtain a favorable judgment in a relevant court and identify appropriate assets of the defaulting government to try to attach in that time period. Moreover, by the time the 'rogue creditor's' court case was actually won, the original loan contracts would have been restructured and the lawsuit would thereby be made moot. Nevertheless, the first stay would have symbolic power, especially with IMF Executive Board approval, marking the start of the process. Subsequent creditor-endorsed stays would signal that the cooperating creditors were working effectively to arrive at a solution to which they would seek to bind all creditors.

17 Why, one might ask, is an abridgement of creditor rights in domestic bankruptcy proceedings acceptable to creditors and the comparable abridgement in the case of a sovereign is not? Lee Buchheit, a well-known attorney in international financial practice, provides an answer: in domestic bankruptcy, the quid pro quo for a stay is that enforceable restrictions are placed on management to prevent it from taking money out of the firm or municipality in various ways, maintaining its status quo as of the time of default. There is no authority to enforce such a quid pro quo on a sovereign, rendering the stay on litigation one-sided. However, governments do bind themselves in treaties so it seems this matter should remain an open question.

18 The IMF staff, concerned about the possibility that overly broad powers could be conferred by a general stay, proposed that the SDRM employ a more limited 'hotchpot rule', which in essence subtracts from a successfully litigating creditor's share of a final group settlement whatever was won through its litigation, neutralizing its gain. The staff coupled this proposal with a supplement, which would enjoin enforcement of individual creditor court actions that would otherwise undermine the collective restructuring agreement (see IMF, 'The Design of the Sovereign Debt Restructuring Mechanism – Further Considerations' (EBS/02/201), 27 November 2002, paras 124–41). The final proposal put to the International Monetary and Financial Committee included a creditor-approved stay as a third option, while noting that a

number of Executive Directors of the IMF preferred a temporary automatic stay and general cessation of payments (see 'Report of the Managing Director to the IMFC on a Statutory Sovereign Debt Restructuring Mechanism' IMFC/Doc/7/03/4, 8 April 2003, para. 7).

19 This is illustrated by the sequence of negotiations and policy initiatives needed to address the 1980s debt crises, and the even longer span of time and greater number of policy iterations to resolve the still ongoing crises of the heavily-indebted poor countries.

20 In addition, a 'sharing clause', if it became standard in bond contracts, as in syndicated bank loan agreements, as noted above, could make a formal stay on litigation unnecessary.

21 The question is well posed in William Bratton and Mitu Gulati, 'Perfect Market Puzzles: Five Observations from the World of Sovereign Debt', *Economic and Political Weekly*, Mumbai, 6 July 2002, pp. 2702–04.

22 See 'Sovereign Debt Restructuring', discussion draft of a joint statement by Emerging Markets Creditors Association, EMTA, Institute of International Finance, International Primary Market Association, International Securities Market Association, Securities Industry Association and The Bond Market Association, 6 December 2002, p. 8 (available at www.emta.org).

23 See IMF, 27 November 2002, op. cit., especially paras 157–168 and 183–208.

24 Ibid., paras 74–82. In its final report to the IMFC, the Fund left the exclusion of bilateral official claims in 'square brackets', meaning not yet agreed and requiring further discussion (see IMF, 8 April 2003, op. cit., para 3(d)).

25 As was the practice under the Bank Advisory Committees in the 1980s, the steering committee would probably set up its own technical economic subcommittee to advise it.

26 For a detailed presentation, see Thomas Fritz and Philipp Hersel, *Fair and Transparent Arbitration Processes: A New Road to Resolve Debt Crises*, Discussion Paper, Berlin and Aachen, August 2002 (see www.blue21.de or www.misereor.de). See also Jubilee Research (New Economics Foundation), Jubilee South and other organizations (important initial and continuing work on the idea has been done by Kunibert Raffer at the University of Vienna).

27 Adopted at the Millennium Summit, New York, 8 September 2000 (see United Nations, General Assembly resolution 55/2).

28 This suggestion speaks to a guideline in the Monterrey Consensus, namely that 'Future reviews of debt sustainability should also bear in mind the impact of debt relief on progress toward the achievement of the development goals in the Millennium Declaration' (United Nations, *Report of the International Conference ...*, para. 49).

29 United Nations, *Report of the International Conference ...*, op. cit., para. 53.

30 IMF, 27 November 2002, op. cit., paras 233–44 and IMF, 8 April 2003, op. cit., para. 13(a).

31 Were such a path taken, the treaty negotiators would do well to start from the detailed work on the SDRM by the IMF Legal Department, as cited herein.

32 When the debtor defaults on an interest payment on a bond, there is first a grace period and then a per cent of the investors (as specified in the bond contract) may 'accelerate' the bond, making it fully due and payable. Other bonds, payments on which are due on other dates, may be brought into play by cross-default clauses, if not by actual default when payment is required. Restructuring all the accelerated bonds at

the same time may then become the practical consequence of *pari passu* and other clauses in the bond contracts.

33 R Glenn Hubbard, 'Enhancing Sovereign Debt Restructuring', remarks at the Conference on the IMF's Sovereign Debt Proposal, American Enterprise Institute, Washington, DC, 7 October 2002.

34 Richard A Gitlin, 'A Proposal: Sovereign Debt Forum', oral presentation at International Conference on Financing for Development Side Event, 'International Insolvency Framework: Advantages for Indebted Southern Countries?' Co-organized by CIDSE/Caritas Internationalis, Church Development Service (EED) and UN Department of Economic and Social Affairs, Monterrey, Mexico, 19 March 2002.

35 Christoph G Paulus, 'A Legal Order for Insolvencies of States', Humboldt University, Berlin, unpublished manuscript, 2002.

Bibliography

Bratton, William and Mitu Gulati, 2002, 'Perfect Market Puzzles: Five Observations from the World of Sovereign Debt', *Economic and Political Weekly* (Mumbai), July 6, pp. 2702–04.

Caplen, Brian, 2000, 'Paris Club Comes Under Attack', *Euromoney*, September, pp. 56–61.

EMTA (Trade Association for the Emerging Markets), 2002, 'Sovereign Debt Restructuring', discussion draft of a joint statement by Emerging Markets Creditors Association, EMTA, Institute of International Finance, International Primary Market Association, International Securities Market Association, Securities Industry Association and The Bond Market Association, December 6 (available at www.emta.org).

EMTA, 2001, 'Burden-Sharing in 2001: Now is the Time to Reform the Paris Club', Policy Paper of EMTA, February 13 (available at www.emta.org).

Fritz, Thomas and Philipp Hersel, 2002, *Fair and Transparent Arbitration Processes: A New Road to Resolve Debt Crises*, Discussion Paper, Berlin and Aachen, August (available at www.blue21.de or www.misereor.de).

Gitlin, Richard A, 2002, 'A Proposal: Sovereign Debt Forum', oral presentation at International Conference on Financing for Development Side Event, 'International Insolvency Framework: Advantages for Indebted Southern Countries?', co-organized by CIDSE/Caritas Internationalis, Church Development Service (EED) and UN Department of Economic and Social Affairs, Monterrey, Mexico, March 19.

Gopinath, Deepak, 2002, 'The Debt-Crisis Crisis', *Institutional Investor*, August, pp. 36-40.

Hubbard, R Glenn, 2002, 'Enchancing Sovereign Debt Restructuring', remarks at the Conference on the IMF's Sovereign Debt Proposal, American Enterprise Institute, Washington, DC, October 7.

IMF, 2003, Communiqué of the International Monetary and Financial Committee (IMFC), Washington, DC, April 12 (available at www.imf.org).

IMF, 2003a, 'Report of the Managing Director to the IMFC on a Statutory Sovereign Debt Restructuring Mechanism', IMFC/Doc/7/03/4, April 8 (available at www.imf.org).

IMF, 2002, 'The Design of the Sovereign Debt Restructuring Mechanism – Further Considerations', EBS/02/201, November 27 (available at www.imf.org).

IMF, 2002a, 'IMF Board Discusses the Good-faith Criterion Under the Fund Policy of Lending into Arrears to Private Creditors', Public Information Note 02/107, September 24 (available at www.imf.org).

IMF, 2001, 'Investor Relations Programs: Report of the Capital Markets Consultative Group (CMCG) Working Group on Creditor-Debtor Relations', June 15 (available at www.imf.org).

IMF, 2000, Communiqué of the International Monetary and Financial Committee (IMFC), Prague, September 24 (available at www.imf.org).

Paulus, Christoph, 2002, 'A Legal Order for Insolvencies of States', Humboldt University, Berlin, unpublished manuscript.

Salmon, Felix, 2001, 'The Buy Side Starts to Bite Back', *Euromoney,* April, pp. 46–61.

Samuels, Barbara 2002, 'Strengthening Information and Analysis in the Global Financial System: a Concrete Set of Proposals', United Nations Department of Economic and Social Affairs, Discussion Paper no. 23, June (available at www.un.org/esa/esa02 dp23.pdf).

United Nations, 2002, 'Monterrey Consensus of the International Conference on Financing for Development', *Report of the International Conference on Financing for Development, Monterrey, Mexico, March 18-22,* (A/CONF.198/11), Chapter I, Resolution 1, Annex (available at www.un.org/esa/ffd).

United Nations, 2000, 'Millennium Declaration' (General Assembly resolution 55/2), adopted at the Millennium Summit, New York, September 8 (available at www.un.org/millennium/declaration/ares552e.pdf).

9

DEVELOPING A GLOBAL PARTNERSHIP FOR DEVELOPMENT*

Martin Khor

Abstract

I present a critical examination of Goal 8 of the Millennium Development Goals (MDG), namely, to 'develop a global partnership for development'. As of November 2002, seven targets were listed under this Goal, as well as seventeen indicators. Given the wide-ranging issues covered under Goal 8, I review only some aspects of the global economic system, their effects on development and what needs to be done to reach Goal 8. The main focus is on the international trade system and the implications of the rules of the World Trade Organization (WTO). I also offer some suggestions on clarifying or adding to the targets and indicators. A key argument of this review is that success in attaining 'global partnership for development' underpins or, at a minimum, is linked with efforts in reaching the other seven MDGs, and thus Goal 8 should be given a high priority and efforts to attain it should focus on getting international economic structures, policies and rules right.

1. Introduction

The origins of the Millennium Development Goals (MDGs) lie in the United Nations Millennium Declaration, which was adopted by all 189 UN Member States on 8 September 2000. The Declaration embodies many commitments for improving the lot of humanity in the new century.[1] Subsequently, the UN Secretariat drew up a list of eight MDGs, each accompanied by specific

---

* A longer version of this paper was originally written for the United Nations Development Programme and published in UNDP's Development Policy Journal, April 2003.

targets and indicators.[2] This paper addresses Goal 8, which is to 'develop a global partnership for development'. As of November 2002, seven targets were listed under Goal 8, as well as 17 indicators. The selection of indicators is subject to further refinement. Goal 8 covers a wide range of issues but this chapter focuses on only some aspects of the global economic system, and mainly on international trade and multilateral rules under the World Trade Organization (WTO).

Goal 8 is crucial, as it is the only development goal that generally and specifically covers international relations. As is generally accepted, successful development efforts require appropriate policies at both the domestic and international levels. International factors have become increasingly important in recent years as a result of globalization. Developing countries have generally become more integrated in the world economy and their development prospects and performance are thus more dependent on global economic structures and trends. More importantly, many policies formerly made solely or primarily at the national level are now significantly influenced or shaped at international fora and by international institutions. This applies especially to those developing countries that depend on the international financial institutions for loans and debt restructuring and have to abide by loan conditionalities. It also applies to most developing countries that are members of the WTO, as they are obliged to align or re-align national laws and policies to conform to the WTO's legally binding agreements. Thus, the 'external economic environment' comprising global economic structures and trends, and the policies determined or influenced by international agencies such as the IMF, the World Bank, the WTO, the UN and such developed-country groupings as the Group of Seven (G7), the Organization for Economic Cooperation and Development (OECD) and bilateral aid agencies has a tremendous impact on a typical developing country.

In the context of the MDGs, the extent to which a developing country is able to make progress on many of the goals (especially Goal 1, to eradicate poverty and hunger, but also Goals 4, 5 and 6 relating to health, and Goal 7 on environmental sustainability) depends not only on domestic policy choices but also on how 'friendly' or 'hostile' the external economic environment is to that country. Four examples illustrate this:

1. The continuous fall in prices of export commodities has caused dramatic income and foreign-exchange losses to many developing countries, and is a major cause of persistent, or increased, poverty at the local-community level.
2. The financial instability and sharp currency fluctuations caused by large inflows and outflows of external funds have pushed many developing

countries (including those considered the most successful among them) into financial and economic crises, with sudden and dramatic increases in poverty.

3. Many developing countries have suffered declines in, or threats to, their industrial jobs and farmers' livelihoods as a result of inappropriate import liberalization policies, which are at least partly attributable to loan conditionalities or multilateral trade rules.

4. Cutbacks in social-sector expenditure, as well as the introduction of the 'user-should-pay' principle, the result of structural adjustment policies in the past, have been identified as significant contributors to the deterioration of social wellbeing of poor and vulnerable groups in several developing countries.

These examples, as well as the continuation of the debt crisis in many countries, show that attempts to improve domestic policies, however exemplary, are insufficient for developing countries' achieving the MDGs. This underscores the importance of developing a 'global partnership for development' to underpin, or at least to accompany, other efforts to attain all the other goals.

Also, in the effort to meet MDG targets, 'getting policies right' is critically important. If economic and social structures are inequitable and if policies (either for preserving the status quo or for reform) are inappropriate, then the mere expansion of funds and programs in a country would not be enough, and may indeed worsen the problems. This applies to structures and policies at both the national and international levels. Efforts to attain Goal 8 for developing a global partnership should therefore, as a priority, focus on getting international economic structures, policies and rules right.

2. Integrating developing countries in the world economy

Perhaps the most important, and most difficult, set of development policies that a developing country must decide on is in the interface between domestic policies and the world economy. Whether, how, when, to what extent, in which sectors and in which sequence to integrate the domestic economy and society with the international economy and society are large questions facing developing countries. In the international discussions on these issues, there is no consensus; instead, there is much debate and much controversy surrounding the definition, nature and consequences of globalization.

The dominant approach of the past two decades, favored by the 'Washington Consensus', or the major developed countries and the agencies under their influence, is that full, rapid and comprehensive integration of developing countries into the global economy is both beneficial and essential for their development. The dominance of this paradigm is now rapidly eroding, owing to the empirical record of developing countries that have followed, or attempted to follow, the policies of rapid liberalization. The East Asian financial crisis of 1997–9 and other subsequent crises (including in Argentina and Uruguay) have undermined the policy prescription that developing countries should rapidly liberalize their financial systems. It is now more widely recognized that financial liberalization is qualitatively different from trade liberalization, and that developing countries should be cautious about how to (or even whether to) open their capital account.

In the area of trade liberalization, empirical evidence demonstrates that excessive import liberalization has caused dislocation to local industries and farms in several developing countries, without increasing export opportunities or performance. There is now an emerging trade-policy paradigm that stresses the importance of addressing other factors, such as the need to tailor the rate of import liberalization to the increase in competitiveness of local firms and the need to increase the supply-side capacity of local firms in order to realize the country's export potential. Failure to address these while engaging in import liberalization can lead to domestic economic dislocation and worsening trade imbalances.[3]

In the area of foreign direct investment, host developing countries are now being cautioned to pursue policies aimed at maximizing the benefits (for example, through equity-sharing and profit-sharing and technology-transfer arrangements) and minimizing the risks (especially of potentially large drains on foreign exchange through high import content and large profit repatriation).

The emerging paradigm is one in which developing countries take a pragmatic approach to globalization and liberalization. It calls for them to be selective and deliberate in choosing how and when, and in which sectors and to what extent, to integrate their domestic economies with the global economy in the areas of finance, trade and investment. This approach recognizes that interaction with the global economy can, potentially significantly, benefit a developing country. However, the terms of interaction are crucial if the potential benefits are to be realized and if damage is to be avoided. Too rapid a rate of integration, or integration in the wrong areas and in the wrong way, can be harmful. For example, excessive dependence on commodity exports, and an increase in export volume when there is a global over-supply of a particular commodity, can be detrimental. Excessive financial liberalization (for example, allowing local institutions to borrow freely from abroad in foreign currency) can lead to a debt repayment crisis if the right regulations and conditions are not in place. The approach of selective integration, done carefully and appropriately, and suited to the particular needs and conditions of a country, is therefore far preferable. It should replace the still-dominant approach of 'big-bang' rapid liberalization, which is carried out inappropriately in a one-size-fits-all manner.

This change in paradigm and approach should first be considered at the national level, when governments choose their development strategy. However, most developing countries do not have the luxury or scope to choose their approach on economic integration because of the determining influence of loan and aid conditionalities, or because of the rules they have agreed to in the WTO. Thus, Millennium Development Goal 8 assumes central importance. In developing a global partnership for development, developing countries should have the right to take an appropriate and pragmatic approach toward selectively integrating their domestic economy with the world economy. Recognition of this right should be the basis for the systems of international trade, finance, investment, aid and intellectual property rights. The policies, rules and conditionalities arising from these systems should reflect the realities facing developing countries, as well as their needs. Without this change in attitude and approach at the international level, it will be difficult, if not impossible, to attain Goal 8 of a global partnership for development; and it would also be difficult for developing countries to attain the other MDGs.

3. Trade, development, and reform of the multilateral trading system

Trade is an important component of development. Ideally, trade and trade policy should serve the needs of development in the context of a county's overall policy framework. Thus, a country needs to 'mainstream development concerns in trade and trade policy'. In practice, development needs are often compromised when a developing country participates in an inappropriate way in international trade (for example, by depending too heavily on export commodities whose prices are on a trend decline) or when domestic policies and laws are amended in line with the country's obligations to meet the rules of the WTO or to meet loan conditionalities (and where aspects of the rules or policy conditionalities are unfavorable to the country's development interests). 'Mainstreaming trade in development', a newly coined slogan among international agencies, can have unintended and adverse effects if the policies underlying trade (or the international trade rules) are inappropriate and damaging to development needs. In considering the policy approach for Goal 8, this distinction between 'mainstreaming development in trade' and 'mainstreaming trade in development' should be kept in mind.

The international trading system has brought benefits in various ways to several countries, especially the developed countries and those developing countries that have managed to take advantage of it. However, the system is also imbalanced in ways that disadvantage many developing countries. Two aspects of the imbalance are the decline in commodity prices and the rules of the WTO.

3.2 The commodities problem

The continuous decline in prices for export commodities is possibly the most important trade issue facing most developing countries. It has led to falling incomes for millions of small commodity producers, and it has deprived developing countries of export earnings and worsened their debt-repayment capacity.

Between the 1960s and the 1980s, attempts to stabilize commodity prices at reasonable levels were perhaps the most concrete manifestation of a 'global partnership for development'. This partnership took the form of several producer–consumer commodity agreements, under the United Nations Conference on Trade and Development (UNCTAD) umbrella, and the establishment of a Common Fund for Commodities. Many agreements succeeded in commodity price stabilization. However, most of the agreements lapsed upon the withdrawal of interest and commitment by the consumer countries. As a result, commodity prices are now determined mainly by the vagaries of demand and supply.

The downgrading of the commodity price problem on the international agenda is unfortunate since the problem has remained just as serious, if not more so. According to UN data, the terms-of-trade of non-fuel commodities vis-à-vis manufactures fell by 52 per cent between 1980 and 1991, with catastrophic effects. A paper by the secretariat of the United Nations Conference on Environment and Development (UNCED) in 1991 shows that for Sub-Saharan Africa, a 28 per cent fall in terms of trade between 1980 and 1989 led to an income loss of $16 billion in 1989 alone. Between 1986–9, Sub-Saharan Africa suffered a $56 billion income loss, or 15–16 per cent of 1987–9 GDP. The UNCED study also shows that for 15 middle-income highly indebted countries, terms of trade declined by 28 per cent between 1980 and 1989, causing an average $45 billion loss each year in the 1986–9 period, or 5–6 per cent of GDP.[4]

In the 1990s, the general level of commodity prices fell even further in relation to manufactures, and many commodity-dependent developing countries have continued to suffer deteriorating terms of trade. According to UNCTAD's *Trade and Development Report, 1999*, oil and non-oil primary commodity prices fell by 16.4 and 33.8 per cent respectively, from the end of 1996 to February 1999.[5] This decline resulted in a cumulative terms-of-trade loss for developing countries of more than 4.5 per cent of income during 1997–8. 'Income losses were greater in the 1990s than in the 1980s not only because of larger terms-of-trade losses, but also because of the increased share of trade in GDP.' Moreover, the prices of some key manufactured products exported by developing countries have also declined. For example, the Republic of Korea experienced a 25 per cent fall in its terms of trade of its manufactured exports between 1995 and 1997, owing to a glut in the world market.[6]

Further demonstrating the great loss of opportunity for growth represented by the fall in terms of trade is the experience of Africa. In 1989, gross domestic saving was 15.8 per cent of the GDP of African countries as a whole and the gross domestic investment rate was 20.4 per cent of GDP.[7] As noted earlier, Sub-Saharan Africa suffered a loss of income attributable to terms-of-trade deterioration equivalent to 15–16 percent of GDP in 1987–9. Taking the 1989 Africa savings rate as the reference, Sub-Saharan African countries in the late 1980s were losing income equivalent to their entire savings level as a result of terms-of-trade deterioration. If the terms of trade had not declined, and if the income lost had been added to savings, the value of savings could have doubled. If such savings had all been invested, investment in the region could have increased by 76 per cent. These tremendous increases in savings and investments could have contributed to significant increases in the overall rates of economic growth.

The world trading system has favored the developed-country exporters of manufactured goods, while proving disadvantageous to the many developing countries whose main exports are raw materials and commodities and whose imports are finished products. Many Southern countries have also lost their ability to produce their own food, as lands were converted to farm export crops that in many cases suffered from instability of price and demand. Moreover, in recent years, even the prices of manufactured products exported by developing countries are declining.

3.2.1 Proposals

1. The decline in commodity prices is the most important factor keeping many developing countries from benefiting from trade. It also reduces the incomes of millions of commodity producers, thus making it difficult to attain Millennium Development Goal 1 (eradicating poverty and hunger). Such huge income losses incurred by poor countries must be stemmed and if possible reversed. Goal 8 should include a target to 'address the problem

of commodity-exporting developing countries through international measures to ensure commodity prices are stabilized at levels enabling adequate incomes for the countries and producers'. Action on commodities was also recognized as necessary for the Implementation Plan of the World Summit on Sustainable Development. One possibility is for countries to initiate a new round of producer–consumer commodity agreements aimed at rationalizing the supply of raw materials (to take into account the need to reduce depletion of non-renewable natural resources) while ensuring fair and sufficient prices (to reflect the ecological and social values of the resources).

2. If it is not possible to initiate joint producer–consumer attempts to improve the commodity situation, producers of export commodities could take their own initiative in rationalizing their global supply so as to better match the profile of global demand. The increase in the price of oil, owing to better coordination among producing countries, clearly illustrates the benefits that producers can derive from greater cooperation. If the developed consumer countries do not wish to participate in joint producer-consumer initiatives, that should not discourage producers from having their own arrangements to improve their commodity-export prices.

3.2.2 Reforms to the WTO system

The nature of the multilateral trading system, as embodied in the WTO, is currently being rethought. Developing-country members of the WTO, many of whom have become disillusioned with various aspects of the system, are carrying out this rethinking. Meanwhile, public-interest groups worldwide are highly critical, and this criticism is growing.

The WTO rules and processes are now widely seen to be imbalanced, with much needing to be done in the next few years to improve the situation.[8] Perhaps the most important decision to be taken is whether in the next few years WTO members elect to do their best to rectify the problems and imbalances in the existing rules and system, or whether the developed countries succeed in adding more new issues (such as investment, competition and government procurement) to the WTO ambit. The addition of these non-trade issues is likely to distort the trading system and aggravate existing imbalances.

Among the concerns of the developing countries are the following issues.

3.2.3 Non-realization of the expected benefits of the Uruguay Round

The developing countries' greatest disappointment with the Uruguay Round is the little progress made by the developed countries in opening their agriculture and textiles markets to their products. In agriculture, tariffs of many agriculture items of interest to developing countries remain prohibitively high (some over 200–300 per cent). Domestic subsidies in the industrial countries of the OECD rose from $275 billion (annual average for base period 1986–8) to $326 billion in 1999,[9] instead of declining as expected, as the increase in permitted subsidies more than offset the decrease in subsidy categories under discipline in the WTO Agriculture Agreement. The recent decisions of the US administration to increase subsidies under the US Farm Bill and of the European Union (EU) leaders to continue its level of subsidies under the Common Agriculture Policy have dashed expectations of a serious reduction in domestic support by the USA and the EU.

In textiles, only very few items exported by developing countries have been taken off the quota list, even though more than half the implementation period (for the phase-out of the restrictions) has passed. According to the International Textiles and Clothing Bureau in June 2000, only a few quota restrictions (13 out of 750 by the USA; 14 out of 219 by the EU; 29 out of 295 by Canada) had been eliminated.[10] This raises doubts as to whether all or most of the quotas will really be removed by 2005 as mandated under the WTO Agreement on Textiles and Clothing.

There is thus an important asymmetry here: the developed countries have not lived up to their liberalization commitments, yet it is assumed that a rapid liberalization of imports and investments is unquestionably beneficial for the developing countries. Developing countries are asked to bear for a little while the pain of rapid adjustment that will surely be 'good for them' after a few years. The developed countries advocating this policy themselves, however, ask for more time to adjust in agriculture and textiles that have enjoyed protection for so many decades.

Developed countries also have tariff peaks and tariff escalation in other products that are of export interest to developing countries. Developing countries have also been concerned about the non-tariff barriers imposed by the developed countries, which have further reduced their exports. These include the use of anti-dumping measures and countervailing duties on the products of developing countries.

The tariff and non-tariff barriers in the North are costly to the developing countries in terms of the potential exports forgone. According to an UNCTAD report:[11] 'Developing countries have been striving hard, often at considerable cost, to integrate more closely into the world economy. But protectionism in the developed countries has prevented them from fully exploiting their exist-ing or potential competitive advantage. In low-technology industries alone, developing countries are missing out on an additional $700 billion in annual export earnings as a result of trade barriers. This represents at least four times the average annual private foreign capital inflows in the 1990s (including foreign direct investment).

3.2.4 Problems faced by developing countries in implementing their WTO obligations

Developing countries have had many problems implementing their obliga-tions under the WTO agreements. The prohibition of investment measures (such as local-content policy) and many types of subsidies (under the trade-related investment measures agreement and the subsidies agreement) have made it harder for developing countries to adopt measures that encourage domestic industry.

The Agriculture Agreement enables the developed countries to maintain high protection while sustaining large subsidies. This enables them to export agriculture products at artificially cheap prices. However, many developing countries have low tariffs (in many cases they were reduced under structural adjustment programs) and low or no domestic subsidies, and are not allowed to increase the tariffs (beyond a certain rate) or increase their subsidies. There is thus a basic imbalance in the Agriculture Agreement. Many developing countries are facing problems associated with having liberalized their agricul-tural imports, as cheaper imports are threatening the viability and livelihoods of small farmers. A Food and Agriculture Organization (FAO) study of the experience of 16 developing countries in implementing the Agriculture Agreement concluded that: 'A common reported concern was with a general trend toward the concentration of farms. In the virtual absence of safety nets, the process also marginalized small producers and added to unemployment and poverty. Similarly, most studies pointed to continued problems of adjust-ment. As an example, the rice and sugar sectors in Senegal were facing difficulties in coping with import competition despite the substantive devalua-tion in 1994.'[12]

An ideal regime of intellectual property rights (IPRs) would strike an appropriate balance between the interests of owners and users of technology, and between the IPR holder and the consumer. The WTO Agreement on Trade-Related Aspects of Intellectual Property Rights (TRIPS), however, has heavily tilted the balance in favor of the IPR holder, causing difficulties for technology users and consumers. The effects of a high-standard IPR regime in developing countries have included:

- high and often exorbitant prices of medicines, reducing consumer access to affordable medicines
- high pricing (due to monopolies created by IPRs) of other consumer items, including computer software
- the patenting by Northern corporations of biological materials originating in the South (often referred to as 'biopiracy')
- higher cost and lower access for developing countries to industrial technology.[13]

The services agreement has many imbalances. Service enterprises in developed countries have far greater capacity to export and to invest abroad, while developing countries' services firms lack the capacity to operate in developed countries; hence, there is an unequal outcome in benefits. The right of capital to move across frontiers (which is favorable to developed countries who are the main providers of capital) is given far more weight than the movement of persons (where developing countries have the advantage). The agreement also puts pressure on developing countries to liberalize various services sectors, which could lead to their smaller local services enterprises losing their market share or even their viability. At the same time, developing countries' service providers are generally unable to penetrate the markets of developed countries.[14]

These problems raise the serious issue of whether developing countries can now, or in future, pursue development strategies or meet their development needs, including industrialization, technology upgrading, development of local industries, food security and maintenance of local farms and agriculture, survival of local service providers and fulfillment of health and medicinal needs. The problems arise from the structural imbalances and weaknesses of the WTO agreements. These imbalances and problems must be addressed with urgency. Surely the WTO was not created to hurt most of its members or deprive them of development?

The developing countries have explained their problems of implementation and advanced their proposals for redressing these in the WTO. These proposals have been taken up under the rubric of 'implementation issues' in the past few years.[15] They have been discussed on numerous occasions in the WTO General Council special sessions on implementation and in various committees and councils. Unfortunately the developed countries have so far not responded positively. Their attitude seems to be that the developing countries entered into legally binding commitments and must abide by them, however painful; any changes require new concessions on their part. Such an attitude does not augur well for the WTO. It implies that the state of imbalance will have to remain, and if developing countries 'pay twice' or 'pay three or four times', the imbalances will become worse and the burden heavier.

3.2.5 Proposals by developed countries to expand the WTO's mandate to 'new issues'

The biggest immediate problem facing the developing countries in the WTO is the immense pressure on them to accept the proposals by developed countries to expand the WTO's mandate to non-trade issues, including establishing new agreements on investment, competition and transparency in government procurement. Developing countries are being asked to accept these new obligations in exchange for developed countries' opening up their agriculture markets or for favorably considering the 'implementation issues'. The new agreements and obligations in these new areas would, however, hurt the developing countries' development prospects. At the same time (given the past poor record of the developed countries), it is uncertain whether the developed countries will really provide more meaningful market access to the developing countries or resolve their implementation problems.

The three new agreements proposed have a common theme: increasing the access of foreign firms to the markets of developing countries. The *investment* agreement aims to expand the right of foreign firms to enter, invest and operate in developing countries with minimum regulation (as performance requirements would be prohibited) and to be given 'national treatment' (treated at least as well as locals). The *competition* agreement is meant to oblige developing countries to adopt competition laws and policies, which would result in 'effective equality of opportunity' for foreign firms vis-à-vis local firms. In effect this would mean that governments would not be able to assist local firms. The agreement on *transparency* in government procurement would be the first stage of an eventual agreement that would grant foreign firms the same right as local firms to bid for the business of government supplies, contracts and projects. These agreements would seriously tie the hands of governments, preventing them from regulating foreign firms and also from providing assistance or preferences to local firms and other productive units. It would severely restrict the ability of developing countries to build the capacity of their domestic sectors, enterprises and farms.[16]

4. Conclusions

In the context of the Millennium Development Goals, there is a clear rationale for improving and reforming the WTO system of multilateral rules and decision-making processes. The developed countries must provide greater opportunities for developing countries to expand their export opportunities. If done properly, this can lead to an increase in export earnings, foreign exchange and income, thus helping provide the extra resources for financing measures to meet the MDGs. Many developing countries will, however, still be unable to exploit the opportunity because of supply-side constraints. On the other hand, the problems suffered by developing countries by the existing agreements must be rectified. Failure to do so can undermine the realization of several of the Development Goals and would hinder Goal 8 (striving for a global partnership for development). The agreement on agriculture, by allowing artificially cheap subsidized imports to threaten small farmers' livelihoods in developing countries, would threaten the realization of Goal 1 (eradicate poverty and hunger). Without a satisfactory clarification or amendment of the TRIPS agreement, access to health care and other services will be curtailed, thus threatening the achievement of Goal 6 (combating HIV/AIDS and other diseases). The pressures to liberalize services under the General Agreement on Trade in Services (GATS) could hurt the access of the public, especially the poor, to such essential services as education (thus affecting Goal 2), health care (thus affecting Goals 4, 5 and 6) and water supply (thus affecting Goal 7).

The following measures would further the goal of developing a real global partnership for development:

1. The developed countries should commit to meaningfully opening their markets to developing countries in sectors, products and services in which the latter are able to benefit. These include textiles, agriculture and products processed from raw materials, as well as labor services. A meaningful expansion of market access for developing countries will provide large opportunities for earning more revenues that could be the basis for significant extra financing for meeting the MDGs.

2. The WTO process of reviewing implementation problems arising from the existing agreements should result in appropriate changes to the rules or authoritative interpretations of the rules that help resolve the imbalances and the problems facing developing countries. For example, the following are among the changes that should be considered:

   • Give developing countries adequate flexibility in implementing their obligations under the Agriculture Agreement on the grounds of food security, defense of rural livelihoods and poverty alleviation. In developing countries, food produced for domestic consumption and the products of small farmers should be exempted from the Agriculture Agreement's disciplines on import liberalization and domestic subsidies.

   • Amend the TRIMs Agreement to provide developing countries the flexibility to continue using trade-related investment measures to meet their development goals. In the Agreement on Trade-Related Investment

Measures (TRIMs), 'investment measures' such as the local-content requirement (obliging firms to use at least a specified minimal amount of local inputs) and foreign-exchange balancing (limiting the import of inputs by firms to a certain percentage of their exports) are prohibited. Such measures were introduced to protect the country's balance of payments, promote local firms and enable more linkages to the local economy. Prohibiting them deprives developing countries of some important policy options for pursuing industrialization.

- Amend the TRIPS Agreement to take into account developmental, social and environmental concerns. For example, full clarification or amendments are still required to ensure that members can effectively take measures to provide medicines at affordable prices. Members should also be allowed to prohibit the patenting of life forms and to protect the traditional knowledge and practices of farmers, indigenous people and local communities. Other amendments are also needed to rebalance the agreement in favor of the interests of consumers and technology users in developing countries. The issue of whether IPRs should be covered at all under the WTO should also be reviewed.

- Services required by the public, and especially by the poor, such as water supply and health care and education, should be exempted from the general rules and the specific sectoral schedules of the GATS.

- Reorient the operational principles and rules of the WTO to give the development principle the highest priority. The preamble to the Marrakesh Agreement recognizes the objective of sustainable development and also the need for positive efforts to ensure the developing countries secure a share in international trade growth commensurate with the needs of their economic development. The objective of development should become the overriding principle guiding the work of the WTO, and its rules and operations should be designed to produce development as the outcome. Since the developing countries form the majority of the WTO membership, the development of these countries should be the first and foremost concern of the WTO. The test of a rule, proposal or policy being considered in the WTO should not be whether it is 'trade distorting', but whether it is 'development distorting'. Since development is the ultimate objective, while reduction of trade barriers is only a means, the need to avoid development distortions should take priority over the avoidance of trade distortion. So-called 'trade distortions' could, in some circumstances, constitute a necessary condition for meeting development objectives. From this perspective, the prevention of development-distorting rules, measures, policies and approaches should be the overriding concern of the WTO.[17]

3. The reorientation of the WTO toward this perspective and approach is essential to achieve progress toward a fair and balanced multilateral trading system, with more benefits than costs for developing countries. Such a reorientation would make the rules and judgment of future proposals more in line with empirical reality and practical necessities. Taking this approach, the goal for developing countries would be to attain 'appropriate liberalization' rather than to aim for 'maximum liberalization'. The rules of WTO should be reviewed to screen out those that are 'development distorting', and a decision could be made that, at the least, developing countries be exempted from having to follow rules or measures that prevent them from meeting their development objectives. These exemptions can be justified on the basis of special and differential treatment.

4. The next phase of the WTO's activities should focus on the above three areas so that the review of existing rules, the realizing of opportunities in the developed countries' markets, and the reorientation of the WTO to developing countries' needs and interests can be carried out. These processes would in themselves be a massive task, requiring the commitment, energy and resources of WTO members. However, this is necessary to build a mutually beneficial multilateral trading system.

5. The proposal to begin negotiations on 'new issues' (especially investment, competition and transparency in government procurement) after the next WTO Ministerial Conference in Cancun in September 2003 should be withdrawn. This would not only distract and detract from the tasks of reform detailed above, but also put new and heavy obligations on developing countries and render the WTO system far more imbalanced.

6. Decision-making in the WTO must be democratized, made more transparent and enable the full participation of developing countries. At present, the system of participation is flawed. The so-called consensus system enables the developed countries to pressure developing countries to accept decisions made by developed countries. Moreover, non-inclusive and non-transparent processes are used, especially surrounding the Ministerial Conferences, during which key decisions are taken. For example, at the Singapore Ministerial Conference in 1996, only 30 countries were invited to the 'informal' meeting where major decisions were made; the remaining countries were asked to accept the decisions on the last night. At the Doha Conference in 2001, the proposals of a majority of developing countries on key subjects were not included in the drafts of the Declaration, despite their objections. This put them at a great disadvantage. The decision-making processes should therefore be reformed, as the absence of reform

makes it difficult or impossible for the other suggested improvements to be achieved. At the least:

- all members must be allowed to be present and participate in meetings
- the views of all members must be adequately reflected in negotiating texts
- pressure should not be applied on members to accept views of other members
- adequate time must be given to all members to consider proposals being put forward
- the practice of holding late-night exclusive meetings at Ministerial Conferences should be discontinued.

7. The scope of the WTO's mandate over issues and the role of other agencies should be revisited. It is misleading to equate the WTO with the 'multilateral trading system', as is often the case in many discussions. In fact, the WTO is both less than and more than the global trade system. There are key issues regarding world trade with which the WTO is not seriously concerned, including low commodity prices. On the other hand, the WTO has become deeply involved in such domestic policy issues as intellectual property laws, domestic investment and subsidy policies. There are also proposals to bring in other non-trade issues including labor and environment standards, as well as investment and competition. The WTO and its predecessor the General Agreement on Trade and Taxes (GATT) have evolved trade principles (such as nondiscrimination, most-favored-nation and national treatment) that were derived in the context of trade in goods. It is by no means assured or agreed that the application of the same principles to areas outside of trade would lead to positive outcomes. Indeed, the incorporation of non-trade issues into the WTO system could distort the work of the WTO itself and the multilateral trading system. Therefore, a fundamental rethinking of the mandate and scope of the WTO is required:

- First, issues that are not trade issues should not be introduced in the WTO as subjects for rules.
- Second, a review should be conducted of current WTO issues to determine whether the WTO is the appropriate venue for them (the obvious issue to consider here is IPRs).

The processes of reviews, reforms and changes suggested above for the WTO are important for contributing to the achievement of Goal 8 of formulating a global partnership for development'. In fact, the above measures could be included as new targets, with accompanying indicators. Within its traditional ambit of trade in goods, the WTO should reorient its primary operational objectives and principles toward development. The imbalances in the agreements relating to goods should be ironed out, with the 're-balancing' designed to meet the development needs of developing countries and to be more in line with the realities of liberalization and development processes. With these changes, the WTO could better play its role in the design and maintenance of fair rules for trade. It would thus contribute toward a balanced and predictable international trading system that is designed to produce and promote development. The WTO, reformed along the lines above, should then be seen as a key component of the international trading system, co-existing, complementing and cooperating with other organizations. Together with these other organizations, the WTO would operate within the framework of the trading system in a true 'global partnership for development'.

Appendix 1

MILLENNIUM DEVELOPMENT GOALS (MDGS)

Goal 1. Eradicate extreme poverty and hunger

Target 1.
Halve, between 1990 and 2015, the proportion of people whose income is less than one dollar a day

Indicators
1. Proportion of population below \$1 (PPP) per day (World Bank)[a]
2. Poverty gap ratio (incidence x depth of poverty) (World Bank)
3. Share of poorest quintile in national consumption (World Bank)

Target 2.
Halve, between 1990 and 2015, the proportion of people who suffer from hunger

Indicators
4. Prevalence of underweight children under five years of age (UNICEF-WHO)
5. Proportion of population below minimum level of dietary energy consumption (FAO)

Goal 2. Achieve universal primary education

Target 3.
Ensure that, by 2015, children everywhere, boys and girls alike, will be able to complete a full course of primary schooling

Indicators
6. Net enrolment ratio in primary education (UNESCO)
7. Proportion of pupils starting grade 1 who reach grade 5 (UNESCO)
8. Literacy rate of 15–24 year olds (UNESCO)

Goal 3. Promote gender equality and empower women

Target 4.
Eliminate gender disparity in primary and secondary education, preferably by 2005, and to all levels of education no later than 2015

Indicators
9. Ratio of girls to boys in primary, secondary and tertiary education (UNESCO)

10. Ratio of literate women to men of 15–24 year olds (UNESCO)

11. Share of women in wage employment in the non-agricultural sector (ILO)

12. Proportion of seats held by women in national parliament (IPU)

Goal 4. Reduce child mortality

Target 5.
Reduce by two thirds, between 1990 and 2015, the under-five mortality rate

Indicators
13. Under-five mortality rate (UNICEF-WHO)

14. Infant mortality rate (UNICEF-WHO)

15. Proportion of 1-year-old children immunized against measles (UNICEF-WHO)

Goal 5. Improve maternal health

Target 6. Reduce by three quarters, between 1990 and 2015, the maternal mortality ratio

Indicators
16. Maternal mortality ratio (UNICEF-WHO)

17. Proportion of births attended by skilled health personnel (UNICEF-WHO)

Goal 6. Combat HIV/AIDS, malaria and other diseases

Target 7
Have halted by 2015 and begun to reverse the spread of HIV/AIDS

Indicators
18. HIV prevalence among 15–24 year old pregnant women (UNAIDS-WHO-UNICEF)

19. Condom use rate of the contraceptive prevalence rate
(UNAIDS-UNICEF-UN Population Division-WHO)[b]
20. Number of children orphaned by HIV/AIDS (UNICEF-UNAIDS)[c]

Target 8.

Have halted by 2015 and begun to reverse the incidence of malaria and other
major diseases

Indicators

21. Prevalence and death rates associated with malaria (WHO)
22. Proportion of population in malaria risk areas using effective
malaria prevention and treatment measures (UNICEF-WHO)[d]
23. Prevalence and death rates associated with tuberculosis (WHO)
24. Proportion of tuberculosis cases detected and cured under directly
observed treatment short course (DOTS) (WHO)

Goal 7. Ensure environmental sustainability

Target 9.

Integrate the principles of sustainable development into country policies and
programmes and reverse the loss of environmental resources

Indicators

25. Proportion of land area covered by forest (FAO)
26. Ratio of area protected to maintain biological diversity to surface area
(UNEP-IUCN)
27. Energy use (kg oil equivalent) per $1 GDP (PPP) (IEA, UNSD, World
Bank)
28. Carbon dioxide emissions (per capita) (UNFCCC, UNSD) and
consumption of ozone-depleting CFCs (ODP tons) (UNEP-Ozone
Secretariat)
29. Proportion of population using solid fuels (WHO)

Target 10.

Halve by 2015 the proportion of people without sustainable access to safe
drinking water

Indicators

30. Proportion of population with sustainable access to an improved water
source, urban and rural (UNICEF-WHO)

Target 11.

By 2020 to have achieved a significant improvement in the lives of at least
100 million slum dwellers

Indicators

31. Proportion of urban population with access to improved sanitation
(UNICEF-WHO)

32. Proportion of households with access to secure tenure
(UN-HABITAT)

Goal 8. Develop a global partnership for development

Indicators for targets 12–15 are given below in a combined list.

Target 12.

Develop further an open, rule-based, predictable, non-discriminatory trading
and financial system

Includes a commitment to good governance, development, and poverty
reduction – both nationally and internationally

Target 13.

Address the special needs of the least developed countries

Includes: tariff and quota-free access for least-developed countries' exports;
enhanced programme of debt relief for HIPCs and cancellation of official
bilateral debt; and more generous ODA for countries committed to poverty
reduction

Target 14.

Address the special needs of landlocked countries and small-island developing
States (through the Programme of Action for the Sustainable Development of
Small Island Developing States and the outcome of the 22nd special session of
the General Assembly)

Target 15.

Deal comprehensively with the debt problems of developing countries
through national and international measures in order to make debt sustainable in the long term

*Some of the indicators listed below are monitored separately for the least developed countries
(LDCs), Africa, landlocked countries and small-island developing states*

Indicators

Official development assistance

33. Net ODA, total and to LDCs, as percentage of OECD/DAC donors'
gross national income (OECD)

34. Proportion of total bilateral, sector-allocable ODA of OECD/DAC
donors to basic social services (basic education, primary health care,
nutrition, safe water and sanitation) (OECD)

35. Proportion of bilateral ODA of OECD/DAC donors that is untied (OECD)

36. ODA received in landlocked countries as proportion of their GNIs (OECD)

37. ODA received in small island developing states as proportion of their GNIs (OECD)

Market access

38. Proportion of total developed-country imports (by value and excluding arms) from developing countries and from LDCs, admitted free of duties (UNCTAD, WTO, WB)

39. Average tariffs imposed by developed countries on agricultural products and textiles and clothing from developing countries (UNCTAD, WTO, WB)

40. Agricultural support estimate for OECD countries as percentage of their GDP (OECD)

41. Proportion of ODA provided to help build trade capacity (WTO, OECD)[e]

Debt sustainability

42. Total number of countries that have reached their HIPC decision points and number that have reached their HIPC completion points (cumulative) (IMF-World Bank) (see indicator 43 below)

43. Debt relief committed under HIPC initiative, US$ (IMF-World Bank)

44. Debt service as a percentage of exports of goods and services (IMF-World Bank)

Target 16.

In cooperation with developing countries, develop and implement strategies for decent and productive work for youth

Indicators

45. Unemployment rate of 15–24 year olds, each sex and total (ILO)[f]

Target 17.

In cooperation with pharmaceutical companies, provide access to affordable essential drugs in developing countries

Indicators

46. Proportion of population with access to affordable essential drugs on a sustainable basis (WHO)

Target 18.

In cooperation with the private sector, make available the benefits of new technologies, especially information and communications

Indicators

47. Telephone lines and cellular subscribers per 100 population (ITU)

48. Personal computers in use per 100 population (ITU) and Internet users per 100 population (ITU)

[a] For monitoring country poverty trends, indicators based on national poverty lines should be used, where available.

[b] Amongst contraceptive methods, only condoms are effective in preventing HIV transmission. The contraceptive prevalence rate is also useful in tracking progress in other health, gender and poverty goals. Because the condom use rate is only measured amongst women in union, it will be supplemented by an indicator on condom use in high-risk situations. These indicators will be augmented with an indicator of knowledge and misconceptions regarding HIV/AIDS by 15–24 year olds (UNICEF-WHO).

[c] To be measured by the ratio of proportion of orphans to non-orphans aged 10–14 who are attending school.

[d] Prevention to be measured by the percentage of under 5s sleeping under insecticide treated bed-nets; treatment to be measured by percentage of under 5s who are appropriately treated.

[e] OECD and WTO are collecting data that will be available from 2001 onwards.

[f] An improved measure of the target is under development by ILO for future years.

Notes

1 United Nations 2001.
2 See appendix.
3 TWN 2001.
4 Khor 1993.
5 UNCTAD 1999a, p. 85.
6 UNCTAD 1999.
7 Khor 1993.
8 Das 1998; 1999.
9 OECD 2000.
10 WTO 2000.
11 UNCTAD 1999.
12 FAO 2000; 2001.
13 Khor 2001.
14 TWN 2001.
15 See WTO 2001c; 2001d; 2001e.
16 Khor 2002.
17 TWN 2001.

Bibliography

Das, Bhagirath Lal, 2002, 'The New WTO Work Program', paper presented at a forum organized by Third World Network in Geneva.

—— 1999, *Some Suggestions for Improvements in the WTO Agreements*, Penang, Third World Network.

—— 1998, *The WTO Agreements: Deficiencies, Imbalances and Required Changes*, Penang, Third World Network.

Food and Agriculture Organization, 2001, *Agriculture, Trade and Food Security, Vol. II*, Rome.

Food and Agriculture Organization, 2000, *Agriculture, Trade and Food Security, Vol. I*, Rome.

Khor, Martin, 2002, 'The WTO, the Post-Doha Agenda and the Future of the Trade System: A Development Perspective', Penang, Third World Network.

—— 2001, 'Rethinking IPRs and the TRIPS Agreement', Penang, Third World Network paper.

—— 2000, *Globalization and the South: Some Critical Issues,* Penang, Third World Network.

——, 1993, 'South-North Resource Flows', Penang, Third World Network.

Organization for Economic Cooperation and Development, 2000, *Agricultural Policies in OECD Countries: Monitoring and Evaluation 2000*, Paris, OECD Secretariat.

Shafaeddin, SM, 1994, *The Impact of Trade Liberalization on Export and GDP Growth in Least Developed Countries*, Discussion Paper no. 85, Geneva, United Nations Conference on Trade and Development.

Third World Network, 2001, 'The Multilateral Trading System: A Development Perspective', report prepared for UNDP.

United Nations, 2002, 'External Debt Crisis and Development: Report of the Secretary General', General Assembly document A/57/253.

United Nations, 2001, 'Road Map Towards the Implementation of the United Nations Millennium Declaration: Report of the Secretary General', General Assembly document A/56/326.

United Nations Conference on Trade and Development, 2002, *Economic Development in Africa: From Adjustment to Poverty Reduction: What Is New?* Geneva, United Nations.

United Nations Conference on Trade and Development, 1999, *Trade and Development Report, 1999,* New York and Geneva, United Nations.

United Nations Development Program, 2002, *Human Development Report 2000*, New York, Oxford University Press.

World Trade Organization, 2001a, 'Ministerial Declaration', adopted 14 November.

—— 2001b, 'Declaration on the TRIPS Agreement and Public Health', adopted 14 November.

—— 2001c, Implementation-Related Issues and Concerns of 14 November.

—— 2001d, 'Compilation of Outstanding Implementation Issues Raised by Members', General Council document JOB(01)152/Rev.1.

—— 2001e, 'Implementation-Related Issues and Concerns', General Council document JOB (01)/14.

—— 2000, 'Statement by Hong Kong, China, at Special Session of the WTO General Council on June 22, 2000, on behalf of International Textiles and Clothing Bureau', Document WT/GC/W/405.

—— 1999, Preparation for the 1999 Ministerial Conference: Ministerial Text, Revised Draft, WTO, Geneva.

10

INTERNATIONAL FINANCIAL INSTITUTIONS AND INTERNATIONAL PUBLIC GOODS: OPERATIONAL IMPLICATIONS FOR THE WORLD BANK

Ravi Kanbur*

Abstract

The global international financial institutions (IFIs) increasingly justify their operations in terms of the provision of international public goods (IPGs). This is partly because the rich countries of the North appear to support expenditures on these IPGs, in contrast to the 'aid fatigue' that afflicts the channeling of country-specific assistance. But do the IFIs necessarily have to be involved in the provision of IPGs? If they do, what are the terms and conditions of that engagement? How does current practice compare to the ideal? And what reforms are needed to move us closer to the ideal? These are the questions I ask in the framework of the theory of international public goods, and in light of the practice of international financial institutions, the World Bank in particular. For the World Bank, I draw a series of specific operational and resource reallocation implications.

1. Introduction

When people talk of the international financial institutions (IFIs), they usually mean the two Bretton Woods institutions, the International Monetary Fund and the World Bank. Of course, strictly speaking, any multilateral organization with financial operations is an IFI – for example, the regional multilateral banks, regional monetary authorities or some agencies of the UN that disburse funding. However, in practice, the term IFIs is understood to mean the two global IFIs – the Fund and the Bank. In recent years there has been growing discussion of the role of these institutions in the provision of international public goods (IPGs). An aid-fatigued public in the rich North, beset by its own internal budgetary problems (for example, the looming social security crisis associated with an aging population) and convinced by tales of waste and corruption in aid flows, has grown weary and wary of conventional country-specific development assistance. In contrast, the notion of IPGs seems attractive to Northern publics – at least, their representatives have adopted the IPG refrain in international fora.[1]

But what exactly is an IPG? Given the 'aura' that the term seems to have developed, there is clearly an incentive to justify any activity by any agency as an IPG, and aid agencies have not been shy in doing this. At its most general level, development in poor countries is being defined as an IPG, and hence an argument for continuing conventional aid – disenchantment with which turned the Northern public to IPGs in the first place. On the other hand, such highly specific activities as research into vaccines for tropical diseases are also being labeled as the provision of an international public good. If we are not careful, everything will be labeled an IPG and the concept will lose not only its analytical edge, but also its capacity to mobilize Northern resources.

This chapter begins by defining IPGs and characterizing their key dimensions. It argues that the concept is subtle and multifaceted, and that in practice there are many different types of IPGs. The mechanisms for provision of these IPGs need to be equally subtle and multifaceted. The IFIs have not been slow off the mark in claiming the mantle of 'IPG providers', but the theory of IPGs provides a framework in which to evaluate the claims of the IFIs for resources in the name of IPGs. I then discuss World Bank practice for specific IPGs and consider reforms to better articulate the comparative advantage of the Bank with the requirements of IPG provision. I conclude by outlining areas for further research and analysis.

2. IPG theory

As noted above, there is an understandable tendency to fit almost any IFI activity under the IPG umbrella. Examples include: financial support for vaccine research; in-house economic research on development; capacity building for research in developing countries; collation and dissemination of research; convening international summits on global pollution; developing international trading mechanisms for national pollution permits; multicountry environmental and water preservation projects; raising money from financial markets at lower cost; disseminating and evaluating information on economic and financial conditions in individual countries; developing and monitoring of banking standards and coordinating aid flows from disparate donors.

It is important at the outset to clarify terms and set up a clear framework for identifying IPGs and their key characteristics.[2] The technical definition of a pure public good is a commodity or activity whose benefits are 'non-rival' and 'non-excludable'. By non-rival is meant that one entity benefiting from it does not diminish the benefit to another entity. Non-excludable means that no entity can in fact be denied the benefit. An international public good is one where the entities in question are conceptualized as nations rather than individuals. Two important points bear making with regard to these two criteria. First, although they help sharpen conceptualization, in most practical cases they will only be met partially. Second, while rivalry can be characterized as a property given by technology, excludability is man-made.

IPGs relate closely to spillover effects or externalities between countries. Consider a collection of nation states that have jurisdictional authority and control over different policy instruments within their own boundaries. However, there are spillover effects of events and policies in one country on other countries, near and far. Civil war in one country sends refugees to near neighbors. Carbon dioxide emissions from one country affect all countries through their impact on global climate. Water use in one country lowers the available water supply for others who share the same water table. Infectious diseases incubated in one place spread to another. Financial contagion, as the name suggests, spreads from country to country; lack of confidence in one country's financial future may unfairly taint other countries belonging to the same group. Activities that mitigate negative externalities and promote positive ones then satisfy the criteria defining IPGs.

All of the above illustrate cross-border externalities, spillovers that are not mediated by competitive markets. Certain key features of these spillovers will be relevant for our discussion of IPGs and IFIs. The first feature to highlight is the spread of the spillover – what sorts of countries are involved at the two ends of the spillover? It is useful to distinguish between spillovers across developing countries only and spillovers that include both developing and developed countries. The next feature to consider is the direction of the spillover – is it unidirectional or does the spillover go both ways? Characterization of this is a subtle and intricate matter and is not independent of the particular circumstances of time and place. The standard example of a multidirectional spillover currently is air pollution, where developed and developing countries are inflicting spillovers on each other. Farm protection policies in North America and the European Union, which create a surplus and depress world prices, are a unidirectional spillover from developed to developing countries. Infectious diseases are in principle multidirectional but in the specific conditions of today the issue is framed as a unidirectional one – poor infectious disease control in developing countries leading (though travel) to spread in developed countries (for example, SARS).

Perhaps the most famous example of a unidirectional spillover, at least as it is portrayed in much of the current discussion, is development itself. This argument is being used with increasing force by donor agencies in general, and the IFIs in particular, to justify maintenance and increase of official development assistance. But at least two caveats must be registered. The first is a certain unease with the 'there's something in it for us' line of argument bolstering the case for development assistance in the face of an aid-fatigued public. While recognizing that this seems to be working at the moment, at least if statements of politicians are anything to go by, it can be argued that this undermines the more solid moral basis for assistance based on a common humanity and alleviating suffering.

The second caveat is perhaps more pertinent for the discussion in this chapter, and is in any case relevant to the critique noted above. This is that the whole argument rests on the assumption that the transfer in question actually makes the recipient better off. The theoretical literature in international economics is replete with analyses showing how the paradox of an immiserizing transfer can occur. Indeed, one can theoretically have a situation where the transfer makes the donor better off and the recipient worse off – and many non-governmental organizations (NGOs) have argued that this is what the aid system, bilateral and multilateral, actually does. The evidence on the efficacy of aid in promoting development is decidedly mixed and, before the IFIs and other agencies are allowed to use the 'development is good for developed countries too' argument, they should be subjected to the scrutiny of whether aid is actually good for development.[3]

This chapter will not elaborate further on the 'development and poverty reduction in poor countries is an IPG' argument. In other words, it will not deal any further with the generalized unidirectional externality from lack of development in poor countries to the well being of rich countries (and other poor countries). Rather, it will focus on more specific activities that (i) although taking place primarily in developed countries, imply a unidirectional positive externality to several developing countries simultaneously, (ii) coordinate multidirectional externalities among groups of developing countries and (iii) benefit developed and developing countries simultaneously, the benefits in all cases being non-rival and non-excludable.

A leading example of the first type of public good is basic research, on tropical agriculture or medicine or even, some would argue, on the development process itself. Examples of the second category of public goods are regional – or sub-regional – level agreements on transport or water. Finally, global mechanisms to control carbon dioxide emissions, or financial contagion, are examples of the third type of public good.

In the case of multidirectional spillovers, whether between developing countries or between developed and developing countries, the central issue is one of coordination failure, each country ignoring the negative consequences of its actions on others. All countries could be better off if they took this into account and coordinated their actions. In this case it is the coordination *mechanism* that is the IPG. Once coordination is in place, countries as a whole benefit, and it is not easy to exclude any one country from this pool of benefit (otherwise why would it want to coordinate?). However, many different types of coordination are possible and these determine not only the total gains but also the division of these gains. There is thus a range of possible IPGs, each with different consequences for different countries.

This last point leads to an important consideration. Coordination mechanisms may satisfy the technical definition of an international public good, but it is important to analyse the distribution of benefits from the coordination – in particular, how they are divided between developing and developed countries. To the extent that the benefits are unevenly divided against developing countries, what we might have is not so much an IPG as a cartel of developed countries pursuing their own interests. This distinction between an IPG and an international cartel is well worth bearing in mind as we move to a discussion of IFI practice.

The final theoretical consideration[4] follows from the principle of subsidiarity. This says that other things being equal, the coordination mechanism must be as close as possible to the jurisdictions being coordinated. Under this rubric, there is a priori no strong argument for a global institution to coordinate the water rights problems of three countries in Africa – rather, an institution as close as possible to the three countries should coordinate. Economies of scale may suggest a regional-level institution to deal with coordination issues between countries in that region, but it is unlikely that they will suggest a global-level institution capable of tackling coordination problems across any group of countries anywhere in the world. Against this argument is one on economies of scope – that IPG issues in a particular sector (for example, health) could best be combined under a single institution such as the World Health Organization (WHO). In practice we may end up with a combination of regional and technical institutions to handle coordination problems within developing countries.[5] But the claims of a global institution to do all jobs should be treated with skepticism.

3. World Bank Practice

How does the actual practice of the IFIs compare to the theory of IPGs? How much of what they do can be faithfully characterized as IPGs? The Bank and the IMF are, of course, complex entities with multifaceted operations in scores of countries and many sectors. They are also controlled primarily by the developed countries, especially by the Group of Seven industrial countries (G7). It is important to bear this political fact in mind and also to be clear about which parts of their operations are being discussed (for example, financial versus research, or country-specific versus multi-country) and the criteria for evaluation. The bulk of the operations of the two institutions are country-specific in nature and this is unlikely to change in the future.

In this chapter we focus on the World Bank. Of its administrative budget of about $1.4 billion in financial year 2001, about half went directly to support country operations ('Regions').[6] If we take away the 'overhead' expenditure of administration, corporate management etc, the share of country operations is even higher. This therefore raises two questions. First, to what extent can their country-specific operations take on the mantle of international public goods? Second, is there a case for a shift to more of their operations being multi-country in nature, and what would this entail? Under multi-country activities, research and dissemination of research (the budget headings of Development Economics and World Bank Institute) account for about $100 million of the total administrative budget. The Development Grant Facility, from which a range of global activities is funded in the form of grants, was approximately $150 million in FY01. 'Networks' account for almost $120 million – it is not clear how much of this allocation is for multi-country activities and how much for supporting country operations. However, if we allocate 1 in 8 (roughly, the ratio of research and dissemination to research, dissemination and country operations) of this to multi-country activities, we get $265 million ($100 million + $150 million + $15 million) as the allocation of the administrative budget to this category, compared to $805m ($700m + $105m) to country-specific activities.[7]

Any evaluation of the Bank will stand and fall, for many years to come, on the efficacy of its country-specific operations. Let us focus, however, on the non-country-specific operations. We start from IPGs for small groups of developing countries and work our way up to global IPGs. What is striking is that multi-country operations across small groups of developing countries facing cross-border externalities are few and far between. To the extent that they exist, they are generally outside the normal realm of Bank instruments, relying on grants from the Bank's net income rather than loans from International Bank of Reconstruction and Development or the International

Development Association. The hugely successful River Blindness project is often cited as an example where the Bank supplied an IPG in which (in concert with other donors) a multi-country project was put into place to counter a vector-borne disease – a classic negative externality across geographically adjacent countries, which benefited these countries in a manner that was at least partly non-rival and non-excludable.[8]

But at least two questions arise in light of the theoretical discussion in the previous section. First, does the Bank necessarily have to be involved in such IPGs? The principle of subsidiarity suggests that regional institutions should prima facie be responsible for these activities. Even if it can be argued that at the time of the project regional institutions in Africa were not strong enough to take over this task, and even if they are not strong enough now, should we not be aiming for a time when they will be capable of supplying such localized IPGs? Second, how, if at all, can the Bank's standard loan instruments be used in the supply of such public goods? To the extent that they cannot, this surely implies a move in the direction of more grant financing from the Bank as a whole. These questions will be taken up in the next section.

Staying with multi-country coordination, let us move to the case where the coordination required is across developing and developed countries – in other words, a truly global coordination mechanism, the supply of which would undoubtedly count as the supply of an IPG. The Bank is involved in a number of these types of exercises. The global coordination (jointly with the IMF) of debt relief for the poorest countries (the Heavily Indebted Poor Country Initiative) is a leading example. It is clear that even for a single debtor country with many creditors there is a major coordination problem in debt relief, since it is in the interest of every creditor to be repaid at the expense of the other creditors. Such coordination mechanisms exist for commercial debt (London club) and official bilateral debt (Paris club); a mechanism is needed to coordinate across these, as well as of course for multilateral debt itself. Some of the debt issues are quite intricate – for example, the Soviet-era debt owed to Russia by African countries, while Russia is itself a debtor to Western nations. The case for coordination is strong but not without questions. Should the Bank be involved at all or should this be left to the IMF? How can either the Bank (or the IMF) be a legitimate coordinator between creditors and debtors when its own debt is at stake?

A second leading example of coordination across developing and developed countries would be the Bank's work on the environment, especially air pollution. Global coordination problems on the use of the seas, on fishing disputes, etc., are dealt with by specialized agencies of the United Nations (UN) and various trade organizations, and the Bank does not play a major role. However, for the case of carbon dioxide emissions or ozone depletion the

Bank has taken a lead role in conjunction with UN agencies such as United Nations Development Program (UNDP) and United Nations Energy Program (UNEP). The Global Environmental Facility (GEF), for example, was incubated in the Bank but is now a separate entity, with the Bank listed as an implementing agency through its regular country operations in countries that participate in GEF projects. This shows another aspect of practice that bears noting. Global coordination will often require country-specific projects. To the extent that the Bank's country programs purposively finance such projects (for example, the Aquatic Biodiversity Conservation project in Bangladesh as a part of the overall objective of global biodiversity conservation), they are part of the supply of IPGs. But this raises yet more questions. What is the trade-off between resources for such projects and resources for national development pure and simple? And is it better to use loan or grant instruments for such projects?

Consider now a non-rival, non-excludable and unidirectional positive externality from activities primarily in the developed countries, or in the IFIs, for developing countries as a whole. One example would be generalized lifting of trade barriers, or immigration restrictions against developing countries by developed ones. But the more commonly discussed examples are basic research – for example, into tropical agriculture, tropical diseases or into the development process itself.

Rather like the River Blindness project, the work of the Consultative Group on International Agricultural Research (CGIAR) is often cited by the Bank as an example of an IPG that it is instrumental in helping to supply. Most evaluations of CGIAR generally applaud its achievements in helping increase agricultural yields in developing countries as a whole. Indeed they call on it to do more, in light of the slowdown in yield growth experienced in the last 15 years. There is a strong argument for increased CGIAR financial support, subject to the usual caveats of institutional reform. By extension, there is strong argument for the Bank to increase its support, which is in the form of grants from its net income. But notice an interesting point. Whatever the Bank's initial role in getting CGIAR off the ground (it can be argued that foundations such as the Rockefeller Foundation played an even more crucial incubating role), its current contribution is essentially that of a financier (through its Development Grant Facility), rather than a provider of substantive input (for example, based on its country operations). This raises again the question of the link between the Bank's role as an IPG provider and its bread and butter country-specific operations.

Similar to the Bank's contribution to the CGIAR, its contribution to various proposed funds for research into diseases prevalent in developing countries satisfies the criteria for helping the supply of an IPG. Basic research that leads to an anti-malaria vaccine, for example, could benefit poor countries enormously. While this benefit will of course depend on the specifics of how the vaccine is disseminated, the output of the research itself is non-rival, and furthermore non-excludable, provided the right institutional framework is in place that does not create private property rights in its findings. As is well known, the development community faces a difficult trade-off between using the private sector's efficiency in pursuing research goals, and giving private property rights on the outcomes as an incentive, since the benefits would not then be non-excludable. There is the added issue that vaccines or treatments for the diseases of poor people may not be profitable enough. One way to square these various circles is the well-discussed device of the Vaccine Purchase Fund. This Fund would act as an incentive to the private sector to do basic research on poor-country diseases and then, effectively, make the findings available (at a price). From the point of view of developing countries, the Vaccine Purchase Fund is indeed an IPG, a positive unidirectional externality from the Fund to the countries as a whole.

But once again the question arises whether there is anything other than the Bank's financing in the final product of the IPG? In the case of the Vaccine Purchase Fund (rather like in the case of the HIPC fund), it is clear that the Bank's 'convening role' has been important. It (along with a small number of individuals and foundations) was able to nurture the basic idea and then expand it to other partners to the point where it could become operational. I will address this convening and incubating role again in the next section.

As a final example of World Bank practice in the supply of IPGs, let us consider its role in producing research on the development process itself. The World Bank, in particular, projects itself as the 'Knowledge Bank', and sees its role as a synthesizer of country-specific development experience for the benefit of all countries – an IPG. While the IMF does not project itself quite so aggressively in this mode, it offers the general experience of its staff in a range of countries to policymakers from specific countries, and it also has a large research department. Taking the World Bank specifically, two major issues are of interest. First is the actual mechanism through which the vast amount of information generated by its operations is synthesized – much is made of the role of new information technology in this process. But secondly there is the issue of how, and in what framework, the synthesis takes place.

Leaving to one side complex technical and institutional issues of managing knowledge flow, the central issue is that frameworks for understanding and interpreting information and knowledge in the development process are contested. In this context, the Bank can take an open stance by allowing a range of issues to be debated and discussed, with dissenting voices invited and given their proper place, or it can present a particular synthesis and stand behind it to the exclusion of other perspectives. In practice the outcome is somewhere in the middle, with a definite stance on some policy issues (for example capital account liberalization until a few years ago, and trade liberalization now), which reflect and are reflected in country specific operations, but a more open stance on others (for example, on reducing gender discrimination).

Is World Bank (and IMF) research an IPG? It is clearly non-rival, in the sense that once the output of the Bank's research goes on to its comprehensive website, access by one person anywhere in the world does not diminish access for another). And the Bank does a very good job in wide dissemination of its findings. It is also non-excludable in the sense that anyone who wishes to have access to the Bank's research can in principle do so. But this is a case where satisfying these technical criteria is not enough – we have to look deeper into the consequences of making this research available widely. The consequences depend upon whether the research is believed, and by whom. To the extent that there is a perception, and perception is what matters, that the research is blinkered and dedicated to showing particular results, it will not have a general impact. In this context, effective mechanisms of collecting, organizing and disseminating information through electronic means can only deepen suspicion. The recent discussion of civil society's deep reservations on the Development Gateway is a case in point.[9]

The central question is whether research in institutions like the Bank, which have to take stances and views on policy in their operations, can ever command wide enough trust to be an IPG. This is in no way to impugn the motives of the many fine individuals who do research in these institutions. But they do face constraints, which is entirely to be expected in an operational organization. The point is not whether there should or should not be a research organization in an operational institution, as any such institution will need a group dedicated to specific analysis and to interacting with outside analyses. The point is rather whether IFI research can claim the mantle of an IPG, and thence the aura and the resources that flow from it in the current climate favoring IPGs. Our conclusion on this is a skeptical one, at least when there is a widespread perception that the research is in service of a particular line or policy stance to the exclusion of others. This is perhaps more likely in social science research where, unlike research in the natural sciences, much of the terrain is contested and there is no uniform, unifying framework in which research and its findings can be assessed.

4. Reform to promote IPGs

Almost by definition, IPGs will tend to be undersupplied in the world. And this undersupply will often hurt developing countries. The World Bank is engaged in a wide variety of activities whose direct (and sometimes indirect) objective is to supply various types of IPGs. Indeed, it (and other international agencies) are using this fact of IPG-related activities to argue for continued support in a climate where conventional development assistance is out of favor. Before this argument is accepted, it is worth asking whether there are reforms that could make the Bank better at supplying IPGs. The theory of IPGs in Section II, and the review of some examples of World Bank practice in Section III suggest some useful directions.

Let us start with the (reasonable) assumption that over the next ten to fifteen years the World Bank will essentially remain an organization whose operations will mainly be country-specific projects and programs. As noted earlier, we do not consider here the argument, increasingly stridently made, that since development itself is an IPG, the Bank's (and other agencies') country programs should be supported as IPGs. Suffice to say that the argument hinges on the efficacy of these country programs in promoting development, and the debate on that will continue. What is important for us here, however, is that the culture of the institution, and the bulk of its detailed knowledge and experience, is and will continue to come from its country operations. Reform of the Bank to promote the supply of IPGs will have to take this basic fact on board, and weave a pragmatic path between current reality and the ideal suggested by the theory of IPGs.

Recalling the discussion of spillovers between adjacent developing countries (Section II), a coordination mechanism requires simultaneous actions by a number of countries, and financing the costs of these actions – as well as the costs of the coordination mechanism itself – is an IPG. The fundamental disconnect between the requirements of the theory and Bank practice is that the Bank (IBRD or IDA) enters into loan agreements with *individual* countries, while what is clearly needed, if the loan route is to be pursued, are creative mechanisms whereby a number of countries can jointly be extended a loan. This expansion of the scope of Bank lending is the first implication of the reasoning developed in this chapter.

To the extent that multi-country loans are difficult to develop and roll out because of structural impediments in a sovereign debt framework, this argues strongly for the development of grant instruments as a *normal* part of the Bank's country operations. There is of course a big debate about whether *all* of the Bank's operations, certainly in the poorest countries, should be on a grant basis. The practicality of financing coordination mechanisms between adjacent developing countries adds its weight to the side of the debate arguing for conversion to grant instruments. Thus, greater use of grants is the second set of operational implications of an IPG-focused look at the World Bank's operations.

The theoretical principle of subsidiarity states that it should ideally be regional-level institutions, not a global institution like the World Bank, that address cross-border spillovers between small numbers of adjacent countries. In the short term there is often a strong argument for continued or even strengthened World Bank involvement in these local-level IPGs. But over the long term there should be a strengthening of regional institutions to deal with these issues through transfer of knowledge and skills. To the extent that the World Bank's financial resources are used for this, they will be helping to supply IPGs indirectly. A similar argument can be made for strengthening sectoral organizations that are currently relatively weak but are needed on IPG issues – health and the World Health Organization (WHO) is an obvious example. Thus a systematic program of strengthening of regional and specific sectoral organizations is the third operational implication of our reasoning.

On basic research into tropical agriculture and tropical diseases, World Bank practice and IPG theory are quite closely aligned; there are spectacular successes in the past and promising avenues being pursued currently. An expansion of financial resources into these operations is strongly suggested. However, there is scope for reform of World Bank practice from a closer examination of theory and practice. First, given that for the foreseeable future the bulk of the Bank's operations will be country-specific, there should be a systematic attempt to feed in the lessons of country practice into these global initiatives – this would give a substantive strategic role to the Bank over and above its financial role. The details need to be worked out, of course, but the key is the word 'systematic' – the use of new technology to collect and collate information and use them to design global initiatives is something at which the Bank should excel.

But the experience of the various successful global initiatives highlights a second issue. In a number of cases the Bank played a central role as a catalyst, using its convening power, and then took a less central role in discussions while perhaps maintaining its financial role intact. This 'entrepreneurial role' of the Bank has been useful in the past and should be maintained and strengthened. This requires a certain amount of 'blue sky thinking' to identify problems and potential solutions, and to start to build a global consensus on the issue. An expanded fund for pursuing such innovative ideas on IPGs, perhaps through an expanded Development Grant Facility, is thus the fourth operational implication of the arguments in this chapter.

As noted in the previous section, the Bank spends significant resources on general social science research into the development process itself and to disseminate the findings of this research. The Bank as a whole no doubt has a huge base of experience to report on from its country operations. The systematic and independent collation of this information would be an IPG. Reform suggests itself first of all in developing mechanisms that will enable raw information to be accessed the world over. New technology holds out some hope in this regard, and the Bank is already moving in this direction. But there is the fundamental problem referred to in the previous two sections. Social science is not like natural science. It is contested terrain to a much greater extent. Moreover, the Bank as a whole cannot possibly be viewed as an independent arbiter of social science research. It is owned by the rich countries and it has operational policies that need to be defended. These features mean that social science research done by the Bank itself cannot fully lay claim to the mantle of an IPG. The issue is seen sharply in much of the 'cross-country regression analysis' done at the Bank. Whatever one's views on the quality of this research, there is weak comparative advantage justification for this type of research to be done at the Bank. It does not rely on information uniquely available to the Bank because of its country operations, nor on methods and techniques that are unique to the Bank. The fifth and final implication of the reasoning in this chapter is that more of the research at the Bank should be farmed out to universities and transparently independent institutions, where at least perceived independence will enhance its value as an IPG.

5. Conclusion

To summarize, the arguments in this paper imply (at least) five changes in the operations of the World Bank:

- the further development of multicountry loan instruments
- a stronger move in the direction of grant instruments, which will mean an increased charge on net income
- the use of grants to support build up of key regional and sectoral organizations
- an increased use of grants to support basic research initiatives, and innovative development of new IPGs, through an expansion of the Development Grant Facility
- a greater farming out of social science research to independent institutions.

This chapter has only begun a systematic and detailed investigation of international aid agencies as suppliers of IPGs. It has focused on the World

Bank, but many other agencies – the IMF and various specialized UN agencies, in particular – can and should be subjected to the same scrutiny. The details of the practice will differ in each case, of course, as will the application of the theory of IPGs. Such analysis will contribute to an overall sense of what resource reallocation is needed in international agencies to address the undersupply of IPGs. At the same time, it will highlight overlaps and duplications in the supply of IPGs – all international agencies are claiming their activities are essential as providers of IPGs, and they cannot all be right.

But the case of the World Bank itself, as the biggest aid agency of all, needs more detailed analysis than has been possible here. We have used broad budget headings to characterize country-specific operations and different types of multi-country operations that could be interpreted, or have been claimed by the Bank, to be IPGs. With the availability of more detailed budgets (more detailed than those available publicly in the Annual Reports), a more careful accounting would be possible to sort out items under country operations that should be reclassified to country-specific operations and vice versa. While this may not lead to a big change in the overall proportions, it is an exercise worth doing. A concomitant of this exercise would be a much more detailed set of operational and resource reallocation implications than the general ones developed here. For example, the overall set of activities currently lumped under Networks, Development Economics and the World Bank Institute need to be examined against the criteria of IPGs. A more detailed conclusion on the research budget could then be reached.

Finally, a 'big' question has been left untouched – the issue of the World Bank (or the IMF) as an IPG per se. The Bank's International Development Association (IDA), for example, coordinates and acts as the channel for aid flows whose origins are not the Bank's own borrowing or its net income. Rather, the flows from donor countries are channeled through this mechanism rather than through direct bilateral arrangements. In this sense IDA provides the IPG and, some argue, because of this mechanism aid flows are greater than they otherwise would be, and hence developing countries benefit as well. This is a different argument from the multi-country activities that IDA funds could support, or the positive externality that country-specific use of IDA funds generates as the country in question develops and grows. Rather, it is that this mechanism for country-specific programs is better than others, better specifically than the alternative of all bilateral flows, and in providing this very mechanism the Bank provides an IPG. In the end, this may turn out to be the strongest IPG argument in favor of the World Bank.

Notes

* This paper was prepared as part of the research program of the Intergovernmental Group of Twenty-Four on International Monetary Affairs and Development (G24), with financial support from the International Development Research Centre of Canada (IDRC). It was first published by UNCTAD as no. 19 of the G24 Discussion Paper Series. The views expressed and the designations and terminology employed are those of the author and do not necessarily reflect the views of the G24, IDRC and UNCTAD. This paper was also presented at the fifth annual conference of the Centre for the Study of Globalisation and Regionalisation, University of Warwick, 15–17 March 2002.

1 The rising interest in the policy arena has led to an explosion of analytical work at the intersection of IPGs and development assistance: see, for example, Jayaraman and Kanbur 1999; Kanbur, Sandler and Morrison 1999; Kaul, Grunberg and Stern 1999; Sagasti and Bezanson 2001; Gerrard, Ferroni and Mody 2001; Arce and Sandler 2002; and Ferroni and Mody 2002

2 A number of studies set out the basic theory of public goods. See for example Cornes and Sandler 1996, or Sandler 1998 or Kanbur, Sandler and Morrison 1999.

3 There is of course a huge literature on aid effectiveness. Some recent examples include Burnside and Dollar 2000; Tarp 2000; and Kanbur 2000.

4 A number of other theoretical considerations will not be considered further in this paper. One example is how exactly actions in different countries contribute to the public good. These issues of the technology of public good provision are dealt with, for example, in Jayaraman and Kanbur 1999; Kanbur, Sandler and Morrison 1999; and Arce and Sandler 2002.

5 This is discussed further in Kanbur 2001.

6 The figures that follow are from the Annual Report of the World Bank 2001, Appendix 1, 'World Bank Expenditures by Program Fiscal 1997–2001'. The table can be downloaded from http://www.worldbank.org/annualreport/2001/pdf/appendix.pdf

7 Of course, this is a rough and ready order-of-magnitude calculation. Sometimes under Development Economics and World Bank Institute will support country operations, just as some times under Regions will support multi-country activities. A more sophisticated analysis can be conducted with more detailed budgetary data.

8 Other initiatives such as the regional Water Initiative for Middle East and North Africa, http://lnweb18.worldbank.org/mna/mena.nsf/Sectors/MNSRE/AA7510D 24BEE223C85256B58005A5026?OpenDocument, are at the stage of seminars and meetings, with 'normal' project activity projected some time into the future.

9 See Wilks 2001 on the Gateway. For a discussion of the pressures on the World Bank from its major shareholder, see Wade 2002.

Bibliography

Arce, M, Daniel G and Sandler, Todd, 2002, *Regional Public Goods: Typologies, Provision, Financing and Development Assistance*, Stockholm, Almkvist and Wiksell International.

Burnside, Craig and Dollar, David, 2000, 'Aid, Policies and Growth', *American Economic Review*, September, pp. 847–68.

Cornes, Richard and Sandler, Todd, 1996, *The Theory of Externalities, Public Goods and Club Goods*, 2nd Edition, Cambridge, Cambridge University Press.

Ferroni, Marco and Mody, Ashoka, 2002, *International Public Goods: Incentives, Measurement and Financing*, Norwell, Ma, Kluwer Academic Publishers.

Gerrard, Christopher D, Ferroni, Marco and Mody, Ashoka, eds, 2001, *Global Public Policies and Programs: Implications for Financing and Evaluation*, Washington DC, The World Bank.

Jayaraman, Rajshri and Kanbur, Ravi, 1999, 'International Public Goods and the Case for Foreign Aid', in Kaul, I, Grunberg, I and Stern, MA, eds, *Global Public Goods: International Cooperation in the 21st Century*, New York, Oxford University Press, pp. 418–35.

Kanbur, Ravi and Sandler, Todd with Morrison, Kevin 1999, *The Future of Development Assistance: Common Pools and International Public Goods*, Washington, DC, John Hopkins Press for the Overseas Development Council.

Kanbur, Ravi, 2000, 'Aid, Conditionality and Debt in Africa', in Tarp, Finn, *Foreign Aid and Development: Lessons Learnt and Directions for the Future*, London, Routledge, pp. 409–22.

—— 'Cross Border Externalities, International Public Goods and Their Implications for Aid Agencies', Cornell working paper, http://aem.cornell.edu/research/research-pdf/wp0103.pdf

Kaul, I, Grunberg, I and Stern, MA, eds, 1999, *Global Public Goods: International Cooperation in the 21st Century*, New York, Oxford University Press.

Sagasti, Francisco and Bezanson, Keith, 2001, *Financing and Providing Global Public Goods: Expectations and Prospects*, Stockholm, Fritzes Kundservice.

Sandler, Todd, 1998, 'Global and Regional Public Goods: A Prognosis for Collective Action', *Fiscal Studies*, vol. 19, no. 3, pp. 221–47.

Tarp, Finn, 2000, *Foreign Aid and Development: Lessons Learnt and Directions for the Future*, London, Routledge.

Wade, Robert, 2002, 'US Hegemony and the World Bank: The Fight over People and Ideas', *Review of International Political Economy*.

Wilks, Alex, 2001 'Development Through the Looking Glass: the World Bank in Cyberspace', Paper prepared for the 6th Oxford Conference on Education and Development, Knowledge Values and Policy, September. http://www.brettonwoodsproject.org/

World Bank, 2001, *Annual Report 2001*, http://www.worldbank.org/annualreport/2001/wbar2001.htm

INDEX

Please note that references to tables are denoted by the letter 't', while references to notes are shown by page number, 'n', and note number.

ERRATA

CHALLENGES TO THE WORLD BANK AND IMF
Developing Country Perspectives

BACK COVER: About the Author: Ariel Buira is Director of the G24 Secretariat. He has been Special Envoy of the President of Mexico for the UN Conference on Financing for Development, Ambassador of Mexico, Member of the Board of Governors of the Bank of Mexico and Executive Director of the IMF.

p. 3, l. 2 'without the benefit of an economics education.'

p. 3, l. 19 'without moral values, or a vision of society.'1

NEW ENDNOTE should read as follows

'In Adam Smith s conception, the invisible hand does not devise the institutions which harness the self-interest of individuals for the social good. On the contrary; he argues that since merchants consider, that they will derive advantage from monopolies and other regulations on trade, as in fact they do, thus "they are always demanding a monopoly against their countrymen". Indeed, Smith believed that, in the pursuit of their self interest, merchants and manufacturers, seek political influence, since "to narrow the competition, is always in the interest of the dealers" and this "must always be against the interest of the public". (A Smith, pp. 266-7, 459,467; *An Enquiry into the Nature and Causes of the Wealth of Nations*, Oxford, Clarendon Press, 1976).

Thus, the invisible hand requires good institutions and laws to regulate the way in which individuals pursue their interests. These institutions and laws are the outcome of policy: in the view of Lord Robbins, the invisible hand "is the hand of the lawgiver, the hand which withdraws from the sphere of the pursuit of self-interest those possibilities which do not harmonize the public good"
(p. 52, *The Theory of Economic Policy in English Classical Political Economy*, Macmillan London, 1952).'

p. 24, l. 34 'as much as 9.2 per cent of total quotas'.